From Ivory Tower
to Glass House

From Ivory Tower to Glass House

STRATEGIES FOR ACADEMIC
LEADERS DURING
TURBULENT TIMES

• • •

Andrew J. Policano

Acclaim for *From Ivory Tower to Glass House*

• • •

"As THE ENVIRONMENT FACING HIGHER education becomes more complex, the model of an academic leader that worked twenty years ago becomes less relevant. Today, leadership skills like strategic prowess, business acumen and political savvy are becoming more critical. The ability to develop a financially sustainable strategy and communicate convincingly with the external constituency is paramount as universities struggle to replace permanently diminished taxpayer support. In this highly readable treatise, Policano provides an excellent examination of the skills and strategies necessary for university leaders to succeed in the current turbulent environment for higher education."

⸙ **Michael Gottfredson**, former President, University of Oregon and former Provost, University of California, Irvine

"Andy Policano has written the comprehensive handbook for leaders in higher education. He reminds us that the "academic" in academic leadership is fading away. The new leadership of higher education will require acumen in strategy, management, finance, human resources, external relations and fundraising."

⸙ **Donna Shalala**, President, The Clinton Foundation, former President, University of Miami, Chancellor Emeritus, University of Wisconsin and former Secretary of Health and Human Services

"*From Ivory Tower to Glass House* offers a provocative and much needed look at higher education and university leadership. Buffeted by diminishing public support and disruptive technologies and contending with faculty attitudes likely to alienate key constituencies, today's leaders need to be financially accountable and to develop sustainable, cost-effective strategies for delivering services. Equally important, they need to communicate these strategies and the rationale for them to an increasingly suspicious public. Policano delivers an excellent and highly readable foundation for any leader as they attempt to navigate today's challenging environment."

   ♦ **George Daly**, Former Dean, Stern School of Business, NYU

"As an economist and three-time dean, Andy Policano provides a holistic view of critical issues facing higher education in the modern era. *From Ivory Tower to Glass House* explores the challenges and opportunities facing university leaders—from balancing affordability and excellence to keeping pace in a highly competitive environment."

   ♦ **Michael Drake**, M.D., President, The Ohio State University

"Higher education is at a crossroads. Strategies that worked just a decade ago no longer apply. Today's university struggles to maintain academic quality against mounting criticism that higher education is too expensive and the value of a college degree is diminishing. Leaders need a blend of skills including academic prowess, a deep sense of business acumen and political savvy. Policano provides an excellent analysis of the skills necessary to succeed; both university leaders and board members will greatly benefit from reading this book."

   ♦ **Ed Fuller**, retired President, Marriott International Lodging and Trustee, Boston University

"This book looks to be right on precisely because Policano defines the problem so well. So much that has been written addresses the wrong problems with ambivalent solutions. This book has also moved from structural diagnosis to the necessity for a new approach to academic leadership within and without higher education rather than a futile dialogue between the two."

- **David Ward**, Chancellor Emeritus, University of Wisconsin Madison and former President, American Council on Education

"Today virtually any new university president has to view their leadership assignment as one of functioning in a "turn around" environment. They will face academic programs that are resistant to change, consumer demand that is increasingly uncertain, high operating costs, new technologies, low cost competitors, diminishing revenue and rapidly changing societal expectations. The skills needed include abilities to plan and implement short and long term strategies, explore financial alternatives, improve deployment of human capital, communicate change imperatives with stakeholders, and develop strategic alliances outside traditional boundaries. Finding university leaders with these skills who are also committed to the core purposes of creation and dissemination of knowledge is not easy. In *From Ivory Tower to Glass House* Policano articulates both the dynamics affecting higher education and the development of skills needed for successful academic leadership in the years ahead. The challenges may seem daunting to some but the opportunities for societal impact will be greater than ever for those who are prepared."

- **Joe Alutto,** former Interim President, Provost and Dean, The Ohio State University

"This book should be required reading for any dean or other academic leader regardless of their tenure in this role. Policano's chapters on development and external relations are based on sound, thoughtful philosophies and realities that focus on institutional priorities and will be most satisfying to alumni volunteers and possible major financial supporters. This book is filled with invaluable advice. In other words—read this book!"

+ **Don Gray,** retired Vice President of Principal Gifts, the University of Wisconsin Foundation.

Contents

Preface

• • •

As a recently promoted full professor of economics at the University of Iowa I was drawn unexpectedly into the role of department chair, with little opportunity to investigate the relevant tradeoffs or expectations. I accepted this three-year position with vows to not let my research suffer, do a credible job and then return to my passions of research and teaching. My path evolved into over thirty years of leadership positions, which were deeply satisfying. Still, within a few months in my first position I was overwhelmed. No one had warned me about the volume of activity that flows through the department chair. Worse yet, no one had offered to educate me on the myriad of mysteries that underlie academic leadership responsibilities. A search for helpful resources uncovered a sparse literature and a few disjoint workshops. Mostly, I relied on the advice of seasoned leaders and the expertise of a skilled administrative assistant. Today more resources are available, but the playing field has shifted. Existing approaches reflect an outmoded leadership style that focuses internally on academic quality within a traditional ivory tower existence. The current environment demands more; leaders must not only understand academic culture but also have a keen sense of strategic planning, financial strategy, fundraising and a host of other skills that are unfamiliar to most faculty. The purpose of this book is to identify and examine current challenges and then provide a skill set for academic leaders to address them.

This book in part builds on many of the concepts developed in *Public No More: A New Path to Excellence for America's Public Universities* co-authored by Gary Fethke. While the focus there is on the changing nature of public higher education, the emphasis of this book is on the choice to pursue a leadership role and the skills necessary to lead an academic unit and implement financially sustainable strategies. The discussion is framed in part by comments drawn from interviews with seasoned academic leaders. During the interviews, I asked "looking back, was this the right choice for you?" The interviewees reflected on their original decision, their career path and what they believed were their greatest challenges, failures and successes. They also commented on the rewards to leadership and the legacy they hope they have left behind. The conversations were illuminating and powerful. For those who take the leap, it should be comforting to know that the vast majority of those interviewed expressed great satisfaction with the path they took; they viewed their experience as provocative, rewarding and fulfilling, although not without abundant challenges. Leadership is not for everyone and not every experience is positive. The intent here is to provide a set of tools to examine the tradeoffs involved, especially in light of the changing higher education environment. The ultimate purpose is to help the next generation of academic leaders achieve the same sense of accomplishment and fulfillment as many who have gone before them.

Andrew J Policano
Irvine, California
January, 2016

Acknowledgements

• • •

I AM DEEPLY GRATEFUL TO Gary Fethke at the University of Iowa for many thought provoking discussions. Gary always has a unique perspective; I have learned much from him and am fortunate for our many years of friendship and collaboration. Valerie Jenness at the University of California Irvine (UC Irvine), showed infinite patience, offering penetrating comments on early drafts and discussing the finer points with me throughout the process. Michael Gottfredson at UC Irvine, provided excellent feedback on several key chapters; his perspective as a former provost and president was especially valuable. I benefitted as well from many conversations with Chuck Martin, Member of the Boards of Trustees of UC Irvine and Chapman University and successful CEO, venture capitalist and entrepreneur whose deep interest in improving higher education is inspirational. Don Gray, retired Vice President of Principal Gifts at the University of Wisconsin Foundation and Ed Fuller, Overseer and former Trustee, Boston University and retired President, Marriott International Lodging provided excellent guidance on the chapters on external relations, development and fundraising.

I am also grateful for insightful comments from Rick Cosier, former Dean of the Krannert School of Management at Purdue University and Howard Thomas, former Dean at Singapore Management University. Many colleagues at UC Irvine provided useful suggestions, especially Judith Stepan-Norris, Vice Provost for Academic Planning, and Emeritus Professor Richard McKenzie. Meredith Michaels, Vice Chancellor and

Chief Financial Officer at UC Irvine, and Jim Pavelko, Assistant Dean for Finance and Administration at the Paul Merage School of Business, were helpful and willing consultants on many of the budgetary issues examined. My superb executive assistant, Lee Anne Maki, provided much needed logistics and my research assistant Jon Mandala spent many hours copy-editing, for which I am very appreciative. Finally, the support provided by the Dean's Leadership Circle Professorship and the Paul Merage School of Business at UC Irvine was instrumental throughout the process.

The book is guided in part by the perspectives gained from formal interviews with a number of highly experienced and successful academic leaders. I would like to thank each of them, listed below, for their wisdom and the generous amount of time each of them spent with me.

- Joe Alutto, former Interim President, Provost and Dean, The Ohio State University.
- Christoph Badelt, former Rector, Vienna University of Business and Economics.
- George Daly, former Dean, McDonough School of Business, Georgetown University, Stern School of Business, NYU, and Tippie School of Business, University of Iowa.
- Philip P. DiStefano, Chancellor, The University of Colorado.
- Michael Drake, M.D., President, The Ohio State University and former Chancellor, UC Irvine.
- Gary Fethke, former Interim President, the University of Iowa and former Dean, Tippie School of Business, University of Iowa.
- Howard Gillman, Chancellor, UC Irvine and former Dean, Dornsife College of Letters, Arts and Sciences, University of Southern California.
- Michael Gottfredson, former President, The University of Oregon and former Provost, UC Irvine.
- Ralph J. Hexter, Provost, University of California, Davis.
- Gerald S, Levey, M.D., Former Vice Chancellor, Medical Sciences and Dean of the David Geffen School of Medicine, UCLA.

* Peter Lorange, President, Lorange Institute of Business and Former President IMD Lausanne.
* Rosemarie Nassif, Director, Catholic Sisters Initiative, Conrad Hilton Foundation, and Former President, Holy Names College.
* Donna Shalala, President and CEO, the Clinton Foundation, former Secretary of Health and Human Services, former President, University of Miami and Chancellor Emeritus, University of Wisconsin.
* David Ward, Chancellor Emeritus, University of Wisconsin Madison and former President American Council on Education.

Finally, as always, my wife Pam is my greatest confidant and constructive critic. She read every word of this manuscript, providing much needed, very adept insight, guidance and support. I could not do this project without her constant enthusiasm.

Introduction

• • •

HIGHER EDUCATION IS FACING UNPRECEDENTED stress. The combined effects of rising tuition, growing student debt and a challenging job market are raising serious concerns about the value of a college degree. At the same time, global competition and technological innovations are disrupting traditional educational models. Universities are under intense scrutiny as students, parents and legislators demand a more efficient, lower cost educational platform. No longer can universities expect to receive support with little accountability. Indeed, the insular ivory tower existence long cherished by universities is rapidly disappearing. This environment requires a radically different strategy, one that is guided by multifaceted leaders who not only understand academic culture but who also have a keen sense of business acumen. The purpose of this book is to both identify and analyze current challenges facing higher education and then to develop the requisite skill set for academic leaders to address them.

Today's university requires leaders who not only understand and appreciate academic values, but who are also well versed in strategy, finance, human resources, external relations and fundraising. Some universities are looking outside academia to find leaders who possess the required background and experience. Faculty members strongly resist this external intervention but who among them is capable and willing to assume a leadership role? Most faculty members do not have the training, experience or even empathy to take on a leadership role, especially one confounded by the current mounting pressures. The discussion analyzes the tradeoffs facing a faculty member who is considering a leadership path and examines the strategies required to succeed in this rapidly changing environment.

A faculty member's career is typically highly insulated and individually driven with little regard for the institution or its issues. How many academic researchers, dedicated teachers or clinicians are willing to at least partially set aside their other activities to pursue a leadership path? The choice is no easy matter and yet universities offer little guidance in succession planning or mentoring for leadership positions. Moreover, traditional faculty members often view academic leadership as a role for less capable researchers or clinicians. Those faculty members who are willing to consider a leadership role face both a negative stigma from colleagues and a difficult path in obtaining the requisite skills. The irony is that even when faculty members gain the appropriate skills and are willing to lead the necessary change, they are unlikely to be selected for such a role by their colleagues in the current resistant culture of strong faculty governance.

One of the most significant challenges confronting universities is the permanently changing financial paradigm. As the subsidy declines for both public and private universities, fewer activities can be funded without generating sufficient revenue to support them. Strategy becomes paramount; questions like where does the department, college or university have a distinct comparative advantage, which activities should be prioritized, which should be subsidized and which activities should the university not do become major considerations. The need to develop a distinctive, financially sustainable strategy is a complex task, one that eludes the training and experience not only of most faculty members but also of many current academic leaders. Some estimates indicate that there are currently over 50,000 academics at US universities who are in leadership positions where they either manage people, financial resources or both.[1] How much training have these individuals had to do so, especially in the specific areas critical to address current challenges?

Interviews with seasoned academic leaders provide insights on both the tradeoffs associated with pursuing a leadership path and creative methods to address the challenges that are likely to arise. This book does not portend to present the definitive approach to the issues discussed; rather, the intent is to provide a basis for comparing different perspectives while offering a plausible path. Existing literature on academic leadership focuses primarily on traditional skills needed in the customary ivory tower academic environment.[2] Little attention is given to developing a distinctive strategy, achieving financial self-reliance, working with external constituents and leading development efforts, all of which are key components of this book.

ORGANIZATION OF THE BOOK

Chapter 1 discusses the environment facing higher education and examines some of the critical issues that university leaders are likely to face. Inevitable tensions arising from current challenges make the decision to embark down a leadership path seem ever more precarious. Anyone considering a leadership role needs to understand the external environment and recognize that these dynamics require an expanded set of leadership skills as compared to those in the past. The dilemma is that the necessary leadership profile has little intersection with the training and experience of most faculty members. This chapter examines the implications for academia as some universities shift leadership to individuals from outside the ivory tower. While faculty resist these appointments, their opposition lacks credibility unless some faculty are willing and capable to step into these roles. Chapter 2 discusses the tradeoffs for a faculty member who is considering a leadership path. This discussion offers a view of the required skills, role and life cycle for leaders.

Once in office, there is little guidance for the life-long academic who is now thrust into a side of the university they have had little opportunity or need to engage. Chapters 3 – 7 provide a description of the responsibilities of academic leaders including strategic planning, financial strategy and implementation, human resource management, and external relations, which spans development, fundraising and alumni activities. Chapter 8 focuses on pragmatic suggestions including how to prioritize and delegate activities, build a team and effectively address difficult personnel issues and crises. Finally, Chapter 9 provides a reflection on the life cycle of an academic leader, including impact, legacy and life after leadership.

CHAPTER 1

The Changing Face Of Higher Education: Who Will Lead?

• • •

The dogmas of the quiet past are inadequate to the stormy present. The occasion is piled high with difficulty, and we must rise - with the occasion. As our case is new, so must we think anew, and act anew.

—ABRAHAM LINCOLN

INTRODUCTION

IN FEBRUARY 2016, YEARS AFTER the drastic funding cuts associated with the Great Recession, the University of California Berkeley announced that it is facing a substantial and growing deficit of $150 million or 6% of its operating budget. How could this happen at the most prestigious public university in the country? A combination of factors including slow economic growth and increasing demands on taxpayer funds are causing permanent shifts in the funding paradigm for higher education. Universities must accept the reality that taxpayer funding has permanently fallen; they need to adopt financially sustainable strategies that respond to constituent needs. Many universities are doing so; they are implementing cost cutting measures and new efficiencies and are developing distinctive strategies with new sources of revenue in a move toward a transformed operating environment. These universities have an opportunity for sustained success within a financially self-reliant framework. Others continue to function as usual, waiting for a return to previous public funding levels. These universities are likely to suffer the same plight as Berkeley.

The environment facing higher education has changed drastically over the last several decades. Significant declines in state subsidies are forcing unpopular increases in tuition and growing student debt. Pressures arising from intense global competition and technological innovations are disrupting traditional educational models. Universities are under intense scrutiny as students, parents and legislators demand a more efficient, lower cost educational platform. Accustomed to receiving resources with little accountability, universities are recognizing that their long cherished ivory tower existence is rapidly disappearing. This chapter examines some of the critical challenges facing universities including declining government support; controversy over who will pay for higher education; the emergence of alternative methods of program delivery; the future of tenure; and the increasing adoption of performance based budgeting.

As current dynamics force needed changes, the question of who should lead universities comes to the forefront. Anyone contemplating a leadership role needs to recognize that the traditional skill set used by academic leaders is no longer sufficient. In addition to an appreciation of academic standards and faculty culture, today's leader needs to be well versed in strategy, finance, human resources, external relations and fundraising. Some universities are looking to government and industry to find leaders who possess the required skill set. Many faculty oppose these outside interventions, but who among them is capable and willing to lead? While the discussion assesses some of the recent non-traditional university appointments, the costs and benefits of opening the ivory tower to outside leadership are not yet fully understood.

The Financing of Higher Education

In late 2014, following an almost 24% decrease in state support between 2007 and 2013 and three years of mandated frozen tuition, the University of California Board of Regents called for a multi-year increase in tuition. The reaction from the state legislature was predictable; Senator Ricardo Lara declared that "...the UC Board of Regents appears to be out of touch with average working-class families" and he called for the legislature to be empowered to veto such increases.[3] This scenario is typical after a decrease in public university support by a state legislature. The regents react by raising tuition to recoup some of the lost revenue. The legislature then blames the regents for raising the student's share of the cost of education, apparently not recognizing that it was their funding cut that made it necessary for the university to do so. Private universities also receive criticism for setting overly high tuition and appealing to an elite set of students. The irony of this banter is that the groups on both sides of the debate desire the same outcome: to ensure the excellence of and access to higher education. Still, this "blame game" continues primarily due to a lack of understanding of the role of the university, the value it brings to society, and the cost and financing of higher education.

Who is at fault? While the media plays a role by not always capturing the full picture, universities themselves do an extraordinarily poor job explaining what they do, how well they do it and why what they do matters. The consequence is that much of the criticism of higher education is based on misperceptions. Whenever tuition increases, there is a public outburst that universities are driving up costs and lower-income students will be not be able to afford higher education. Much of this criticism derives from confusion between the price of education, which is related to tuition, and the cost of education, which includes faculty, facility and overhead expenses. The fact is that universities have done reasonably well at containing costs.[4] Still, someone has to pay. The contentious issue facing universities is not whether higher education is important but rather, who will bear the brunt of its cost. When a state legislature decreases public university funding, it is reducing the taxpayer's share of the cost and deciding that students and their families should pay more. Even so, over 65% of college students in the U.S. receive financial aid; when tuition increases, most universities allocate a greater proportion of the increased revenue to lower income students. As discussed below, a higher tuition, higher financial aid model can actually enhance access.[5]

Universities should be repeatedly communicating these facts and clearly articulating the value of higher education. While attempting to convince state legislatures and the federal government to restore lost funding, universities also need to recognize that there are many demands on scarce resources. Governments at all levels are facing pressures from many sources including public pension liabilities, health care, funding for K – 12 education and unfortunately, growing needs from an aging, overcrowded prison system. Legislators making allocations based on alternative uses of funds do recognize that higher education is important, but how critical are its funding needs relative to these other priorities?

Funding issues are especially problematic for state legislatures during recessions. Every recession since the 1980's has caused states to scramble to make cuts in areas where there is discretion; public higher education is a major target. Although there is some recovery when a recession ends, since 1988 the percent of higher education funding per student full-time-equivalent (FTE) has been in long-term decline. The Great Recession in 2008 was no different as state legislatures decreased university funding dramatically. In 2012, according to the Pew Foundation, state governments decreased spending by $8 billion compared to 2011; much of the decline came from cuts to education. With the improvement of the US economy in 2013 and 2014, overall state and local funding for higher education increased, rising 5.7 percent in 2014. While this funding has provided some relief, the overall level is still below inflation adjusted 2008 - 2011 levels. According to the State Higher Education Executive Officers Association, where public subsidies covered almost three-quarters of operating costs in the 1980s, the share is now closer to half.[6]

Universities need to accept the fact that public funding has permanently fallen. With a plethora of demands on government revenues and slow economic growth, the ability of taxpayers to fund the majority of the cost of higher education has diminished. The future of higher education is promising for those universities that adapt to the current reality.

The alternative is not rosy for those who choose to continue to operate in a model that hopes for a return to past levels of public support. Some department chairs and deans continue to view their role as negotiating with the administration to obtain more resources. Some presidents and chancellors continue to work diligently to convince governors and legislatures to restore permanent funding. These leaders will likely lead their unit or institution down an unsustainable path. One only needs to examine the events at UC Berkeley to witness the consequence of waiting for funding to be restored to previous levels. Some university battles with the legislature can yield short-term benefits, but the question is whether universities are fighting the right war. In each case, when some funding was restored, it came either as temporary funding or as part of an agreement not to increase tuition. The most feasible path to financial self-reliance involves developing a distinct strategy that responds to constituent needs and is funded in large measure by increasing tuition. The war that is worth fighting is one that convinces legislators to allow a rise in tuition with a return to financial aid that enables access for low-income students.

Examples: Public Universities

In a recent conversation with a senior faculty member at a research-intense university, he complained that the president of the university was urging all departments to hire more adjunct faculty. He also expressed concern that the dean was proposing that rewards should place greater emphasis on teaching and that more revenue producing programs should be developed. Even today, over eight years after the Great Recession, many faculty have yet to recognize the extent to which their world is changing. Lack of knowledge of the external environment creates a perception that local problems are idiosyncratic. Tensions arise because constituents battle to gain a larger share of a pie that doesn't exist. Understanding current challenges aligns constituents to address shared concerns. Leaders should have a deep appreciation of the external environment and should educate the faculty on the issues facing higher education. In that vein, the following examples provide a brief synopsis of recent actions in several states.

Arizona Public University System

The plight of the Arizona public university system provides an excellent example of many of the tenets described both here and in Fethke and Policano (2012). Historically, the tuition structure in the Arizona Regents Universities was among the lowest of all state universities. As recently as 2000, resident tuition at Arizona State University was $2,272.[7] The Great Recession initiated tuition increases that ended this tradition of highly subsidized education. Public funding for higher education fell by one-third between 2009 and 2015 and the relationship between the legislature and the university system took a predictable turn for the worse. One legislator complained that too many people pursue college and that increasing appropriations is not the solution to help these individuals get jobs.[8]

As reported by The College Board, in response to the cuts, in-state tuition and fees in Arizona increased 70 percent when adjusted for inflation between the academic years 2008-09 and 2013-14.[9] The national average was 27 percent. The negative correlation between state funding and tuition continued with further budget cuts to the university system in 2015. According to Arizona Board of Regents President Eileen Klein, the cuts to university budgets amounted to 63% of all the hard cuts that were necessary to balance the state budget.[10] To negate the budget cuts the Regents proposed a 4.1% tuition increase. The result is that over the past decade, tuition has increased 120%, when adjusted for inflation.[11] To the casual observer the increase may seem shocking, but one needs to consider the low tuition base. The cost of maintaining artificially low tuition is that the percentage increase required to offset a cut in public funding is substantial.

Implications from Arizona: Slow economic growth combined with growing financial demands of other priorities imply that first, there is little hope of a return to previous funding levels for higher education, and second, the outlook for any significant increase in public funding is highly unlikely. The Board of Regents has responded appropriately with higher tuition and a return to aid, which is the most realistic path to financial sustainability.

UNIVERSITY OF CALIFORNIA

Governor Brown has consistently opposed tuition increases at the University of California (UC) in an attempt to maximize access for lower income students. The resulting pattern, which is what occurred in response to the Regents' request for a tuition increase in 2014, is that the UC System settles for an appropriation in lieu of a tuition increase. Not only was the increase woefully short of replacing previously cut funding, but also for 2015 and 2016, the agreement includes a commitment to increase enrollment with insufficient state funding to do so.

Arguments against tuition increases in the UC are generally based on access for low-income students. But these arguments are flawed: access for lower income students to the UC System is supported through the UC Blue and Gold Opportunity Program. Any California resident student admitted to the UC System whose family income is less than $80,000 receives financial support that covers tuition and fees from multiple sources. Additional aid for books and supplies is available for students who need these funds. Access to the UC is provided for these students with little financial burden to their families. The UC is also phasing in a Middle Class Scholarship program where the maximum amount of an award in 2017-18 will be: (a) 40 percent of system-wide tuition and fees for students with family income up to $100,000, and (b) between 10 percent and 40 percent of system-wide tuition and fees for students with family income up to $150,000 per year (based on a sliding scale).

Implications from California: While additional cost containment measures should continue to be implemented, holding tuition well below the cost of providing education eventually causes a deterioration of quality. The UC System is one of the premier research university systems in the world. The Legislature chose to fully fund the budget request from the California State System in 2015 while declining to do so for the University of California System. Providing education at a top research institution is not inexpensive. The legislature and governor are indicating that taxpayers are no longer willing to pay a significant premium for this research intensity. What adjustments should the UC System and other universities adopt?[12] One path, described in an example later in this chapter, is to increase tuition, using the financial aid programs described above to ensure access. Moreover, as will be examined in Chapters 3 and 4, universities need to develop financially sustainable strategies that establish affordable priorities.

UNIVERSITY OF IOWA

Iowa's Governor Terry Branstad has repeatedly argued against tuition increases. In 2015 the university system prepared for a third consecutive year of an undergraduate tuition freeze. The flagship of the system, the University of Iowa (UI), has steadily increased non-resident enrollment, which reached almost 46% in 2014. The two research universities, UI and Iowa State University (ISU) have historically received a combined 80% of the state allocation, while the University of Northern Iowa (UNI) received about 20%. Recent controversy has surrounded a seemingly mechanical formulaic allocation of funds and a disparity in the proportion of funds allocated relative to the number of resident enrollees. In 2014, the University of Iowa received 46% of the general operating funds allocated to the system, while educating 34% of the Iowans registered. ISU received 36% while educating 43%, and UNI received 18% while educating 23%.

In 2014, an Iowa Blue Ribbon Commission proposed a more discretionary formula based on resident enrollees and several outcome measures including graduation rates and placement. A major component of the proposal was a uniform subsidy for each resident student regardless of major or enrollment as an undergraduate, graduate or professional student. As pointed out by Fethke (2014), the proposal would incentivize the enrollment of resident undergraduates and penalize the two research universities by underfunding their more costly graduate and professional programs. Eventually, the Legislature tabled a decision on the recommendation but did approve a reallocation of some funding from UI and ISU to UNI. At the same time, the Legislature mandated that tuition remain frozen and provided no new funding in 2015, urging the university to implement the suggestions of outside consultants who identified $50 million in cost cutting efficiencies.

Implications from Iowa: The situation in Iowa mirrors that in many other states. Legislators and the governor would like to see low tuition, low subsidy, high enrollment of residents, and enhanced access for low-income individuals and minorities. The challenge is obvious; who is going to pay for this utopia? The implication of the reduction in funding combined with frozen tuition and penalized non-resident enrollment is an inevitable decrease in quality. Moreover, in Iowa, the Legislature's decision to reallocate funds from the two research universities to UNI shows their preference to allocate taxpayer funds for resident undergraduate education rather than for graduate and professional education and research.

The use of outside consulting firms to uncover efficiencies reflects a growing trend. Universities can become more efficient but achieving efficiencies takes time, usually involving staff layoffs; purchase, development and implementation of complex software; and hiring individuals with different skill sets. Inevitably, the costs of implementing these efficiencies are underestimated and the benefits are overestimated. Efficiency strategies are important but realistic timetables and financial estimates are critical for their success. Apparently, in an attempt to bring a more business like approach to the university, the Iowa Board of Regents in 2015 selected an executive, Bruce Harreld with experience at Boston Market and IBM as its President. The implications of this strategy are discussed in a later section in this chapter.

Louisiana State University

In the spring, 2015 Louisiana's Legislature, faced with a significant budget shortfall, proposed a budget that included a worst-case scenario cut of 82% for the university system. One reaction by Louisiana State University in April 2015 was to begin an examination of the process for declaring financial exigency. Technically, financial exigency resembles bankruptcy but a declaration of bankruptcy, under Federal Law, would make the institution ineligible for the receipt of government-backed financial aid for students. Financial exigency provides a legal method to change contracts or other financial obligations, including allowing the prerogative of laying off tenured professors and eliminating programs or departments.

When publically confronted, President and Chancellor F. King Alexander indicated that the University had not filed for exigency but that every avenue for reacting to the proposed cuts was being explored. The situation in Louisiana resembles that in numerous states where the Legislature declares that there will be cuts to higher education and at the same time they berate the university for increasing tuition. Between 2009 and 2014, state funding fell by 55 percent, a drop of $90 million. In reaction, tuition and fees climbed by 61 percent. While tuition rose by a larger percentage increase than the percentage decline in spending, the percentage increase in tuition appears relatively high because it is computed from a low base. Total university revenue from tuition and the state subsidy had fallen; LSU would be squeezed to its limit with the new proposed cuts. President Alexander shrewdly documented the consequences of doing so, while articulating the benefits of higher education.[13] In the end, in June, 2015 the Legislature passed a budget that restored the university's funding to the level of the previous year.

Implications from Louisiana State: The long term issues still remain. The battle will continue to be fought in subsequent years as the growth in demands on state funds exceeds the growth in revenues it can realistically generate. The only way to sustain the quality of higher education is to: first, assess the cost structure and continue to implement efficiencies; second, determine the cost of the level of quality that the university aspires to; and finally, price the cost of education to fund that level of quality. The long-term solution is once again to raise tuition to cover this cost and subsidize students who have the ability, but not the resources to attend.

University of Wisconsin

In June 2015, the state legislature passed a budget that cut funding to the University of Wisconsin System by $250 million. In July, the Regents budget approved a reduction in funding to the flagship Madison campus of nearly $59 million. Rebecca Blank, Chancellor of the University of Wisconsin Madison indicated that the one-year cut would include an additional $23 million from a previous reduction that had temporarily been covered out of reserves.[14] Increases in non-resident tuition were approved allowing the potential for some increase in revenue to offset the state budget cuts. In addition to the budget cuts, Governor Scott Walker included a provision for the modification of rules under which tenured faculty could be dismissed. Previously, statutory language governed the circumstances under which faculty could be terminated, which include just cause or financial emergency. This language is now part of Regent policy.

Implications from Wisconsin: In addition to the now common case of cuts and legislative battles over finances, Governor Scott Walker forced a change in rules over dismissal of tenured faculty. Who should have the ability to dismiss a tenured faculty member and what are legal grounds upon which to do so? These issues are discussed in a separate section below.

PERFORMANCE BASED BUDGETING

Historically, public universities became accustomed to receiving funds based on full-time equivalent enrollment at the beginning of the academic year. While universities are concerned about student performance and graduation rates, incentives to improve either of these objectives do not explicitly enter into a funding model based solely on entry enrollment. Many states are now modifying this framework by adding additional performance based goals to determine funding allocations. According to the National Conference of State Legislatures, as of early 2015 the performance based budgeted activity across the US includes thirty states that have already adopted some form of performance based model and four others that are in the process of implementing this type of budgeting system. [15] In each case, some portion of the allocation is based on indicators including resident enrollment, course completion, time to degree, transfer rates, the number of degrees awarded, and low-income and minority graduates.

In theory, providing incentives to reward actions that accomplish societal goals should result in desirable outcomes. The challenge is to determine what the socially optimal goals should be. State legislators continue to believe that their university is a closed system that should educate a local population for the local economy; as such, resident enrollment is a key factor in allocations. The reality is that the major universities in every state are global institutions. They attract students from all over the world and graduates often choose to live and work outside the state. The provincial view of the university as primarily benefiting the state is no longer valid. Eventually, legislators will recognize that they cannot exert significant financial or other control over the future course of their state's university system; rather increasingly competitive global markets determine not only the fate of state universities but also on a larger scale, the fate of state economies. While resident enrollment may not be the best performance measure, other measures can help to incentivize efficiency and desirable outcomes. Some of these include graduation rates, diversity measures, time-to-degree and course completion.

Example: Performance Based Budgeting in Ohio

In 2015, Ohio adopted a new funding model based on the number of students who pass courses and graduate rather than on student head count. Wright State and Central State reacted by raising admission standards, which provoked criticism that disadvantaged students would be denied access. The intent of including performance measures is to increase student success; one consequence is that to do so, colleges attempt to enter a more highly qualified student body. If the result is to deny admission to a cohort of students who are unlikely to graduate, then the ultimate outcome is likely to avoid a number of negative consequences. Students who enter but drop out usually have a burden of outstanding loans, which is not a desirable outcome for either the student or society. With six-year graduation rates in Ohio ranging from 22% to 83%, adding graduation rates to the funding model makes sense. Over time, society is likely to gain from a better-prepared entry class, a more efficient learning environment and a smaller burden of student debt. Hopefully, students who are denied admission follow a more productive path through either the community college system with the possibility of transfer into a four year university, or skill-based education and preparation for employment.

The Future of Tenure

Legislative deliberations concerning the financial strife faced by universities often include criticism of the tenure system. A common belief is that tenure is the cause of inflated costs and low productivity. Movements to make it easier to dismiss tenured faculty are increasing. In Wisconsin,

Governor Scott Walker proposed what appears to be a relaxation of the rules for terminating a tenured faculty member. Newly adopted language authorizes the Regents to lay off tenured faculty under a broader set of circumstances than previously existed. Although faculty have expressed great concern, University of Wisconsin Chancellor Blank has argued that the new description is consistent with policies at peer universities.[16]

How should an academic leader respond to critics who argue that giving jobs for life decreases productivity and flexibility? First, it is useful to explain why tenure exists. In 1915, the newly formed American Association of University Professors (AAUP) described the purpose of tenure as a way to protect academic freedom.[17] During the late 19th and early 20th centuries a number of highly publicized cases involved governing boards and administrations that dismissed faculty members who held controversial views. With the protection of a tenured position, faculty members are able to conduct research on controversial issues with the potential to obtain results that could run counter to the beliefs of other faculty, politicians, donors and other external constituents. While the above rationalizes why the tenure system exists, it is also important to explain what the tenure system is *not* intended to do. The tenure system is not designed to protect incompetent or unfit faculty. Reviews of tenured faculty are required at most universities and while rarely used, there is a legal pathway for dismissal of non-performing tenured faculty. Tenure does not protect faculty members from being fired; the intent is to prevent faculty from being fired for the wrong reasons.

Tenure plays a critical role in assuring the richness and quality of the faculty. When recruiting faculty members from other universities and attempting to retain top faculty, tenure is an integral component of the negotiations. Competition, as in any labor market, requires aggressive salary and support packages. Companies offer a variety of mechanisms to retain the best performers; golden handcuffs is a commonly used practice. For universities, tenure provides one such mechanism. Still, while the tenure system provides benefits, there are also substantial costs associated with a lifetime employment contract. Moreover, some less productive faculty undoubtedly hide behind the veil of tenure. Dismissing a tenured faculty member involves a long, often distasteful process that universities tend to avoid. Perhaps some faculty would be more accountable if they felt that underperformance could result in more punitive measures such as decreased compensation or, in extreme cases, the loss of employment. Some of these issues are discussed below and in Chapter 4.

Tenured faculty are the highest salaried faculty; the most productive are sought after by other universities and they command aggressive compensation. Granting tenure turns a variable cost into a fixed cost and implies a significant expense for the university over the lifetime of the faculty member. There are few organizations that are more effective at turning variable costs into fixed costs than universities. This cost is especially large given that universities typically do not have mandatory retirement policies. As Joe Alutto, former Provost at Ohio State pointed out each tenure decision involves a commitment of about 30-40 years of increasing cost, which is especially risky in an environment experiencing a long term decline in public funding. If not doing so already, universities should be applying more scrutiny to tenure decisions, especially for cases that are on the margin.

Universities have been more carefully weighing the benefits and costs of hiring tenure track or tenured faculty versus lecturers and adjuncts. Over the past 30 years, the substantial increase in the use of non-research instructional faculty has caused a significant reduction in the centrality of tenure. According to the National Center for Education Statistics, during the 1970's full-time faculty members who were either tenured or tenure track made up 55 percent of the teaching faculty.[18] By 2013, as reported by AAUP, the fraction of tenured or tenure track faculty had fallen to only about 25 percent of the teaching faculty. The increased use of graduate students and non-tenure track faculty has been astounding.[19] Is reducing the centrality of tenure in academia socially optimal? Tenure is certainly a key component of a highly vibrant research intense faculty. Still, someone needs to pay for the faculty and the research infrastructure. The decrease in state appropriations combined with the effects of sequestration on federal research funding are signals that the taxpayer believes too much academic research is being conducted. Perhaps this is the case. Beyond the top 100 institutions how much more research does society need? What is the value of this work relative to its cost?

In 2012, the International Association of Scientific, Technical and Medical Publishers (STM) released a report with publication data from nearly 66% of all journal articles and tens of thousands of monographs and reference works. STM members include professional societies, university presses, private companies, and others. The report indicates that there were about 28,100 scholarly peer-reviewed journals in 2012, collectively publishing about 1.8 to 1.9 million articles per year. Even if one stretched the number of fields to as many as 200, the implication is that there are about 9,000 articles published in each field each year. How many of these articles have an impact? How many are even read by other academics in the field?

The public's revealed preference is signaled through reduced taxpayer support. What are reasonable reactions to secure additional research funding? Universities have reduced instructional cost by increasing the use of less expensive instructional faculty and expanding distance education options. Another possibility is to ask students to pay for a larger share of the cost of research. But how many students are willing to pay higher tuition so that the faculty can teach less to do more research? Universities are also attempting to increase funding from both donors and technology transfer, but as will be discussed in Chapter 4, these sources are unlikely to yield the substantial amounts required to support research infrastructure.

Chapter 3 describes a more promising solution in which universities strategically assess their research capabilities and then support those areas that have the greatest potential to make a significant impact. Critics of this approach argue that the fruits of fundamental research are difficult to predict. Major discoveries sometimes occur by accident when the researcher is looking for something different. Basic research can bear fruits that were not perceived at the time the research was conducted. But usually it is the top research investigators who have these "accidents" and then recognize their potential. The point is to invest in the best people in the most potentially productive areas. Many universities can have research programs but few can afford to conduct path-breaking work in every area of discovery. Claims in university vision statements to aspire to be "in the top" across the board are mostly vacuous. Priorities need to be established.

As universities follow the above path the implication for the future composition of the faculty is a continued increase in non-research faculty who deliver the bulk of the teaching mission. This cohort will surround a smaller core of research faculty who are carefully and strategically chosen. Tenure decisions will be much more stringent; quality and centrality of mission will both be major considerations. While research will continue to be conducted across the university, a smaller number of carefully chosen areas will be supported at a level consistent with achieving true distinction.

Digital Transformation: Distance Education

The underpinnings of the global economy are dramatically shifting due to the impact of digital transformation. The ability to build, share and leverage knowledge is replacing the ownership or control of assets as the primary source of competitive advantage. How do these changes affect higher education? Although distance education has received heightened attention since the development of Mass-Open-On-Line-Courses (MOOCs), the concept of separating learning from live instruction dates back hundreds of years. On-line learning is a relatively more recent phenomenon, but videos and other distance methods have been utilized for several decades. So why have MOOCs caused so much awareness as well as controversy? The concept of educating thousands if not hundreds of thousands of students with one MOOC course has caused legislators to salivate and faculty members to palpitate. Legislators see the potential for ample cost savings while faculty wonder how the demand for in-person teaching will be affected. The issue is whether on-line learning will be an effective alternative to traditional teaching or its ultimate replacement. As is the case for most comparisons of extreme options, the answer is likely to lie somewhere in between.

Most courses today use some form of on-line learning; readings, materials and exercises are routinely posted electronically. Courses have chat rooms, digitally recorded versions of live lectures and, in some cases, access to live classes on-line for students who cannot attend specific sessions. The emphasis on assessment of learning in higher education has become a significant issue with respect to distance education. A report by the Department of Education in 2009 finds that students who were enrolled in part of a class on-line performed better on average than students who participated in the same course via traditional teaching methods. The study indicates that a hybrid course like that described above provides the most advantageous learning environment.[20] These results coincide with a popular emerging view that hybrid solutions provide the best of both possible worlds by "flipping the learning environment." This approach, popularized by the Khan Academy, allows students to learn basic material on-line at their own pace and to choose alternative learning paths.[21] This self-learning is combined with the power of in class, in person discussion where critical thinking and problem solving skills can be developed. This model of flipping the learning environment is becoming more prevalent throughout all levels of education.

Overall, the jury is still out on the effectiveness of a pure on-line experience. The editors of the DOE study indicate that their results may derive from factors other than the delivery method including differences in content, pedagogy and learning time. The main variables could be the quality of the instructor, the specific course content and the extent to which the course layout accommodates different learning styles. Within a decade the most likely model is one in which standard introductory courses are taught by a small number of the most gifted faculty across the globe via distance media. On-line courses from faculty at the top universities can be more effective and desirable than sitting in a live course at a lesser-known institution with hundreds of other students. A hybrid approach is likely to be used for many upper level courses, while a pure in-class experience remains the best platform for courses that require more class interaction, personalized experiences and a small, intimate learning environment. In-residence college education is not likely to disappear but it will transform into a more flexible model allowing students the ability to choose their learning mode, shorten their time on campus and either graduate earlier or undertake additional learning opportunities.

The Changing Landscape of Higher Education

How have recent events affected the higher education landscape and what are their likely impacts going forward? First, waning public funding has already had dramatic effects. Although media rankings are far from perfect indicators of quality, their long-term trends can be revealing. In 1988, three of the top ten universities in the US News & World Report ranking of the best U.S. universities were public. In 2015 there were *no* public universities in the top ten and only one in the top twenty. Why? Private universities charge a tuition rate that approximates their cost subsidized by significant donations from loyal alumni. Public universities set tuition below cost with the hope that state funding and other revenue sources make up the difference. Traditionally, public university alumni contributed less support, believing that their tax dollars provided sufficient funding. Declining public support combined with limits on tuition increases has resulted in a strengthening of elite private universities relative to publics. As described above, even the most respected public university in the country, UC Berkeley, is suffering budget shortfalls, years after the drastic cuts associated with the Great Recession.[22] This scenario is creating considerable controversy concerning access and the role of higher education in addressing social goals.

Public university challenges and possible solutions: State budget processes provide little warning of final allocations. When cuts to public universities are announced, the only immediately possible reaction is to decrease variable cost. Course offerings are reduced, open full-time positions remain unfilled and campus services are cut. Part of this cost reduction reflects increases in efficiency but inevitably, cost reductions also result in a decrease in quality.[23] Larger class sizes, decreased student infrastructure, increased use of part-time instructors and a less competitive faculty support structure diminish the ability to maintain quality. Longer term reactions by public universities need to recognize that the decrease in state funding is permanent. They should be developing a distinctive strategy that is financially sustainable; if they do not, the separation between privates and publics will continue to grow. Lower tier publics will find it increasingly difficult to recruit and retain top faculty and students; some may eventually disappear as market forces reduce their competitiveness.

A variety of obstacles limit the ability of public universities to obtain financial self-reliance. Some of these barriers include limits on tuition, controversy over non-resident enrollment, required homogeneity across a university system, and criticism associated with the corporatization of the university. Each of these issues is discussed briefly below.

Tuition constraints: In spite of a waning subsidy, tuition increases are constrained by the legislature and public opinion. In addition to cost-cutting measures, universities seek to replace some of this lost revenue by admitting higher paying non-residents and in many cases, by raising non-resident tuition. Neighboring states typically do the same. This beggar-thy-neighbor strategy inflates costs for non-residents and can actually result in denying access to qualified residents. In California, after the number of resident students that the state will support has been enrolled, higher paying non-residents are admitted. Even though there are qualified residents who are willing to pay non-resident tuition, University of California Board of Regent policy forbids allowing residents to do so. Some of these students then become non-resident students in other states. Paradoxically, the attempt by the Regents to provide access via a low tuition policy actually denies access to this cohort of students. Moreover, universities that are increasing non-resident enrollment also suffer the wrath of legislators who apparently never connect the fact that they incentivized this activity when they approved a cut in state funding, while mandating restraints in resident tuition increases.

Required homogeneity: The standard practice in many public university systems is that all campuses are required to adopt the same admissions standards and charge the same tuition in spite of very different missions, cost structures and willingness to pay by students. In California, for example, does it make sense that a student who is contemplating either UC Berkeley or UC Merced faces the same price for each? Each university in the system should aspire to compete against a different set of peers and to develop a mission, vision and positioning strategy that are unique to their current and potential core strengths. Forcing admissions and pricing homogeneity across a university system decreases the ability of the flagship universities to enhance quality while hampering the ability of the other universities to attain their true distinction.

Corporatization: A further barrier is created through criticism by some traditional faculty members of efforts to increase donations from corporations. These faculty fear that that the university is "selling out' to the business community and is slowly relinquishing control of academic decisions to outside influence. An additional challenge is the bureaucratic university approval process that slows entrepreneurial initiatives to develop revenue generating degree programs that are offered either off campus, in the evenings, on weekends or via distance education. Some faculty members resist supporting these attempts, still expecting that the state should pay for new programs. Finally, while the future of higher education most certainly lies in a hybrid model that combines distance and in-class experiences, faculty adoption of these methods has been slower than warranted in the current environment.

With all of the above constraints and challenges, the best path to financial sustainability is through first, implementing a strategic planning process that determines the most cost effective way to deliver the desired level of quality and next, adjusting undergraduate tuition to cover the large share of that cost. The exact path to doing so is complex. A proposal for adjustments to the structure of tuition in a university system is described below.

A path to financial sustainability: One solution for setting tuition, a version of which is suggested in Fethke and Policano (2012) is based on the fundamental law of efficiency in competitive markets: price (tuition) should be set equal to the marginal cost of educating a student. While this solution is appealing, it raises several challenges. First, constituents need to determine and agree on the minimum cost for a particular level of quality. Next, whatever the cost, the efficient solution of marginal cost pricing does not usually provide an equitable outcome. It is highly likely that the resulting tuition is prohibitive for a portion of the population. To reach a more equitable outcome, a portion of tuition revenue should be set aside for financial aid to be awarded to capable students whose families cannot afford to pay for their education. In addition, state and federal subsidies for financial aid are likely to be needed to further promote access. Finally, universities have an expensive fixed infrastructure; marginal cost pricing is not likely to provide sufficient revenue to cover the fixed cost associated with buildings and equipment. The state must still play a role in funding capital expenditures.

EXAMPLE: ACHIEVING EFFICIENCY AND EQUITY IN A PUBLIC UNIVERSITY SYSTEM

The following describes a framework for a public university system that can preserve academic quality while providing access to qualified students of lower economic means:

1. To determine a realistic cost per FTE, each university should choose a group of peer schools and determine the average cost per FTE across this peer group. These data, which are collected by College Measures,[24] provide a detailed break down of how the cost

is allocated across instruction, student services, academic support, operations and maintenance, and institutional support. Distance education models should be incorporated into the determination of the most efficient way to deliver the curriculum. A determination should be made of which services to outsource. It can be useful to contract an outside consulting service that has performed similar cost assessments on other campuses. Those areas whose cost is significantly above the average can be penalized unless there is a viable justification. [25]

2. The Regents or other governing body of the system should recognize that each campus has a different cost structure and faces a different student demand in terms of willingness to pay. The governing body should allow differential tuitions across the system such that the subsidy plus tuition covers a cost-based level of expenditure per student that is unique to each campus. For example, in the University of California System, Berkeley, UCLA and UC San Diego would likely charge the highest tuitions and UC Merced the lowest.

3. Financial aid per student should be determined on a sliding scale based on the student's ability to pay with the goal to provide flexible opportunities for qualified students. A portion of tuition should be set aside to provide financial aid for qualified low income students. Federal and state funding is likely to be needed to supplement financial aid. Still, constraints may be binding. Given the increasing demands on taxpayer funds, admitting all qualified lower and middle-class resident students at no or a reduced charge may require more funds than can be realistically provided. Net tuition will need to increase for upper income class students and for some middle-income class students. A sliding scale for financial aid for middle income class students will protect them from a too burdensome increase in net tuition.

4. After taking into account the cost-adjusted resident subsidy, resident and non-resident tuitions should be approximately the same. If each campus receives about the same tuition revenue per student

regardless of residency, admissions decisions can be based on quality and academic fit of the applicant. Access would increase for residents, whose tuition net of in-state financial aid would still be lower than non-residents.

5. Each campus should allow differential tuition or fees across academic majors to reflect the differences in cost of delivery and student willingness to pay, thereby eliminating inefficient and often unfair subsidies from one set of students to another. Currently, students in low-cost majors like English subsidize students in high cost majors like Engineering. Differential tuition or fees would make the tuition structure more equitable.

Implementing the above steps can lead to a financially solvent system with increased efficiency. Tuition plus the appropriation is set to cover the university's cost of operation. Tuition revenue captured by each university combined with an appropriation that reflects differences in costs and student needs provides incentives for each campus to achieve their specific quality goals. Those campuses that display inefficiencies are penalized while those that are high quality and productive are rewarded. A financially sustainable level of access can be determined by a commitment of funds by the state and federal governments. Capital appropriations for maintenance of current plant and equipment plus building needs for enrollment growth still need to be financed through public appropriation.

Can the above model work in practice? Ultimate success requires acceptance to change and effective execution, both of which can be difficult to attain in the current academic and political environment. What is clear, especially from UC Berkeley's recent financial woes, is that the current low-tuition, low-subsidy model provides little hope of preserving the quality of the world's most prominent universities.

Small liberal arts colleges: There are over 500 liberal arts colleges in the US. The defining feature of these colleges is that they offer a smaller and more personalized learning experience than can be provided by large comprehensive universities. Some are historically black colleges, faith-based and/or single-sex campuses. Many focus on developing a niche that is usually centered on an innovative undergraduate curriculum. Many times located in a small town, these schools provide an almost mystical environment that is beloved by alumni, current students, staff and faculty. What does their future hold? In some cases, these smaller colleges are losing their market. Even without the heavy cost of an infrastructure for faculty research, the revenue obtained from a small student base compared to the large fixed operating cost creates financial stress. Tuition tends to be high and the overall cost of attending can be beyond the reach of many families. With ample distance education opportunities, there is a gloomy future for schools outside the top-tier that lack a sizeable endowment, loyal alumni base, attractive location and distinct competitive advantage.

EXAMPLE: SWEET BRIAR COLLEGE

In March 2015, the then Board and President of Sweet Briar College, a small liberal arts college for women in Virginia, announced that the school was shutting its doors due to insurmountable financial challenges.[26] As described by Jacobs (2015) the decision was made based on several trends including the declining number of female students interested in all-women colleges and the dwindling number of students overall interested in small, rural liberal arts colleges. Subsequently, with the support of alumni from across the country a nonprofit organization, Saving Sweet Briar, was created to mount a campaign to sustain the college. Through legal action and with the appointment of a new board and president, the college declared that it would stay open.

Given the external factors that have diminished Sweet Briar's traditional market niche, it can be challenging to create a new atmosphere that attracts a sufficient number of students to be viable. Biemiller (2015) describes the difficulties that are confronting many small colleges. Wilson, in Chambersburg, Pa., faced a similar issue in 1979, when it closed due to enrollment problems and then later on reopened. Today, Wilson's fiscal status is improving through a number of innovations, the most significant of which is to abandon its long-held women only policy. Antioch University reopened in 2011 after a three-year closure in a resurrection driven by alumni. In a search of alternative revenue streams, Antioch, has opened a wellness center that sells memberships to local residents, reopened its theater, and is exploring a residential retirement community for individuals who want to live near a college atmosphere.

To succeed, small colleges need a competitive niche that appeals to students combined with a wealthy, supportive alumni base and a sizeable endowment. Creating entrepreneurial funding streams through ventures into the community, developing creative programming and distance education, and implementing effective cost controls can provide a solid basis for sustainability. Still, inevitably, the future is unlikely to support the number of small private colleges and universities that exist today.

DIVERSITY: A CRITICAL ONGOING ISSUE

While the focus in this chapter is on new issues facing higher education, one of the most critical ongoing issues is the lack of diversity of the student, staff and faculty across virtually all universities. Challenges remain even after decades of programs designed to enhance the participation of minority groups. Some bold initiatives are underway; for example Brown University recently announced that it will spend $100 million to promote diversity and inclusion; Yale University committed $50 million for similar efforts; Johns Hopkins committed $25 million and the University of Cincinnati allocated $40 million. While these efforts are laudatory the key question concerns how these resources will be deployed. A central goal of all of these initiatives appears to be to increase the university's recruitment of faculty from underrepresented groups. At least one of the universities has indicated that it will attempt to hire top minority faculty from other universities and will increase salaries to do so. The problem is that unless there are national efforts to increase the size of the pool, these initiatives can only succeed by increasing the diversity of one university at the expense of another, which can be more harmful than helpful. If universities concentrate efforts only on their own diversity goals, they will regrettably miss an important opportunity to address the national challenges associated with achieving diversity and inclusion across all universities.

University leaders need to take responsibility for increasing the size of the national pool of qualified minority students and faculty; the substantial funding being made available can have its greatest impact on diversity by doing so. A key initiative should be to increase the numbers of underrepresented students who complete high school and continue their education to pursue a college degree. Minority students need faculty role models; unfortunately, if universities continue to focus only on their own diversity initiatives, they will continue to struggle in their attempts to diversify the faculty.

One of the most successful diversity initiatives in higher education, the PhD Project, initiated a program over 20 years ago designed to increase the diversity of doctoral faculty in business schools.[27] The vision of the PhD Project is to increase the diversity of the faculty, who in turn will work to attract a more diverse student body and encourage their students to pursue leadership roles in society. The impact of the PhD Project on the composition of the faculty in business schools has been astounding. Their efforts have more than quadrupled the number of minority business faculty, from 294 to 1,302, with another 309 doctoral students in the pipeline. The effect has been to lift faculty diversity for hundreds of universities. Other disciplines should follow a path similar to that of the PhD Project. Diversity is a fundamental goal of higher education; every leader should be deeply committed to reducing the extent of racial and ethnic disparity that continues to exist in many universities throughout the U.S.[28]

Who Should Lead?

In the face of the challenges described above, who is best qualified to lead universities into the future? As the landscape continues to become more complex, leadership skills like political savvy, strategic prowess, business acumen and charisma become more critical. Given the paucity of these skills among the faculty, some universities are looking outside academia for the next generation of leaders. Is this movement indicative of a growing trend? Will importing leadership from outside the ivory tower lead to a more viable strategy with innovations that are less likely to occur otherwise?

Two high profile atypical leadership appointments occurred in 2013. Mitch Daniels, former Governor of Indiana began as President of Purdue University and Janet Napolitano, former Governor of Arizona was selected to lead the University of California System. Other former governors who have led universities include David Boren of Oklahoma and Richard Celeste of Ohio. These appointments have a plausible rationale: Governors have ample experience leading a complex, politically charged organization, communicating with a diverse set of constituents and negotiating budget allocations with state legislators. Both Texas and Iowa have taken even more dramatic approaches. In January 2015, William "Bill" McRaven, a retired four-star admiral, Navy SEAL and Commander of the U.S. Special Operations Command became Chancellor of The University of Texas System. In February 2015, the Iowa Board of Regents selected former executive Bruce Harreld as President of the University of Iowa. Harreld's credentials include an MBA, experience as a senior level executive at IBM and Boston Market, and teaching as an adjunct professor at Harvard. Both McRaven and Harreld have backgrounds that are far from the traditional resume of a university president.

What level of success can be expected when someone with little academic background steps into a resistant culture laden with staunch faculty governance? Harreld is arriving into an already charged environment; the University of Iowa (UI) Faculty Senate and student government voiced "no confidence" votes against the Iowa Board of Regents after the decision was made to appoint him. While the choice of a non-traditional candidate at Iowa may be warranted to address current funding and competitive issues, many believe that the selection process excluded faculty and student input. Perhaps if the process were more deliberate, Harreld would not be facing the long uphill battle that now confronts him.

Janet Napolitano has had a reasonable level of accomplishment but, not surprisingly, she faced challenges initially concerning the intricacies of how universities operate and the nature of faculty culture and governance. She has encountered typical resistance in the California Legislature, especially when attempting to convince the legislators that research and quality matter. In a bold move, she confronted Governor Brown by convincing the Regents in 2014 to vote for a much needed tuition increase. The Legislature and Governor later agreed to provide a four percent increase in university funding in exchange for keeping tuition constant. They also agreed to a one-time allocation to alleviate some of the unfunded liability in the university's pension plan but with significant caveats to change the retirement system. Still, even with these allocations, the final result falls far short of replacing the significant funding decrease of the Great Recession. Moreover, the Legislature showed its lack of appreciation for a research-based university when it fully funded the budget request from the California State System but did not do the same for the University of California.

Mitch Daniels was a respected, popular governor who was re-elected for a second term. His selection as President of Purdue was controversial because as Governor he appointed eight of the ten Trustees who later elected him as the university's president. Critics claimed a conflict of interest but a state investigation found no violation of the Indiana Code of Ethics.[29] In the face of additional criticism that he lacked an academic background, he immediately accused the university of levying unnecessary increases in tuition designed to generate whatever level of revenue it wanted to spend.[30] He froze tuition and reduced meal plan and textbook costs, thereby lowering the total cost of attending Purdue and the total debt of the student body. In 2013, Daniels introduced "Purdue Moves," a plan to provide new investments in research including 165 new faculty.[31] In 2014, he announced two $500,000 awards; one for the first academic unit that developed a 3-year degree program and the other for the first unit to develop a competency based degree program.

Some of the actions taken by Napolitano and Daniels have been impressive and bold. Daniels froze tuition before the legislature had voted on the allocation to the university. He empathizes with the plight of legislators who are choosing between many worthy funding requests that total well above available revenues. Napolitano and Daniels do not shy away from placing innovations in front of the faculty and they move ahead in spite of imbedded traditions and culture. In some ways, they are fearless change agents. While they understand that their popularity and eventual tenure may be challenged, they are willing to put themselves at risk. Academics in leadership positions are typically less bold; they choose to move slowly in deference to faculty culture and traditions, and they tend to shy away from innovation that may endanger their length of term in office.

Several of Daniel's highly publicized actions at Purdue involve measures that are neither unique nor do they require action by a non-traditional head of the university. Efficiency measures in areas outside the academic core have taken place at all universities. Moreover, organizations don't rise to greatness through cost cutting. After the fat is gone, revenue growth and right sizing become critical. Universities need to identify their distinction and decide which areas to support and which areas to cut as part of a financially sustainable strategy. Difficult decisions need to be made that are likely to create significant unrest. While Daniels has presented a plan for academic innovation, neither Napolitano nor Daniels have yet to determine what the university should *not* do, which very well could be the most challenging issue facing universities into the future.

Can the non-academic leader model work? Several of the interviewees offered their perspective on the implications of nontraditional appointments of university presidents. Gary Fethke, former Interim President at Iowa, observed that atypical university leaders like Napolitano and Daniels can communicate in a way that escapes most academics. They do not always address external constituents with a declaration that "academic values" must be defended as if these values obviously deserve to be funded. They are more effective with external groups because they understand external cultures; it is easier to convince someone if you understand their environment. Many academics have beautiful rhetoric that can often leave people bewildered. Chancellor Howard Gillman of UC Irvine compared the top position at a major university to that of a politician in office; both individuals need to prove themselves repeatedly. In his view, with a multitude of constituents to please, being a university president is very much like running for office every day. Perhaps this analogy is useful in understanding why former governors have the potential to excel in the role as a university leader. They have ample experience dealing with the complex slate of activities being addressed by state legislatures. They understand conflict, tradeoffs and how to skillfully articulate the message of the university to a diverse constituency, artfully gaining support in doing so.

A model that seems to be working in California and Indiana, and before them with David Boren as President of the University of Oklahoma is to combine the external expertise of a seasoned politician with the academic experience of a faculty member who has ample leadership background. A former governor who assumes the role of university president can focus on the interactions with external constituency and can provide leadership on operational efficiency and cost cutting measures. A well-respected faculty member can take on the role of provost and chief academic officer. With a keen appreciation of faculty governance and culture, the provost can provide the main conduit to the faculty.

Daniels and Napolitano have followed the above model. While they seem to be having reasonable success, there are some who believe this separation of duties is not a good idea, even if both leaders are faculty members. Donna Shalala believes that the president and the provost should work almost as an interchangeable team. Each should understand and know the role of the other so well that constituents see a seamless leadership team and always receive a consistent message. Still, a blend of different perspectives and skills across leaders drawn from different worlds may be a model that can also work. In the case of the University of Iowa, it will soon be seen whether an executive, who is neither a politician, academic or local favorite is too far removed from the traditional model to be able to succeed in the role of university president.

Summary and Conclusions

The future of higher education is a precarious one that is laced with challenges ranging from funding issues to intensifying competition from global competitors and the emergence of alternative methods of delivery. Effective leadership at the department, school and university levels is ever more significant during these periods of stress. Understanding the issues facing higher education becomes critical; leaders who are embedded in a disappearing model of highly subsidized higher education are likely to mired in a conundrum of reduced resources and competitive decline. Meaningful solutions require an integral knowledge of the challenges facing higher education and the ability to devise entrepreneurial solutions for long-term financial sustainability. A well-positioned financially self-reliant strategy will define the university of the future.

The dilemma facing higher education is that the changes necessary to address the current environment do not mesh well with traditional academic culture. The ivory tower existence focuses on academic quality and depends on heavy public subsidization; accountability and efficiency are not primary concerns. Faculty members are generally not well versed in the skills necessary to invoke the innovations necessary to address current challenges. Moreover, those faculty who gain the requisite background and are capable of implementing a financially sustainable strategy are unlikely to be chosen for such a role in the current culture of resistant faculty governance. The result is that external oversight boards are exerting greater control and appointing non-academic leaders even though the long-term consequences of doing so are not yet fully understood.

Key Takeaways: Chapter 1

- Someone has to pay to cover the cost of higher education. Legislatures that decrease public university funding are decreasing the taxpayer's share of the cost and deciding that students and their families should pay more.

- The contentious issue is not whether higher education is important but rather who is going to bear the brunt of its cost.

- Battles for increased funding with the legislature can yield short-term benefits, but are universities fighting the right war? The war worth fighting is one that convinces legislators to allow a rise in tuition with a return to financial aid that enables access.

- Lack of knowledge of the external environment creates a perception that local problems are idiosyncratic. Uninformed constituents battle to gain an increased share of a pie that doesn't exist. Communicating the challenges confronting all universities draws constituents together to address shared concerns.

- Tenure does not protect faculty members from being fired; the intent is to prevent faculty from being fired for the wrong reasons.

- There are few organizations that are more effective at turning variable costs into fixed costs than universities.

- Few universities can afford to conduct path-breaking work in every area of discovery. Aspirations to be "among the top twenty" are mostly vacuous. Priorities need to be established.

- The concept of educating thousands of students with one MOOC course has caused legislators to salivate and faculty members to palpitate.

- Public universities that are increasing non-resident enrollment are criticized by legislators who apparently never connect that the decrease in support that they approved incentivizes this activity.

- A low-tuition policy incentivizes UC schools to enter higher paying non-residents, even when some resident students are willing to pay out-of-state tuition. The UC Regents mandated low in-state tuition actually denies access to these qualified resident students.

* Admissions and pricing homogeneity across a public university system decreases the ability of the flagship universities to maintain and enhance quality while hampering the ability of other campuses to attain their true distinction.

* Non-traditional university leaders do not shy away from placing innovations in front of the faculty. They move ahead in spite of imbedded traditions.

* Academics in leadership positions tend to move slowly, defending faculty culture and avoiding confrontation that may put their position at risk.

* A well-positioned financially self-reliant strategy will define the university of the future.

CHAPTER 2

Choosing an Academic Leadership Path: Tradeoffs and Expectations

• • •

Some are born great, some achieve greatness, and
some have greatness thrust upon them.

—WILLIAM SHAKESPEARE

INTRODUCTION

UNIVERSITIES EXHIBIT A STRONG SENSE of faculty governance and leadership. After all, who better to understand academic rigor and culture than doctoral faculty? But the current environment demands more. Universities have become complex entities that struggle to maintain academic values while reacting to pressures to become more efficient, innovative and entrepreneurial. The traditional ivory tower focus on academic quality is no longer sufficient. Today's leaders must be proficient strategists who have the ability to develop and implement financially sustainable strategies that are accountable to societal needs. While faculty resist looking outside academia for leaders with the requisite skills, the dilemma is that most faculty members lack the background and experience necessary to address the current mounting pressures.

At some point in their career, almost all faculty members are confronted with a decision to alter their focus away from research, teaching and/or clinical practice to accept a leadership role. Assessing both the tradeoffs involved and one's leadership ability can be challenging. Most faculty are unfamiliar with the language and issues of management; they typically have given little thought to pursuing a career path other than the one envisioned during their doctoral education. Moreover, universities exert extraordinarily little effort to nurture leadership talent in the faculty. Those who have such leanings are often reluctant to express their interests. George Daly, dean emeritus at NYU, Georgetown and Iowa, referred to a perverse mindset where many faculty believe that anyone can do administrative work and they view taking on a leadership role as a waste of time and talent. When a faculty member has a leadership opportunity, not only are the factors unfamiliar and difficult to assess, the opportunity can be clouded with negative perspectives from faculty colleagues.

This chapter explores the issues that a faculty member faces when presented with a leadership opportunity. Primary considerations include whether the individual is well suited to take on such a role and, if so, deciding the best time to pursue such a position. The discussion applies to a wide range of positions including department chair, associate dean, center or institute director, dean or a higher-level position. Still, every leadership position is different and while some of the required skills are generic, not all are transferable. Many of the skills needed to be a university president differ, for example, from those needed to be a department chair or program director. The discussion does not attempt to duplicate the vast literature on leadership but instead focuses on the requisite profile of a leader within the confines of university culture and hierarchy. As such, the analysis is based in part on the perspectives gained from interviews with academic leaders.

Department chairs and others who decide to pursue a higher-level university position are likely to find the interview process to be challenging. Search committees reflect a broad spectrum of interests from across the campus. The majority of the committee members are faculty who invariably want to protect their turf. With a culture of strong, resistant faculty governance, any candidate who too aggressively expresses the need for change and provides too much detail concerning how it will be accomplished is unlikely to be selected to do so. The discussion offers a pragmatic view of each step in the search process with suggestions to help navigate the application, interview and negotiation stages. The chapter concludes with an overview of what to expect in a leadership position. The interviewees' comments revealed a common pattern of experiences as they progressed through their term in office in each position they held. Their descriptions characterized several phases of leadership, with each phase reflecting changes in their environment and different levels of accomplishment. The examination of these phases provides a broad foundation for the in depth analysis of various facets of leadership presented in the remainder of the book.

When is the right time?

Very few individuals pursue doctoral studies with the intent to enter into an academic leadership position, yet few escape without having to serve in administrative role at some point in their career. When is the right time to consider such a role? The answer varies. Some faculty start almost immediately out of graduate school, usually as a director or co-director of a research project or institute. More typically, according to a study by Gmelch and Miskin (2004), faculty who move into a meaningful administrative role do so on average about sixteen years into their academic career. Their work reveals that the most frequently cited motivations to accept the first role, in this case as department chair, are a desire for personal development and a reaction to being drafted by colleagues. Their data indicate that the position as department chair lasts an average of six years before the individual either returns to the faculty or assumes another role. For those who pursued positions beyond their first role, the average was about six years in that role before returning to the faculty.

The interviews revealed a variety of experiences leading to the first administrative position. An overwhelming majority of the interviewees were not at that time actually seeking a leadership path. Two examples (paraphrased) are as follows:

- *When I received my doctorate I was asked to co-direct a research institute that provided funding to support research in my area. I found this opportunity to be beneficial for my research career but I also found that I had some ability to create a vision, develop a path to get there and convince others to follow.*
(Michael Gottfredson, whose leadership roles span more than 25 years as a vice provost, provost and then president.)

- *I had the great fortune to have early success in my research career when I published what quickly became a highly recognized book followed by string of other publications. This period allowed me to gain a full understanding of the challenges of an academic career. When I was asked to become involved and eventually take on leadership roles I felt more apt to accept given my already well-established research program.*
(David Ward, whose leadership roles span almost thirty years as dean, provost and chancellor.)

Determining the best time to take on a leadership role varies across individuals, reflecting different personal preferences. Still, the interviewees suggested that the most common reasons why individuals choose to pass on or delay a leadership opportunity include the desire to build and spend time with family and the reluctance to sacrifice a strong research program.

WHAT FEATURES CHARACTERIZE THE "RIGHT" PERSON?

Many of the interviewees had experiences similar to the two examples above. Colleagues recognize desirable characteristics in certain individuals and call on them for a leadership role as the opportunity aris-es. When contemplating whether or not to serve, it is natural for indi-viduals to ask, "Am I the right person?" The thought process invariably leads to the perennial question, "Are leaders born or made?" While there are many views on the issue, both the vast research literature on this sub-ject as well as the interviews suggest that the answer is a bit of both.[32] As summarized in Table 2.1, the initial traits that are recognized by others tend to be mostly natural or generic—these include intelligence, curios-ity, clarity, empathy, a pleasant easy-going nature, honesty, a good sense of humor and very importantly, a passion to make a difference.[33] These characteristics can serve well for the typical first administrative posi-tion, which is usually a department chair, center or program director or associate dean.

The characteristics of individuals who sustain success and move into a prolonged term or increasingly complex positions tend to be more ac-quired than natural. Running any organization effectively is a challeng-ing task. It can hardly be expected that individuals would be born with the skills necessary to do so. Critical skills here include the ability to develop and implement a vision, prioritize initiatives, make tough deci-sions, develop financial and human resource strategies, and generate ex-citement and support from others, both internally and externally. These skills can be learned and, along with already established traits, can be honed over time.

Taking on a complex leadership position entails making personal sacrifices. The first requirement is that the faculty member must be able to leave their outward ego behind. Rather than primarily con-centrating on personal success, the focus now becomes fostering and delighting in the success of others. Jack Welch often explains that ef-fective leaders possess the "generosity gene."[34] They relish and can't wait for others to succeed. They strive to ensure that each individual understands both their role in achieving the vision, and important-ly, how they personally can benefit if the organization is successful.

Individuals who possess the generosity gene have the potential to grow, excel and rise to positions of greater leadership. Jim Collins, in his book *Good to Great*, finds that great companies without exception have leaders who exhibit a combination of personal humility and personal will.[35] It is not the case that they have no ego but they deflect accolades to others and they channel their energy and ambition primarily to the organization. The more the leader places the success of others above personal success, the more others become inspired to share ideas and contribute positively to innovations.

In contrast, some individuals suffer from the "I" syndrome; they have an unquenchable desire to be recognized and take credit. Those individuals who seek primarily personal reward rarely receive the recognition they believe they deserve, nor are they likely to leave behind a lasting positive legacy. Bear Bryant, long time football coach of the University of Alabama explained the leader's role as follows:

> *"If anything goes bad, I did it.*
> *If anything goes semi-good, we did it.*
> *If anything goes really good, then you did it."*

Effective leaders monitor progress on both implementation of key actions and the development of the individuals accomplishing them. They measure their own success not primarily by the personal accolades of their journey but rather by the successes of the people they helped to develop along the way. But being supportive does not mean shying away from making tough decisions. Establishing priorities and upholding standards requires consistency and the ability to say no, especially under challenging circumstances. Good leadership only occurs when results, not effort are rewarded. Emphasizing what is important, making difficult tradeoffs and rewarding excellent performance motivates individuals to achieve their potential. The leader is watched with great scrutiny. Decision-making based on relentless adhesion to the mission establishes a clear indication of what really matters and creates a unified purpose.

TABLE 2.1 Traits of Successful Leaders

Natural	Acquired
Clarity	Ability to make tough decisions
Collegiality	Crisis management
Curiosity	Financial savvy
Empathy	Fundraising
Honesty	Human resource intelligence
Intelligence	Political savvy and sensitivity
Passion	Public relations and public speaking
Sense of humor	Strategic thinking and vision

One frequent rationale among the interviewees for accepting a leadership role was dissatisfaction with the current reality. Great leaders have a passion to change the institution and make a difference. They observe "low lying fruit" and innovations that are necessary to address critical issues but are not being implemented by current leadership. A characteristic of successful leaders is that they have the ability to look at the same data as everyone else and see something radically different. Where others see limitations and impossibilities, effective leaders see opportunity. In addition to identifying and forming the vision, effective leaders have a blend of talents that facilitate implementation of the vision. Many individuals have vision; ideas are plentiful. But as Benjamin Franklin perceived over two centuries ago, "vision without implementation is hallucination." Effective leaders recognize that others have skills that they do not possess and that successes will depend on the formation and cooperation of a team. They have the ability to motivate and excite others. They harness the best talents of all to accomplish the vision and recognize and reward effective performance.

Tradeoffs

Some of the tradeoffs associated with a leadership position, such as a decrease in the amount of time for research, teaching and life balance, are seemingly straightforward. What tends to be underestimated is the *extent* of commitment, especially if the objective is to affect lasting positive change. A major impediment is faculty culture. Imbued with a tradition of shared governance and independence, faculty members are accustomed to receiving support for their research and teaching with limited accountability. In the face of increasing global competitiveness, declining resources and evolving technologies, faculty are being asked to change rapidly and adapt to a different set of rules. To deal with the inevitable tensions, academic leaders need to devote considerable time and demonstrate ample interpersonal skill, willingness to compromise and calm persistence.

Many academic departments rotate the position of department chair, with senior faculty members serving a two or three year term. The temporary nature of the position creates the connotation among the faculty that the position is a necessary chore where everyone "takes their turn." Most faculty can do so without appreciable sacrifice in other areas. A decrease in teaching load combined with a focus on completing research in progress and collaboration with co-authors allows for continued research productivity, although often at a slower pace. Most of the individuals interviewed felt that the impact on their research was not significant during their first administrative position. Indeed, some felt they were able to continue their research throughout most of their career. Many mentioned the benefit of collaborating with co-authors and doctoral students. Ralph Hexter, Provost at the University of California Davis explained how employing a post-doc allows him to focus on the substance of his research while the post-doc works on both the substance and supporting activities. Joe Alutto, former Provost and Interim President at Ohio State maintained a productive research path while working with a highly valued co-author. Others had similar experiences but almost all felt that the ability to work at the frontier of their discipline dissipates over time the longer one remains on a leadership path.

Attempting to "make a difference," especially at higher-level positions requires a substantially higher degree of commitment. Over the past two decades, the positions of dean, provost, vice chancellor and president or chancellor have become increasingly more complex. Today, these positions combine a traditional focus on academic mission with fundraising, entrepreneurial activities, public relations, marketing and a myriad of other externally focused initiatives. Deciding to pursue a position at this level makes little sense if the individual is not fully committed to making sacrifices in other areas. There are exceptions depending on the nature of the position and the individual. Some positions can be less intense reflecting, for example, the size of the unit or the mission of the university. Some individuals, including iconic academic leaders like Richard Cyert, Howard Bowen and Clark Kerr were able to maintain active research programs throughout their career. But for most high-level positions and for most individuals some tradeoff, whether it is in research productivity, life balance or elsewhere, inevitably has to be made.

Pursuing the next level of leadership

Success at mid-level management is not always a good predictor of success at higher levels. Very few department chairs, even the most effective, make excellent presidents. The skill sets do intersect but the overlap is small because the activities are vastly different. Still, successful leaders at lower levels are naturally nominated for higher-level positions. The interviewees recognized that each higher-level position entails an increasingly complex set of responsibilities and a deeper commitment. When confronted with such an opportunity, the primary question they examined was "where can I make the greatest impact during the remainder of my career?" They realized that at a later stage in their career it would be difficult to achieve the impact and success they would have aspired to if they resumed their research program. They chose to pursue a leadership path because they believed that their ultimate contribution would be greater.

Looking back, an overwhelming majority of the interviewees felt that they had chosen the right path. They expressed a great deal of satisfaction in their leadership roles and they felt a great sense of pride in their accomplishments to affect meaningful, lasting change. Still, some leaders find the challenges of bureaucracy and faculty culture to be overly frustrating and relentless. Some agonize when things go wrong; they develop insecurities and take only modest pleasure when things go well. For these individuals, a return to the comfort of a more controllable, individually focused academic career can be very appealing. Positions as dean and especially, as president or chancellor can involve isolated, underappreciated experiences with heavy scrutiny from the academic senate, other groups on campus and the press. These higher-level positions are challenging and all-consuming. Taking such a path requires acquiring the appropriate skill set and experience, developing an intimate understanding of the external environment and analyzing carefully the issues and politics faced by the university. If the candidate is well prepared and capable, as the interviewees indicated, a leadership path can be very fulfilling. Still, there are bound to be many challenges along the way.

THE DYNAMIC OF AN ACADEMIC SEARCH PROCESS

After careful consideration, if the individual decides to pursue the next level of leadership, the first hurdle is the often confusing dynamic of an academic search process.[36] Search processes differ depending on the level of the position. An internal search for a department chair typically entails a call to the faculty for nominations followed by interviews of interested faculty, a faculty vote and a recommendation to the dean who makes the final choice. Most internal searches for associate deans and center or institute directors follow a similar pattern. External searches for dean, provost and president and sometimes directors of interdisciplinary institutes are more complex. Some dean searches, especially in the areas of law, medicine, business and engineering employ outside search firms. Searches for the position of president or chancellor and provost almost always use executive search firms.

The search firm organizes the process, solicits nominations and aides in initial screenings and due diligence. The role of the firm can range from providing minor support to essentially running the search, depending on the experience of the both the unit and the search committee chair.

The committee usually includes faculty, staff, academic senate members, students, alumni, external constituents and an individual who holds or has held a similar position. At the outset, the search committee develops the position description and establishes expectations for the responsibilities of its members. The position is announced, the description is disseminated broadly and nominations are solicited. In the first round many applicants are dismissed immediately and the committee narrows the list to about a dozen applicants. These individuals are invited for what has become known as an "airport" interview because applicants are flown in for a brief visit and airports serve as a convenient meeting place. The term "confidential" interview is also widely used as it more accurately reflects the nature of the meeting. A concerted effort is made to keep the list of candidates confidential until the top three to five finalists are determined. If the names of candidates are disclosed too early in the process, these individuals can be placed in an awkward and potentially damaging situation. Top candidates usually already hold key positions; if word gets back to their campus that they are entertaining other positions, their credibility and loyalty at home are threatened. They often decline nominations if they cannot be assured that confidentiality will be maintained until the final short list of candidates is chosen. By that time, the candidate can inform appropriate individuals and explain the situation.

The committee develops a list of questions and the same list is posed to each candidate, usually with members of the committee assigned to ask specific questions. This standardization of the interview allows easier comparison of candidate performance and traits during subsequent committee deliberations. The university and/or search firm conduct due diligence by contacting references provided by the candidate, committee members and the search firm. The candidate is typically given the opportunity to inform each of the references that the committee may reach out to them. In some cases, the candidate may request that an individual not be contacted until a later stage in the process. Again the goal is to avoid placing the candidate in a compromising position. Individuals who have worked closely with the candidate provide a valuable perspective on the effectiveness, impact and integrity of the applicant. After the airport interviews the committee shortens the list to usually three to five candidates who are then invited individually for a several day visit to the campus. Each candidate meets with relevant faculty, staff and students as well as university and external leaders. Input is then requested from all parties who have interacted with the candidates.

The search committee then identifies the finalists whose names are forwarded to the individual who has the responsibility of making the final selection. In the case of chairs, associate deans or college center directors, the final choice rests in the hands of the dean; in the case of deans, university-wide centers and higher-level positions, the final choice rests with the provost. For university presidents or chancellors, the university's governing body makes the final selection. At private universities, the governing body is generally a board of trustees; for public universities it is usually the office of the president (or chancellor) of the university system with approval by a board of regents. Rather than requesting a ranking of the finalists, some decision-makers prefer to meet with the committee and allow each member to reflect on each of the candidates.

Once the offer is made a negotiation process follows between the appropriate university official and the candidate. If the offer is accepted, the final step involves publicity. Given the current ease of distributing news rapidly via web sites and other digital media, it is critical for the chosen candidate to quickly inform the relevant parties.

NAVIGATING THE SEARCH PROCESS: THE CANDIDATE'S PERSPECTIVE

The culture and operation of a search committee can be difficult for the candidate to decipher. Committee members may view the ability to uncover and anticipate some of the key issues to be part of the candidate's "test." The process is similar to that of running for an elected political office in the sense that the committee members represent a broad spectrum of interests. The majority of the search committee is typically comprised by faculty members, many of who are disciplinary focused and determined to defend their own turf; student and alumni representatives have their own distinct agendas; and the external members on the committee are often seeking bold leadership and change. The higher the level of the position, the more disparate are the interests of the committee members and the more precarious it becomes for the candidate to openly express strong opinions. The dilemma is that with a resistant faculty culture, any candidate that too aggressively proposes the innovations necessary to address current pressures is unlikely to be chosen. To have an impact one has to be selected; to be selected one has to be pragmatic. Being politically sensitive while being honest is challenging, but skillful leaders master the ability to tell truth to power and can do so in a way that does not turn away the majority of stakeholders. The following suggestions are intended to help the candidate navigate effectively through each step of the search process.

The application process: Anyone who intends to pursue a leadership position beyond the level of an academic department can benefit from first serving on a search committee for a higher-level position. If the opportunity has not arisen, it is useful to consult with faculty members who have done so. Moreover, aspiring leaders should develop a network through attendance at conferences and involvement with national and international professional associations. This network expands opportunities both to learn about position openings and identify mentors. Seasoned mentors are critical in guiding a new candidate through a search process. Even seemingly straightforward activities like how to initiate the application process have subtle nuances. For example, some search committees tend to discount individuals who apply directly rather than being nominated by a third party. This "Groucho Marx syndrome" (why would we want to hire anyone who is *that* eager to come here?) may seem shallow but actually does have some rationale. Required broad dissemination of ads generates numerous applications, many of which are from individuals who do not meet the qualifications.

Nominations from experienced, well-respected individuals provide a credible filter and carry a heavy weight in committee deliberations. The candidate's first step in the process should be to seek advice from mentors; a supportive mentor usually offers to nominate the individual without being prompted. The candidate should provide an updated vita, the job description and cover letter that will be submitted to the search committee. Offering a few bullet points that the mentor can choose to include in the nomination letter is helpful and appreciated.

The candidate should strategically prepare the materials submitted to the committee. The vita and cover letter are critical. Documenting voluminous achievements with little connection to the position can frustrate the committee. Members are likely to conclude that the candidate either lacks an understanding of the required attributes or worse yet, doesn't possess them. The candidate should update, reorganize and edit the vita to best present the background, experience and accomplishments that are most relevant for the position. Next, cover letters that show little effort by the candidate to research the environment and gain an understanding of the position are discounted heavily. The result can be that the committee perceives a lack of sincere interest and quickly dismisses the candidate. To best deliver an impactful message, the candidate's cover letter should:

* Express that it is an honor to be nominated and considered;
* Show respect and admiration for the institution and unit;
* Humbly explain accomplishments;
* Demonstrate a careful examination of the position, environment and status of the unit and institution;
* Explain at a high level how their background, experience and personal situation match both the needs of the institution and a personal career path.

The candidate's cover letter should **not**:

* Overuse "I";
* Take too much personal credit for accomplishments;
* Provide detailed solutions to issues at the recruiting institution;
* Be overly verbose.

<u>Preparing for the confidential "airport" interview:</u> Preparing for the confidential interview would seem to be fairly straightforward. Still, given the diverse composition of the committee and the complex issues in the current environment, the individual should carefully study and understand the dynamic of the interview. Anyone who has served on a number of search committees has almost certainly witnessed candidates who commit "interview suicide" primarily due to lack of appropriate preparation. Helpful steps include researching the background of the committee members, developing an understanding of the external environment, the unit and university, identifying the questions that are likely to be posed, and preparing succinct, but substantive and politically sensitive responses.

The search committee chair typically offers an opportunity for a conversation before the interview. Other committee members may also contact the candidate. It is generally not a good idea for the candidate to make unsolicited calls or contacts with the members. Consulting with colleagues who have experienced this type of process can be helpful, but the candidate should be careful not to place too much weight on comments concerning specific aspects of what the committee may be seeking. The strategy and intent of the committee and university leadership are held close to the vest; only generic updates are provided publicly. Someone who is not on the committee can lead the candidate astray.

The candidate should visualize the desired end result of the interview; what image and key takeaways would the individual like to establish in the eyes of the search committee? At a high level, a search committee tends to assess whether or not the candidate possesses the following qualities:

1. Vision, passion and creativity;
2. A keen sense of the external environment, the issues facing the university and what the position entails;
3. The ability to excel in the role;
4. Political savvy;
5. Energy and a results driven orientation;
6. A caring, supportive attitude toward people;
7. The ability to multi-task but delegate; and
8. A relaxed, confident attitude.

The confidential interview is usually scheduled for about two hours. It often begins with a request for the candidate to make an opening statement. Next, a carefully structured list of questions is posed; usually questions are rotated around the table to allow each member to have a somewhat one-on-one interaction with the candidate. Most committees share the questions with the candidates prior to the visit. The interview typically concludes with the candidate being asked if there are any questions for the committee.

Typical interview questions include:

1. Our strategic plan calls for the following: (one or two themes are highlighted.) How would you proceed to ensure that this vision is attained? Or more generally, "What is your vision for the school, college or university." What are the most critical factors in the external environment that can impact our strategy? (The discussion about vision, mission, strategy and implementation can be expressed in two or three questions, which can consume a good portion of the meeting.)
2. In your view what are our major strengths?
3. In your view, where do the major challenges lie in achieving our vision?

4. What is your view on interdisciplinary work? How have you fostered collaboration across departments and colleges? Describe one or more specific interdisciplinary initiatives in which you have played a major role.

5. What experience have you had with programs and initiatives to encourage diversity? What programs do you think would work here?

6. Describe your leadership style. What do you consider to be your strengths? What areas do you feel you could improve?

7. Describe one major initiative you led that you view as a major success. Also describe one initiative that did not go as well as you would have liked. What are the major lessons you took away from these experiences?

8. Describe your experience with overseeing complex budgets and devising a financial strategy.

9. Describe your experience working with external constituents including alumni, the broader community and the media.

10. Describe your experience with development. What is your approach to fundraising and how successful do you feel you have been?

11. Do you have any questions that you would like to ask us?

<u>During the confidential interview</u>: The candidate should recognize that actions are being observed carefully even upon entering the room. Candidates who walk around the room, shake hands and engage each member personally immediately establish a rapport. In turn, the candidate should observe the committee members, especially paying careful attention to body language when responding to questions. Some candidates almost immediately commit "interview suicide." The usual cause is a long, meandering opening statement that reflects poor judgment with some combination of too much bravado, too little enthusiasm and a general lack of preparation. When this happens, the resulting dynamic is acutely

noticeable. Committee members begin to fidget; they simplify their questions and they avoid follow up discussion in an attempt to graciously end the interview as quickly as possible.

If the candidate senses a loss of interest, one strategy is to attempt to win back the committee's attention by recognizing the faux pas. Apologizing, perhaps in a semi-humorous way, for the overanxious response and then promising a return to a more normal style of brevity with substance can hopefully restore the pace of the interview. Better yet, the candidate should understand the causes of interview suicide and avoid them from the outset. The list below identifies both some pitfalls that can cause a poor interview and some pointers that can aide the effectiveness of the interaction.

INTERVIEW PITFALLS

1. A long-winded, meandering opening statement and/or heavily detailed responses to questions;
2. The "I" syndrome and too much bravado;
3. Lack of knowledge of major strengths and general attributes of the university and unit;
4. Not knowing the members of the search committee;
5. Lackluster attitude;
6. Not demonstrating a sincere interest in the position; and
7. Too aggressively offering opinions and solutions, especially before all the facts are known.

INTERVIEW POSITIVES

1. Brevity with substance;
2. A high degree of confidence without excessive bravado;
3. A lively, gracious personality with an intelligent sense of humor;

4. Demonstration of serious preparation combined with thoughtful spontaneous comments;
5. An understanding of the strengths of the university and unit;
6. A genuine passion for the vision and potential of the unit; and
7. An affinity for working with students, alumni, faculty, staff, donors and the broader community.
8. Personalization of the process by referring to each committee member by name and mentioning their work or background if relevant in answering questions; and
9. A politically sensitive but informative discussion of the issues facing higher education and how they apply to this school, college or university.

As described above, the higher the level of the position, the more diverse are constituent groups and the more important it becomes to be politically sensitive when expressing strong opinions. While the candidate should honestly discuss personal beliefs and values, expressing opinions too strongly can create unnecessary opposition. The candidate should prepare responses to expected questions to provide substantive comments in a logical, strategic way. It is useful to frame the issues from a broad perspective without identifying specific actions. Candidates rarely have sufficient information to delineate a detailed plan; it is usually best to admit this reality as a way to buffer responses to questions asking for such detail.

Example: Being honest but pragmatic

A search committee that is seeking a new president at a research-intense university is likely to pose a question along the following lines: With a reduced taxpayer subsidy, especially for federally funded research grants, the university needs to decide which areas will continue to be supported and which will need to reduce their scope. From what you know about our university which areas do you think we should prioritize?

Response from candidate A (forceful and direct): The reality is that very few research universities can continue to provide the level of support for research they provided even a decade ago. As president I will oversee a process to decide which areas to cut and which to continue to support. Obviously, the research being done at this university has been very successful and we need to find funds to ensure its continued success. One way to do so is to identify the areas that have been less productive and lower their support for faculty and infrastructure.

Response from candidate B (action oriented but politically sensitive): The truth is I do not yet have enough information to answer that question. I need to learn a lot more and listen to a cross section of individuals on this campus and in this community to gain more insight on what this university is now, what it wants to be and what it could be. Don't get me wrong; the reality is that very few research universities can continue to provide the level of support for research as they did even a decade ago. Scope is a big issue. Priorities have to be set and tough decisions have to be made. But, I have no preconceived notion of what the outcome of these decisions will be. We will determine the future of this university together through a transparent process with excellent governance and oversight.

The goals of both candidates' plans are similar but the search committee is unlikely to provide the opportunity for candidate A to achieve them. After the confidential interview, the search committee identifies a short list of candidates who are invited individually for a campus visit. The groups involved can include (a) faculty, students and staff in the potential department home of the candidate, (b) administrators in similar positions across the university and others who interact with the person in this position, (c) external constituents including alumni, donors and university board members, and (d) the person to whom the position reports. The preparation for and lessons learned from the airport interview provide valuable input for much of the interaction on the campus visit.

THE NEGOTIATION PROCESS

<u>Salary and compensation packages</u>: Most of the seasoned leaders who were interviewed indicated that salary was not the top priority nor was it a stumbling block during the negotiation processes that they experienced. The university identifies the normal range for the position, the candidate researches salaries for similar positions and a comparison is made to the candidate's current income. Based on this data, an agreement is reached. The overall package can also include moving costs, research support, a housing allowance, a compensating factor if retirement benefits are being sacrificed at the current institution, and if relevant, football, basketball or other sporting activity season's tickets. A critical component of the package is the support provided upon leaving the position. If the term is five years, it is reasonable to request at least a half-year sabbatical. After seven or more years, a full year is typical. In either case, even after the conclusion of the sabbatical both additional financial and time support can be appropriate. Reduced teaching and a research fund provide an opportunity for the leader who has now returned to the faculty to rebuild a research program. Also, there should be an agreement about the faculty salary that will be in effect once the administrative salary is no longer relevant.

<u>Support for the unit</u>: For deans and chairs, the most critical factor in establishing credibility with constituents at a new institution relates to the outcome of the negotiation process for the unit. Faculty and staff expect new leadership to garner additional resources. Suboptimal negotiation outcomes can be detrimental to morale and undermine even the most visionary plans. Poor results can occur for a variety of reasons including bad timing, negotiating for the wrong items and miscommunication concerning the details of the commitment.

The candidate's negotiation leverage is greatest during the recruiting process. Once the offer is accepted the urgency vanishes for the administration to react in a timely and meaningful way. Identifying the highest priority items can be a difficult exercise, especially for an external candidate. Consulting with the incumbent and other senior leaders is critical. It can be especially important to prioritize requests not only by the unit's greatest needs but also by the greatest difficulty in obtaining approval within the normal bureaucratic process. The recruiting period may be the only time to obtain timely consent for highly valued initiatives that at other times would end up buried in multiple layers of a bureaucratic approval process. Examples of items that could be on this list include new senior or chaired faculty positions and corresponding start up packages, revenue splits or allocations for existing or developing programs and space.

Finally, and perhaps most significant, any commitments made during the negotiation process should be confirmed in writing. A well-known warning, attributed to Samuel Goldwyn, is that "a verbal contract isn't worth the paper it is written on." Still, in the excitement of taking on a new role, it is easy to see why details of commitments can be lost in conversation.

WHAT TO EXPECT: THE PHASES OF AN ACADEMIC LEADERSHIP POSITION

The interviewees discussed how the perspective of their position and performance evolved over time as they adjusted to constituent inputs and a changing internal and external environment. Their reflections describe a typical cycle, shown in Figure 2.1, with several phases that are common in the experiences of many leaders. Understanding the implications of these phases becomes more critical as the complexity and scope of responsibilities expands; still it is useful to discuss them before taking on the first higher-level position. The following sets a foundation for the discussion of the dynamics of leadership positions throughout the book.

Naiveté: Naiveté is a powerful force for leading change. Frequently, research breakthroughs in one discipline are driven by faculty members from another discipline who are not constrained by embedded thought processes and paradigms. The same is true of leadership. The longer one is in office the more one recognizes and learns about the obstacles that can thwart major change. New leaders who have a powerful vision and do not see constraints can often accomplish initiatives that others previously argued could not be done.

<u>Honeymoon</u>: Naiveté is usually accompanied by a honeymoon period during which individuals who helped recruit the leader combine with fervent institutional patrons to offer support. The honeymoon phase is usually longer for an external rather than an internal candidate. Internal candidates have baggage; the faculty has preconceived notions of their strengths and weaknesses. In either case, if major initiatives remain unaccomplished during the honeymoon phase it may be difficult to have an overall significant impact. The ability to affect major change can wane over time. Effective leadership requires setting priorities and sometimes saying no to individuals whose ideas have merit but do not add sufficient value to the mission. Over time, resistance naturally builds from those who have not felt supported; for some leaders the longer is their time in office, the greater is the resistance to change.

FIGURE 2.1 Phases of Academic Leadership

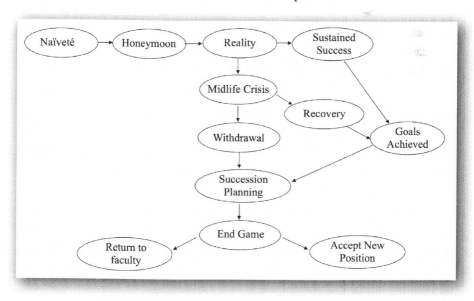

<u>Reality</u>: Successful leaders recognize that they need to move quickly but carefully on significant issues early in their tenure. They understand the need to produce visible results. Highly recognized successes during the honeymoon phase are critical to not only accomplish a vision but also to sustain support through rough patches that may develop during the later stages in office. During the first few months, the new leader should listen carefully to as many constituents as practically possible. While allowing others to do most of the talking, effective leaders plant seeds, enlist support and empower a strong enough team to help implement the new paradigm. They create a sense of urgency that motivates individuals to seek and accept change. They publicly recognize others for results that add value to achieving the vision. Several interviewees suggested that one indicator of success is the extent to which others take ownership of the leader's initiatives and describe and support them as if the ideas were their own.

<u>Mid-life crisis or "What can go wrong?"</u> A new leader's first year is often characterized by a sense of euphoria due to a mix of naiveté and support through the honeymoon phase. During the following years the initial euphoria wanes. Years three and four provide a critical test; once the honeymoon is over, is the organization still behind the leader? If not, leaders can sometimes suffer through a mid-life crisis where mounting challenges take a significant toll and former cooperative supporters become harder to find. This pattern is especially likely if the new leader has not taken advantage of the honeymoon period to achieve early successes.

Even highly capable individuals can falter for a variety of reasons. Some situations are unavoidable due to environmental factors; others are self-made. Recent funding downturns driven by external factors can adversely affect any administration. Political challenges can develop that are embedded from previous administrations. If the prior leader had a prolonged, successful tenure and especially if the individual is still present and intrusive, even a deeply passionate, talented new leader can have limited ability to affect change.

EXAMPLES: THE CHALLENGE OF FOLLOWING A LONG-STANDING LEADER.

A successful dean at a large public university stepped down after over 25 years in office. In his last few years he had become more and more dictatorial trying to preserve all he had done in spite of criticism from those who felt the need for change. When he was finally convinced to retire, he chose an office directly across from the new dean's office and was constantly offering advice and defending his previous decisions. This behavior played a significant role in the short tenure of the next two deans. The loss in progress for the school was significant, especially as this occurred during a period of ample funding and fundraising in the area at this and most other universities.

• • •

Rosemarie Nassif in her first presidency, followed a president who had held the office for over twenty years. Supporters of the former president continued to serve in various positions during her tenure. She readily admitted that as a new president, she had much to learn, which in some ways allowed an already complex and challenging dynamic to gain more power. Eventually, she felt that there were too many barriers for her to lead significant progress and she decided to re-boot in a new environment. She accepting a position as President of Holy Names College, where she enjoyed a long tenure and was able to exert a lasting positive impact. Her first presidency served as a learning experience that helped her to flourish in a different setting.

• • •

As the above two examples indicate, it can be difficult to follow a long-standing leader. In some cases, the best strategy for the individual can be to seek a different opportunity elsewhere. From the standpoint of the institution, although the tenure of the immediate successor is often short term, this period can be a necessary step that allows for the transition to the next longer lasting period of leadership. Challenges can also develop if the next layer of university leadership changes early in a new leader's tenure. Negotiations and commitments may not survive as the priorities of new university leaders shift. In addition, self-made problems can develop due to a variety of factors including (a) an overly ambitious plan that attempts too much too soon; (b) frequent reference by the new leader to the way "it" was done at the former institution; and (c) poor negotiations during the recruiting process. If the new leader is too aggressive without taking sufficient time to actively listen and gain the support of key constituents, overall enthusiasm can quickly wane. As a mentor of one of the interviewee's wisely advised, "never let your vision outpace your relationships." Finally, when the new leader frequently implies that their former institution "had a better way," the main impact is to demoralize the staff and faculty. No one wants to repeatedly hear that their university and methods are inferior.

Withdrawal: It is not always easy to identify that a mid-life crisis is occurring. While it is important for leaders to have an accurate assessment of both their performance and how others perceive them, many individuals are reluctant to perform the assessments necessary to do so. Universities typically conduct a five-year review of key administrators but much can happen in five years. There are observable symptoms of underlying stress. Everyone naturally gravitates toward activities they enjoy and avoids tasks that are not pleasurable. Individuals suffering through a mid-life crisis tend to withdraw. Either they choose to work more often at home or they travel frequently. They find that the more distant they are from the office, the easier it is to gain acceptance. It is less difficult to please alumni, donors or conference participants away from home than it is to deal with challenging issues on campus. When a leader is more absent than present, in all likelihood something is amiss.

<u>Recovery</u>: Is it possible to recover from a mid-life crisis? Most of the interviewees indicated that they endured rough patches and were able to recover and continue with a successful term in office. A key step is to form an inner advisory group, a "kitchen cabinet," with influential constituents. Openness and honesty, not only with the inner group but also with all constituents are critical factors in rebuilding confidence. Frank conversations can elicit support; the kitchen cabinet can help form pragmatic solutions to address problem areas while providing overall guidance. A few meaningful successes combined with transparency are significant steps that can help restore a positive atmosphere.

<u>Sustained success</u>: Many leaders achieve a sustained term in office with few mishaps along the way. They key question is whether or not they have been successful. Some leaders implicitly define success as survival; their main motivation is to remain in the position and do no damage. They believe that they can do so by always attempting to achieve consensus. They painstakingly gather the viewpoints of all constituents and then act on initiatives in a way that will upset the fewest individuals. While this strategy may be comfortable for the individual, it is rarely good for the institution. Significant achievement requires substantive change. A natural resistance to change means that achieving consensus leads to maintenance of the status quo. As an example, two of the most significant challenges facing universities today are declining public support and emerging technologies. Plausible reactions include increased faculty accountability and workload with required course redesign in a new technological framework. It is highly likely that many faculty and staff will resist these changes. Achieving consensus is this environment can result in serious competitive decline.

Effective academic leaders strive for alignment, not consensus. Affecting significant change in any organization is a time consuming and highly complex activity, but it is even more so in the face of a resistant system of faculty governance. Politically adept strategies require ample thought, considerable personal involvement on the part of the leader and solid support from a core of key constituents. Alignment rather than consensus implies that some opposition will continue even after significant initiatives are achieved. Moreover, the need to prioritize activities implies saying no to individuals whose ideas may have merit but are not adopted because they do not add sufficient value. These consequences of effective leadership are not comfortable for many individuals. Over time, resistance can build. Even visionary leaders can sometimes find themselves on a razor's edge between supporters and detractors. As the interviewees indicated, the higher the level of the position, the more lonely and isolated it can become. Still, the ultimate goal should be to make a significant difference that has lasting positive impact; the path to achieve this impact entails establishing priorities and making difficult decisions. A key measure of success is how effective the leader is in doing so.

Succession planning: One of the idiosyncrasies of academic institutions is that the incumbent plays only a minor role in aiding the university to identify and select the next leader. Frequently, the custom in business is that the current CEO can groom internal candidates and provide significant input to the choice of a successor. In contrast, the incumbent university administrator is generally discouraged or even forbidden to take too active a role in the search process. Still, all leaders have a responsibility to identify and develop appropriate individuals for leadership roles, even though they may not be grooming the person to take over their position.

End game: A now famous story about "the three letters" provides some insight concerning the sometimes difficult decision concerning when to step down. On the first day in office a new dean found three numbered envelopes from the former dean with instructions to open the envelopes in sequence when the new dean experienced the first, second and third crisis. When the first crisis occurred, the dean opened the first letter, which read: "Blame me. Tell everyone that I left you with this situation and that you will address the issues. The dean followed the advice and things went well. After the second crisis, the dean opened the next letter and it read:

"Take the blame up front. Tell everyone that the situation is your fault and you will do your best to minimize the damage." Again, the advice was prudent and succeeded when put into action. Finally, after the third crisis, the dean opened the final letter, which read: "Write three letters."

One takeaway from the above story is that when things are going poorly, there are limits to the controversy that any leader can or should endure. Sometimes even the best of individuals can get caught in an untenable situation that can shorten the tenure in office. Unanticipated significant budget cuts, a change in higher-level leadership or other external factors over which the individual has little control can diminish the probability of success for any leader. If that is the case and if there is little hope to change the course, the individual should seriously consider stepping down. The longer that negative elements are allowed to dwell, the more they will grow and the more antagonistic the environment will become. Oliver Cromwell's purported statement to Parliament in 1653 captures how resentment builds if unwelcomed leaders linger in office too long: "You have sat here too long for any good that you have been doing. Depart I say and let us have done with you. In the name of God, go!" No one should reach that point.

Even when the individual is successful, an overly long tenure in office is not healthy for either the individual or the institution. While there are examples of long-term effective academic leaders, this scenario is not the norm. One of the interviewees related a conversation that occurred between him and the president of the university after he had just accepted an offer as dean. The president asked how long the individual wanted to hold the position. He responded "anywhere from ten minutes to ten years." If it isn't working, then why stay on, especially if there is an option to return to the faculty. At the other extreme, some individuals who achieve early successes stay in office too long. One danger is that the individual's identity primarily derives from holding the position. The individual may possess limited alternative career options and perceives that there is little hope to continue a professional life in a respected way without the title. If staying in office becomes the leader's primary goal, avoidance of controversial issues becomes a key objective. The ability to negotiate on behalf of the unit dwindles. Innovation is lost and the institution suffers.

For many leaders, the effectiveness of the time in office follows a concave function with successes accelerating initially and then slowing over time as a natural resistance to change develops and honeymoon support wanes. Too long a tenure can result in stagnation. While ten years may not be appropriate in all situations, the point is that whether things are going poorly or superbly there is a "right time" to step down. Others should be allowed to come forward with a renewed energy, a new set of ideas and very importantly the naiveté to attempt what can no longer be done in the current administration.

What is the usual path followed by effective leaders? After considerable consultation, they quickly develop a strategic plan with clearly articulated goals, a time line for achieving those goals and a sustainable financial model. They create a sense of urgency, empower a carefully chosen group to carry forward the vision, affect short-term meaningful results and systematically communicate and recognize the efforts of those who have played critical roles. After a significant portion of the plan is accomplished, the decision is made to either initiate another strategic burst or to discuss a process for stepping down with the administration.

How should one behave when the time comes to step down? After a public announcement is made, the leader has limited authority. Constituents now recognize the short time remaining in office and they are not willing to exert the effort and resources to support initiatives that have an uncertain future. It is healthy to have a quick turnover to new leadership. The incumbent leader can lose focus on the current agenda and naturally turn to future considerations and next career steps. Other than a few transitional meetings, the former leader should "get out of Dodge fast." After all, how can the new leader develop a different vision that may dramatically change existing priorities if the former leader is still sitting at the table?

A valued role for the former leader is to be available but not visible once new leadership is in place. Effective leaders understand the wealth of knowledge possessed by the former administration. Joe Alutto, a seasoned leader as Dean, Provost and Interim President at Ohio State University observed that too often new leaders fail to learn from those who previously held the position. Sometimes ego gets in the way; they don't want to be seen as weak by asking for advice. In contrast, the most successful leaders recognize the value in seeking out guidance, advice and most of all, nuance. Both the new and former leader understand that their conversations are infrequent and not highly visible. New leaders must be seen as in charge. They should forge a new path, one that builds on but is not constrained by the past. As successful leaders step down, they recognize that many of their initiatives will not last forever. As the environment changes, modifying past strategies and forming new ones are critical steps for sustaining success.

Summary and Conclusions

It is not an easy decision for a successful faculty member to abandon, at least partially, a research, teaching or clinical career path to pursue a leadership position. Anyone considering a leadership role should first and foremost have a passion to make a difference. But to do so the individual should also be willing to

- Obtain the business acumen and skills necessary to address critical issues in the current environment;
- Set priorities and make difficult decisions;
- Subdue their own ego for the sake of the greater good;
- Delight in rewarding and recognizing others;
- Put themselves at risk;
- Actively listen to ideas and learn from constructive criticism;
- Hire the best talent and build on the strengths of others;
- Take responsibility, especially when others cast blame; and
- Give lower priority to their former activities in research, teaching or practice to take on the challenges and issues of the institution.

Leadership positions can involve significant personal tradeoffs. The amount and flexibility of time are widely recognized as key factors. Still, the tendency is to underestimate the extent of each that is necessary, especially if the goal is to truly make a difference. The higher the level of the position, the more significant and the more permanent is the commitment to a leadership role. Most of the interviewees indicated that there was a time in their career when they reached "a point of no return" where resuming their former level of prominence in research or clinical practice would have been extremely difficult.

Looking back, the majority of the interviewees were highly satisfied with the path they had chosen. They felt they grew significantly, both professionally and personally in each position. Still, they cautioned that high-level positions, such as dean, provost and president can be all consuming and relentlessly challenging. Successful department chairs should not assume that the skills and leadership style that served them well in their current role are sufficient to address the multitude of confounding issues at higher levels of leadership. Today's leader must possess a blend of academic prowess, business acumen and political savvy combined with a passion to implement significant change. Leaders must also be prepared for constant scrutiny from the press, student groups, the academic senate and others.

While the interviewees recommended that gifted faculty members consider a leadership path, they also provided a realistic assessment of the personal toll implied by the challenges ahead. An external environment demanding change and an internal environment resisting it can lead to a frustrating, underappreciated existence. Academic leadership involves a higher degree of persuasion than leadership positions in other organizations. Faculty members usually do not want to be led. Many are argumentative, assertive, and convinced of their own intellectual superiority. Saying no to a renowned academic who may have little respect for the leader is challenging. A strategy that identifies priorities with focused and measurable actions and outcomes is essential to allow the leader to be guided by the plan and not by personalities.

Leadership is not for everyone; indeed, any academic seasoned leader has witnessed others who attempted leadership roles but ultimately decided, with relief, to return to a faculty position. Still, those who relish taking on challenging situations and working to forge creative solutions are likely to succeed and have a long-lasting positive impact. The interviewees expressed great pride in their impact on the institutions they served and even more importantly, on the people they have helped along the way.

Key Takeaways: Chapter 2

Leadership

* Successful leaders look at the same data as everyone else and see something radically different. Where others see limitations and impossibilities, they see opportunity.
* Great leaders measure their success not by personal accolades but rather by the successes of the people they helped to develop and grow along the way.
* "Vision without implementation is hallucination." (Benjamin Franklin)
* An external environment demanding change and an internal environment resisting it can lead to a frustrating, underappreciated existence.

The Search Process

* The dilemma is that with a resistant faculty culture, any candidate that too aggressively proposes to implement the changes necessary is unlikely to be chosen.
* Being politically sensitive during the interview process while being honest is challenging, but skillful leaders can tell truth to power in such a way as to not turn away the majority of their constituents.
* Top external candidates often decline nominations if they cannot be assured that confidentiality will be maintained until the final short list of candidates is chosen.
* Documenting voluminous achievements that have little relevance can cause the committee to conclude that the candidate either didn't consider the required attributes or worse yet, doesn't possess them.

* Some candidates almost immediately commit "interview suicide" by opening with a long, meandering statement that reflects poor judgment, too much bravado, and a lack of preparation.
* Negotiation leverage is greatest during the recruiting process. Prioritize requests not only by the unit's greatest needs but also by the greatest difficulty in obtaining approval within the normal bureaucratic process.

PHASES OF LEADERSHIP

* Naiveté is a powerful force for leading change. New leaders who are not constrained by embedded thought processes and paradigms can accomplish what others previously argued could not be done.
* One indicator of success is the extent to which others take ownership of the new leader's initiatives and support them as if the ideas were their own.
* Resistance to change means that achieving consensus leads to maintenance of the status quo. Effective leaders strive for alignment, not consensus.
* If staying in office is the leader's primary goal, avoidance of controversy is a key objective. The ability to negotiate on behalf of the unit dwindles. Innovation is lost and the institution suffers.
* A valued role for the former leader is to be available but not visible. The new leader should forge a new path; one that builds on but is not constrained by the past.
* When successful leaders step down, they recognize that many of their initiatives will not last forever. As the environment changes, modifying past strategies and forming new ones are critical steps for sustaining success.

CHAPTER 3

Vision, Mission, Strategy and Financial Sustainability

• • •

The greater danger lies not in setting our aim too high and falling
short, but in setting our aim too low and achieving our marks.

—MICHAELANGELO

INTRODUCTION

WHEN A FACULTY MEMBER MOVES into a leadership role, strategic planning is often neither a high priority nor a welcomed idea. A new leader usually has little experience in formulating strategy and may doubt the benefit of such an exercise. Moreover, the leader's desire to gain favor makes it challenging to engage in a process that many faculty feel has little value. Rewarded primarily for research and teaching, most faculty view strategic planning as a poor use of time with long, poorly organized meetings, endless distribution of materials and little follow through to invoke meaningful change. Indeed, the danger of initiating a process is that what the faculty fears actually occurs. Poor implementation can cause even passionate individuals to become disinterested or even cynical; the damage that results cannot easily be undone. Still, successfully competing in today's turbulent environment requires a bold action that many universities have yet to take: the development of a distinctive vision and mission with a financially sustainable strategic plan. Doing so effectively requires an engaged faculty.

The purpose of this chapter is to first explain the importance of strategic planning and then to provide a framework that allows the academic leader to successfully engage all participants in a meaningful process. A university-wide exercise is developed that allows each area to articulate its strategy, assess its current status and describe its aspiration. An example is presented that explains how a typical academic department can shape its vision, mission and strategy in this context. Finally, some conclusions are drawn.

WHY UNIVERSITIES NEED STRATEGIC PLANNING

Strategically identifying both priorities and realistic funding sources is especially critical during periods of financial stress. Many universities have reacted to the changing financial paradigm, not by focusing on efforts to become financially more self-reliant, but rather by increasing politically charged lobbying efforts. These efforts, which attempt to convince state legislatures and the federal government to restore lost funding, have fallen mostly on deaf ears. Why? There are many demands on scarce resources; allocations need to be based on analysis of the value of alternative uses of funds. Taxpayers, through decreased public funding are signaling that they value other initiatives above higher education. Universities need to accept the reality that public funding has permanently fallen. They should devote less effort to lobbying and more to developing a distinct, financially sustainable mission that is aligned with the needs of their constituents. Universities need to demonstrate that they are part of the solution, not part of the problem.

A lack of strategic thinking is readily apparent at most universities. Too little attention is given to basic issues like which initiatives should be prioritized, who the university should serve, how outcomes should be measured and how or, or even worse if, the necessary funding can be obtained. One consequence is that universities devote too little effort to explaining what they do, how well they do it and why what they do matters. Constituents who are asked to fund the university's activities demand and deserve accountability; they need to know both how their resources are being deployed and the impact of the activities they fund. Legislators seek initiatives that result in the most effective use of taxpayer funds; donors search for opportunities where their contributions can have the greatest impact; and students seek universities that provide the best return on their tuition dollars. These groups have choices and can take their support and tuition dollars elsewhere. A lack of strategic planning not only limits the effectiveness and potential value that a university can attain, it also puts the university's current support at risk.

This following analysis describes a framework that an academic leader can apply to the development of a vision, mission, positioning statement and financial strategy.[37] The intent is not to provide a comprehensive examination of strategic planning. A vast literature lays this foundation with ample application for strategy formation and implementation.[38] Rather, the focus here is on developing a strategy that addresses the turbulent forces facing higher education. Not all universities can or should respond to these forces in the same way. The underlying commonality is that the financial paradigm has changed drastically and a university's vision should reflect both individual and societal priorities in a sufficiently compelling way to induce constituents to provide funding for its activities.

A critical challenge for academic leaders is to maintain support from key constituents during a transition to financial self-reliance. In the process developed here, the leader provides an opportunity for every academic area to aspire to any level of quality it chooses. But, financial realities must be recognized. Each area presents its strategy, impact and quality along with a financial plan explaining how it intends to fund its proposed activities. All relevant constituents examine each plan and prioritize activities based on quality assessments and budgetary constraints. It is likely that some areas are not able to self-fund the proposed activities and need to request a subsidy. The academic leader should, ex-ante, work with the faculty to establish decision-making rules to prioritize which areas to subsidize. A basic tenet for any prioritization should be that if collectively, students, donors, taxpayers, external granting agencies and other academic areas via subsidy are not willing to fund the proposed activities, then society is indicating that it values other activities more highly. In this case, the affected areas need to either alter their plan to be less ambitious or ask whether the activity is worth continuing at any level.

The need to prioritize is being resisted strongly by those academic areas that are least able to attract constituents who are willing to fund their activities. But as Meredith Michaels, Chief Financial Officer at UC Irvine aptly observed, "most universities can do almost anything, but they cannot do everything." Prioritization is a necessity. In areas where there is little demand for what is being offered, external factors are forcing a decline in their resource base. In other areas where there is sufficient demand, sometimes a complacency or hostility to a market-based approach obstructs the area from building a supporting constituency. In this case, the eventuality of a declining resource base is a self-inflicted wound.

DEVELOPING A DISTINCTIVE VISION: THE ROLE OF THE ACADEMIC LEADER

One of the primary responsibilities of an academic leader is to define reality. The best way to do so is to engage faculty, students, staff and external constituents in discussions concerning the current environment, while building the case for an urgent need for action. All constituents should understand the critical need for the university to develop and implement a financially sustainable strategic plan that addresses societal needs. Key steps are to first convincingly communicate the value of the exercise and then to maintain involvement of all constituents throughout the process. Transparency of measures and decision rules with concrete actions and results are necessary ingredients for success. A strategic planning process is not without its challenges and some leaders may decide that the cost is too high. Those individuals who view their role as "taking their turn" may choose not to endure the time commitment and stress associated with the difficult choices that need to be made. After all, prioritizing some areas means other areas will be supported at lower levels. Undoubtedly, not all parties will be satisfied and tensions will develop. In spite of these challenges, those leaders whose ambition is to leave a lasting, positive impact embrace strategic planning as a productive and beneficial tool for invoking meaningful change.

One way to explain the value of strategic planning is to recognize the damage that can occur in its absence. Most universities do have articulate, well-intentioned mission and vision statements but they primarily are a set of aspirational bullets, giving the impression that the university serves every constituency and seeks to be truly distinguished in everything it does.[39] This idealistic rhetoric is characteristic of organizations that lack a rigorous strategic planning process. With little guidance on what the university should prioritize and, just as importantly, on what the university should not do, poor resource allocation decisions are made. Especially damaging effects occur during periods of budget shortfalls when with few agreed upon priorities, universities continue to subsidize activities that are not highly valued by students, donors or others. The resources to do so derive primarily from more productive, higher quality areas. Over time, this misallocation of resources eats away at the excellence of the university.

Examples: The dangers of non-strategic thinking

One of the interviewees from a large public research university described the following scenario, which occurred after he stepped down from a leadership position and returned to the faculty. At the first faculty meeting he attended, the agenda included deciding how many doctoral students to admit for the next fall. A long discussion ensued on whether the department should admit 12 or 14 students. The arguments made for a larger versus smaller entering class were mostly ethereal points about the critical nature of the research in certain areas and how important it was to train more faculty in those areas. The discussion continued on with no apparent resolution in sight.

After "biting his tongue" for an hour or so, the former leader politely apologized that he did not know some of the basic performance data for the program. He asked what percent of the students in the program completed their doctorate over the last five years and where they had been placed. The response came in dribs and drabs with stories about individual students. No one had a complete picture. He then asked how many doctoral students were currently enrolled and how they were dispersed across years in the program. Once again, no one knew the overall picture. He also wondered whether some faculty members were chairing numerous dissertation committees, and if so, perhaps the department should not accept additional students in overburdened areas. Again there was no real response. He continued with a question about the average time students were taking to complete the degree. No surprise, no one really knew. And finally, he inquired whether the department could fund 14 students, or for that matter, if there were sufficient funds for 12 students. Not to worry, he was told; whatever the department decided, the chair would go to the dean and they would somehow find the money.

This lack of strategic thinking in departments hinders the overall performance of the university. The following similar discussion was described by another interviewee who also held a leadership position at a large research intense university. At a meeting of the academic council, attended by the deans and chaired by the provost, the graduate school dean led a discussion of how financial aid and research and teaching assistants would be allocated across departments. The materials distributed for the meeting included a table of data from doctoral programs across the university. While the focus of the graduate dean was on financial support, one of the deans noticed that the data included time to degree. He inquired whether the data for the History Department, which had an average time to degree of ten years, was accurate. The response was that it was indeed correct and that the faculty in that area believes that everyone who enters the program should complete the doctorate no matter how long it takes.

A vigorous discussion ensued concerning the cost implications and whether it was in the best interest of the students to be allowed to linger in the program for so long. Other departments with a long time to degree were also scrutinized. The main issue concerned whether students are being served well if few constraints are placed on their progress while they continue to receive financial support throughout the program. A major reason for a long time to degree is a lack of sufficient placement opportunities. Is it appropriate for the university to accept students into a doctoral program in areas where it is known that there are few job prospects? If support is provided for students in areas where there is oversupply, these resources are being denied to other areas where there is a greater need and opportunities are more plentiful.

The above scenario occurred during a period of budget cuts; the financial stress caused the group to think more strategically. Over the next six months, the university established time to degree guidelines in each area and restricted both financial aid and subsidized graduate student housing beyond the normal time to degree. At a subsequent meeting, the dean of Humanities, a historian, requested that no additional doctoral support be given to the History Department until the current oversupply of students achieved a higher degree of placement success. The dean openly agreed that it was both unethical and too costly to enter new students who after ten years of study were likely to still have limited job prospects.

The above examples provide just a glimpse of the misallocations that arise in the absence of both strategic planning and transparent metrics to track progress. At a large comprehensive university, many such examples exist. Misallocations within departments can aggregate to exert a substantial negative impact on the quality of the university as a whole.

GUIDING PRINCIPLES IN A STRATEGIC PLANNING PROCESS

<u>Engaging the faculty</u>: In a recent conversation with a senior faculty member, he lamented that it used to be the case that society valued higher education. He yearned for "the good old days" when people recognized the broadly shared benefits that universities provide. Now, he argued, "they" don't allocate sufficient funding; they think that the return to the student is sufficient and the student should pay. These comments were a bit surprising, as they were made by a highly recognized researcher who had previously shown little interest in most issues facing the university. But he then revealed that he had recently felt the brunt of sequestration through a decrease in his external grant support. Clearly, he stated, society no longer appreciates the value of basic research.

The plight of this individual and many other faculty members is symptomatic of a resistant faculty culture combined with the changing funding paradigm for higher education. Faculty members are often embedded in specialized study and seek acceptance primarily from colleagues in their subspecialty. When funding is available, they sense little need to be connected to a broader mission. The leader can gain credibility for needed changes by explaining how external factors directly affect the faculty's wellbeing. Cuts in federal funding for academic research are signaling taxpayer discontent that research conducted by universities is not meeting the needs of society. The decline in public funding provides an opportunity for the academic leader to raise the faculty's interest in discussions concerning how the university will be funded in the future, which areas will be prioritized, and the interface between these issues and the overall strategic direction of the university. More generally, to engage the faculty, the academic leader should articulate how the results of a strategic planning exercise can affect both faculty support and the quality and future of the university. To put it simply, the leader owes it to the faculty to explain why change is good and what's in it for them.

Peter Lorange, President of the Lorange Institute of Business in Zurich, recommends engaging the faculty in a meaningful way by asking each individual to write a memo, ten pages or less, describing what they feel is most and least important among all current and potential initiatives in a department or at the level of the university. In this way, in addition to obtaining strategic input, the leader can gain a deeper understanding of the perspective of each individual. The exercise also sends a message that the leader respects the faculty's ideas and preferences.

<u>Communicate the components of a strategic-planning process</u>: The road map for strategic planning at each university differs depending on specific characteristics and circumstances in each environment. To initiate the process, the role of the academic leader is to communicate the value of the process and describe the steps involved. Next, the leader should

- assign primary responsibility for each step to an individual or committee, and
- establish a timetable with sufficient checks to ensure adequate progress.

The following outline provides an example that can be modified to apply in specific settings:

I. *Assess the external environment*
   <u>Identify and communicate:</u>
   a. The external forces that have a significant effect on higher education;
   b. The competitive environment, how it is changing and how it affects support for research and teaching; and
   c. Constituent needs, both externally and internally.

II. *Develop a mission, vision and positioning strategy*
Identify and communicate:
   a. A peer group of similar departments;
   b. An aspirational group;
   c. An assessment of quality relative to peers;
   d. A set of performance metrics that can be validated externally;
   e. Niches and areas of comparative advantage relative to peers;
   f. Prioritize by classifying sub-areas that can be
      i. Best in class;
      ii. Very good to excellent; and
      iii. Good enough.
   g. Assessment of the realistic scope of the area;
      i. Determine what the area should not do.

III. *Develop a financial strategy*
   a. Determine how much it will cost to achieve the vision;
   b. Identify realistic sources of revenue; and
   c. Modify the positioning strategy and overall plan as necessary to ensure the strategy is financially sustainable.

IV. *Effectively implement and communicate the plan*
   a. Align incentives for innovation and efficiency;
   b. Provide financial transparency;
   c. Solicit input and communicate progress regularly; and
   d. In every decision, relentlessly pursue the vision.

V. *Assess progress and modify priorities and actions as necessary*
   a. Review outcomes based on the performance metrics;
   b. Uncover gaps between performance and plan; and
   c. Modify priorities and actions as needed.

A successful strategic planning process results in a set of integrated strategic choices that position the university relative to its peers and aspirational groups to establish a competitive advantage. Some key choices that define the university's positioning strategy include:

- Student quality: admissions standards and enrollment;
- Tuition setting and financial aid;
- Quality of instruction and depth and quality of student infrastructure;
- Quality of faculty and areas of academic distinction;
- Program scope; and
- Depth of interaction with alumni and the external community.

Positioning strategy: As an example of a positioning strategy, the University of Phoenix maximizes market share by adopting liberal admission standards and offering programs that can be taken at the convenience of the student, anywhere at anytime. At the other end of the spectrum, elite private universities choose to charge high tuition and be very selective while awarding substantial financial aid. They devote significant funding to the learning environment and make investments in targeted academic areas to reach true distinction. They highly value and allocate significant resources to alumni interactions and development. In contrast, many comprehensive research-intense publics choose not to prioritize, even while struggling financially in a framework of low tuition and declining public subsidy. The consequence is that many offer too broad a scope, frequently promising activities beyond their capabilities while underfunding important areas such as the infrastructure for student learning, advising and career services.

STRATEGY FOR A COMPREHENSIVE RESEARCH INTENSE PUBLIC UNIVERSITY

Although the following discussion focuses on a comprehensive research intense public university, the methodology also applies to a broad range of academic settings and can be adapted appropriately.[40] The analysis first examines a university-wide perspective and then develops a vision, mission and positioning statement for a typical research-intense academic department. This example is then referred to in other applications throughout the remainder of the book. In a public university system, critical decisions like setting tuition, admissions requirements and enrollment are usually made for all system universities by an overriding board of governors or regents. As pointed out in Chapter 1 this required homogeneity constrains both the potential and effectiveness of the individual universities.[41] A growing number of publics have separate governing boards that allow them to develop strategies that diverge from others within the system. The presumption here is that external pressures will force most public university systems over time to allow more local discretion over key decisions. While each university is required to respond to externally determined policies and mandates, they are presumed here to have discretion to develop a distinct mission, set campus priorities and entrepreneurially obtain and allocate resources.

The impact of recent budget cuts has been especially challenging at research intense universities due to the significant expense associated with laboratory space and equipment, reduced teaching loads, overhead, doctoral programs, research assistants, post-doctorates, support staff, travel, supplies and other ancillary support items. External research grants and state subsidy have historically funded a large portion of the cost. As this funding has declined, universities have attempted to preserve the research environment in part by decreasing costs of both instructional and support services. Increased use of adjuncts, larger class sizes, use of distance education and many cost saving efficiencies have been introduced at most universities. Still, the reality is that universities cannot afford to conduct the same level of path-breaking research in as many areas as they did ten years ago. Some prioritization needs to take place. A major purpose of a strategic planning exercise is to assess which activities contribute toward achieving the university's vision. Doing so naturally leads to prioritization and helps to guide the allocation of resources. The steps involved in a typical strategic planning process are as follows:

<u>Assess the external environment</u>: The first step is to examine the external environment. What are key challenges affecting the U.S. and the world? What are the forces driving the future of higher education? How are the university's competitors reacting to these forces? What are the trends in enrollment? An impediment for academic leaders is that because most universities are heavily dependent on faculty governance, reaction to changing external dynamics can involve a long, deliberate process.[42] One role for the leader is to communicate a sense of urgency, recognizing full well that some faculty members may never be swayed. As discussed in Chapter 2, one way to gain momentum is to seek alignment from a core of well-respected supporters rather than attempting to gain broad consensus from the entire group.

Academic leaders can gain support for new strategic initiatives by providing inducements for the faculty to address the above issues in their research, teaching and service activities. Several federal granting agencies are now attempting to direct research toward social challenges by requiring that investigators describe the potential practical application before projects can be funded. There are pressures as well to redesign the learning environment to incorporate different delivery methods and reduce time to graduation. Requests for enhanced operating efficiency, serving the community and accountability are also becoming increasingly important factors. While the leader can identify these forces and provide support for the faculty to address them, the question remains as to how to prioritize the many possible paths. With all of the demands on their physical, human and financial resources, it is critical for universities to identify the intersection between the areas where they are most capable of adding significant value and those that are deemed most important by society.

● ● ●

TABLE 3.1 Steps in a Strategic Planning Process

1. Assess the external environment.
2. Develop a mission, vision and positioning strategy.
3. Develop a financial strategy.

4. Effectively implement and communicate the plan.
5. Assess and modify priorities and actions as necessary.

• • •

To provide a context for how external forces shape strategy, assume that the following items have been identified as having a significant impact on the environment: (a) digital transformation and cyber security: (b) changing demographics; (c) emerging economies; (d) terrorism; (e) sustainability; and (f) growing public debt. The academic leader should communicate these factors to the faculty and request that each area examine how its expertise can be applied to better understand and address them. Most issues can involve analysis from multiple disciplines. For example, digital transformation spans computer science, engineering, the social sciences, business, law and other fields. An aging demographic, which involves many issues including health care, public policy and burgeoning public debt crosses many disciplines including the social sciences, medicine, the biological sciences, computer science and the humanities. It is often the case that multidisciplinary collaboration is minimal, primarily because the collective benefit of pursuing this type of effort is greater than the value to each discipline. In these cases, a role for academic leaders develops to provide incentives to support prioritized multidisciplinary efforts that might otherwise not be pursued. Leaders should uncover those areas where the university's expertise is particularly well suited to address specific societal needs. These areas can define a set of strategic priorities that academic units can identify and address through relevant research and curriculum initiatives.

Lead the development of the vision, mission and financial strategy: If well conceived, a university's vision and mission statements identify priorities and guide strategic decisions and budget allocations. Once developed, all actions should then support and enhance the vision. In contrast, many universities have adopted mission and vision statements that, while well written and well intentioned, are indistinguishable from one another.[43]

These statements are often too broad in scope, promising activities beyond capabilities and attempting to respond to too large an audience. Such statements are vacuous. A mission statement should not imply that the university serves everyone; nor should it be so general as to give the impression that university likes every idea. A mission statement that promises everything prioritizes nothing. When the public subsidy was large, sufficient funding was available to support a broad level of activity with a lack of prioritization. When financial constraints are binding, the lack of guidance concerning what is important leads to misallocation of resources and over time erodes the excellence of the university.

Over the past several decades as public support for higher education has waned, many universities have wandered beyond their original mission. They find themselves increasingly in the medical clinic, hospital, sports, entertainment, hotel and restaurant businesses while trying to produce basic research and educate the next generation. The tendency to meander beyond the core competency is a symptom of organizations that lack a distinctive mission. Without clear priorities, universities have difficulty deciding what not to do. The result is that they continue activities that are not highly valued by students, taxpayers, donors, external granting agencies or others even in the face of declining support. Priorities need to be established and tough decisions need to be made. The first step in this process is to develop vision and mission statements that consider financial realities. The process should be based on two fundamental principles:

* *Without a financial plan, strategy is meaningless, and*
* *Without strategic priorities, budget allocations are meaningless.*

A strategy without a financial plan is bound to be ineffective and its implementation can endanger the university's credibility and competitiveness. Without a distinctive vision that guides strategic priorities, budget allocations rest on historical trends. The inevitable result is that high quality, productive areas subsidize low quality, inefficient areas. Over time the lack of incentive for productive areas causes them to emulate less productive areas, thereby reaping rewards with less effort. The ultimate result is a broad diminution of quality across the university.

Universities often employ a "build it and they will come" mentality, moving ahead with projects based on an unrealistic hope that funding will appear. New buildings are commissioned and new schools and programs are initiated with little regard to realistic sources of revenue. Eventually, when revenues fall short, the reality sets in that "hope" is not a strategy. A financial strategy places a reality check on the organization's aspirations by first determining the cost associated with achieving the vision and then by identifying the sources for the required revenue. For any academic unit, the usual sources of funds are (a) public subsidy (b) tuition and fees, (c) external research grants, (d) entrepreneurial income from non-credit programs and other activities and (e) income from current and endowed gifts. If the strategic planning process works well, as shown in Chapter 7, the development strategy flows directly from the financial strategy. The potential for each funding source to generate significant additional revenue is examined in Chapter 4.

A Suggested Strategic Planning Exercise: Engaging the entire university in strategic planning in a logically consistent way to obtain meaningful outcomes is no easy task. The approach developed here, which builds on an example in Fethke and Policano (2012), is overseen by the provost and is based on transparency of metrics, decision rules and outcomes. An appropriately modified process can be used by a school or college where it would be overseen by the dean, or by a department where it would be overseen by the department chair or head. Tensions develop in any strategic planning process because various constituencies have different priorities. In addition to faculty support, a provost, president and some deans seek support from an external constituency that aligns with student desires for a high quality undergraduate education, excellence in teaching and advising and preparation for a career. In contrast, the faculty primarily seeks more support for research, less time in the classroom, fewer service activities and more faculty positions allocated to their area.

The disparity in constituent priorities creates challenges for all leaders, but they are especially acute for department chairs and deans who are often caught in the middle between their department or college and the central administration. The closer the leader is to the faculty who are affected by outcomes of the process, the more difficult it becomes for the leader to make critical choices. A dean should seek guidance from the provost and similarly, a department chair should consult the dean, before embarking on an exercise that is likely to have mixed acceptance by the faculty. Alignment with the next layer of leadership is critical before the controversial decisions are made. It is never a good idea for a leader to make bold decisions, only to end up alone to bear the consequences.

The steps in a strategic planning process conducted by the provost are:

* The provost distributes a description of the process and meets with the deans, department chairs and the academic senate to discuss the details and address any questions;
* Each academic area develops a strategic plan following an agreed upon template; an example is provided in Table 3.2;
* A major part of the plan includes an assessment of quality of the unit and an accounting of the net revenue its activities generate;
* Executive summaries of the plans are distributed;
* The executive summaries are evaluated by committees in the Academic Senate, Department Chairs, Deans, the Provost and the Chancellor who provide their personal assessment of each area according to the categories identified in Table 3.3 below;
* The vision and mission are modified to incorporate the areas of distinction identified in the process;
* Allocations are made based on the outcome of the exercise using the methodology described later in this chapter;
* Relentless pursuit of the vision is followed in assessing new initiatives;

❋ At the end of the process, the provost issues a university-wide request for proposals to incentivize cross-functional collaboration on the study of the prioritized external forces.

While many organizations would likely consider an area-by-area assessment of quality and productivity to be part of its normal routine, universities rarely conduct this type of campus-wide analysis. Academic areas are reviewed regularly, usually in five to seven year increments but these reviews are focused on the discipline under review with little regard to the overall strategy of the university or the financial viability of the unit. Universities tend to avoid open analysis and communication of assessment of quality, which implies that whatever priorities are established are opaque. When university leaders fail to identify the metrics upon which priorities are established, the allocation of resources becomes largely a mystery. This environment leads to game playing, mistrust and frustration.

● ● ●

TABLE 3.2 Template: Department Strategic Plan

Mission:	Statement of purpose: conveys why the area exists.
Vision:	Compelling aspirational statement of what the area will become in five to ten years.
Assessment:	Current status of research and degree programs including actual and desired enrollments, quality indicators and performance metrics (discussed below).
Peer departments:	(List three to five)
Aspirational departments:	(List three to five)
Aspiration:	Explain the gaps between the current status and aspiration and what actions will be necessary to close the gaps.

External forces:

Explain how the department is contributing or has the potential to contribute to the thematic approach established by the university based on external forces. Describe any additional external forces that the department faces and potential reactions.

Financial Plan:

In collaboration with the university budget office, compute the current net revenue contribution of the department. Determine the funding necessary to achieve the vision and the sources of additional funding.

• • •

The lack of a rigorous planning process is evident when reading the vision and mission statements for any randomly selected set of comprehensive public universities. They include amorphous phrases like "we will be a leading university in research and teaching" with little mention of the performance metrics by which "leading" would be measured or how the plan would be funded. It is not financially possible for all but a handful of universities to be "leading " in all the academic disciplines it offers. Yet, many universities aspire to do so.

Today's environment requires a more accountable approach like the one described above, where a rigorous process enables assessment of the quality and net contribution of all areas based on agreed upon performance metrics. A key tenet is that any academic area is welcome to propose a plan that aspires to any level of quality that the area chooses. The academic substance of the plan is paramount. But there are two qualifiers: first, the broad constituency of the university must review and assess the plan for its worthiness and alignment with the mission of the university, and second, someone must be willing to pay for the implied initiatives.

After the relevant groups have completed their assessments of each area, the next steps are captured in Table 3.3, which provides a decision matrix for determining allocations. Those areas that have the highest quality and net revenue contribution receive the highest priority, while those areas with the lowest quality and smallest contribution receive a low priority. If an area is deemed to be academically excellent but does not have sufficient financial support from constituents (students, taxpayers, donors and granting agencies) then the deans and provost can decide whether or not to subsidize the area. If they decline to do so, the area needs to adjust its plan to become less ambitious. The ultimate result is a prioritization that identifies the areas in which the university will be truly distinguished, very good or "good enough." Prioritizing in this way, allows the university to match critical constituent needs to areas that are judged to exhibit both high quality and financial sustainability.

How realistic is it to implement the above exercise at a large public university? Given the likely reaction of the faculty one might conclude that would not be possible. Actually, as described below an exercise very similar to the one above took place at the University of California Irvine.

Example: The University of California, Irvine

In 2011, Provost Michael Gottfredson introduced a strategic exercise similar to the one described above at a meeting of the academic deans. The immediate reaction was one of astonishment. Several deans argued that the exercise was too invasive and would cause too much controversy. Provost Gottfredson was unrelenting and declared that the exercise would be done. One of the deans then suggested that the exercise be undertaken without announcing it to the faculty. The Provost indicated that one key purpose of the exercise was to involve as many faculty members as possible; in fact, he argued, the success of the full implementation of the process requires an engaged faculty. This exercise provides an excellent example of the transition from ivory tower to glass house. Faculty members who have focused on their own career in a sheltered environment must now recognize and be more accountable to the broader missions of the university and society.

Why was there such reluctance to this type of exercise at UC Irvine and for that matter why have more universities not moved in this direction? Faculty governance certainly plays a role. Traditionally, strategic direction and evaluation of programs have rested in the hands of the faculty with performance metrics driven primarily by academic performance. Faculty culture is based to a large extent on strong beliefs in specific paradigms within sub disciplines. In many areas, there are deeply seated historical tensions between faculty members that reflect different approaches, with each believing that their paradigm provides greater inherent value. It is understandable that academic leaders are reluctant to open up this can of worms, especially with no apparent way to measure the philosophical benefits of alternative approaches. The solution is to measure value by someone's willingness to pay. Even if academic quality is high, the absence of an expression of value by students, via tuition, taxpayers, donors, external agencies or other areas of the university via subsidy, indicates a low prioritization by society. Each unit can present its assessment of the value of the area and its quality, but value must be externally validated by someone's willingness to provide funding for the activity.

TABLE 3.3 Assessment and Decision Matrix

QUALITY NET REVENUE CONTRIBUTION	Top 20%	Middle (metrics chosen by each unit)	Bottom 20%
Positive	Above average increase (or no decrease)	Average increase (or decrease)	Enhance quality
Negative	Subsidize	Examine centrality to mission	Downsize or eliminate

After the deans at UC Irvine accepted the reality that the exercise would in fact be implemented, the discussion turned to identification of the metrics upon which quality should be judged. A compelling argument was made that each area should choose its own metrics. If metrics were dictated by the administration, any area could argue that the set chosen does not fit their particular discipline. In the end it was decided that an assessment of the area based on standard performance metrics would be required but areas would be permitted to include additional metrics if they could justify their relevance. Importantly, an external validation of the department's self assessment of quality was also required.

The results of this exercise were fascinating. There was remarkable homogeneity in the ratings of the academic disciplines by all groups that evaluated the individual department plans. The vast majority of areas were perceived to be very good to excellent and these were rated in the middle 60%. It was also clear which areas were truly distinguished and these were placed in the top 20%. Finally, there was little disagreement in identifying the areas that were not high quality and/or not making a positive net contribution. Despite their differences of opinion and their different interests, the faculty, the academic senate and the administration were able to commonly define "excellence." A key aspect of the exercise was that the assessors' use of the matrix in Table 3.3 provided a methodology for prioritization by creating a distribution of the areas by quality and net revenue. The outcome for resource allocation was that in a year of an overall cut in state funding, those areas at the top received no cut; those in the middle received an average cut and those in the bottom received an above average decrease. Provost Gottfredson also advised those areas in the bottom cohort to revise their plan by adopting a variety of actions including reorganization, delivering the curriculum more efficiently and reducing scope.

The example below illustrates how a typical department could respond to the above call for a strategic plan. Before embarking on the exercise, a department chair should consider how others reviewing the plan would react to various scenarios. How should the department position its vision, mission and aspirations within the context of the university-wide assessment of the plan? While there is always a temptation to set high goals, the aspiration must be sufficiently within reach and the financial needs and sources must be sufficiently realistic to garner the necessary support. Moreover, participants leading their own strategic planning exercise also judge the plans of every other department. In this way, the exercise places a reality check on the department's self-assessment, aspiration and financial plan that allows a more truthful and productive sharing of information and more effective decision-making.

EXAMPLE: STRATEGIC PLANNING IN A HYPOTHETICAL DEPARTMENT OF ECONOMICS

Mission: To discover innovative approaches that address critical societal challenges through public policy formulation; and to disseminate a broad knowledge of economics to students and others, with specific emphasis on macroeconomic and public policies.

Vision: To enhance overall economic wellbeing through break-through research and creative public policy solutions emanating from a truly distinguished faculty, students and alumni.

Assessment: The department is recognized among the top 40 economics departments overall and in the top 20 in public policy based on the following measures: (supporting data would be provided)

   * Publications in leading journals;
   * Citations;
   * Faculty members of editorial boards;
   * Faculty recipients of national awards;

* Placement of doctoral students;
* Alumni success; and
* External grant funding.

Degree programs would be described here with actual and desired enrollments and quality metrics.

Peer departments:

* Michigan State
* University of North Carolina
* Illinois
* Arizona

Aspirational departments:

* Minnesota
* Wisconsin
* UCLA
* UC San Diego

Aspirational statement:

We will continue to provide top quality education and research across the broad field of economics. We will become distinguished in the areas of public policy, especially focused on health, energy, and macroeconomic policy. We are already highly recognized in these areas based on the measures described above. Our alumni hold distinguished positions in public policy, are leading experts in their fields and have expressed significant interest in helping to achieve our goals. This focus coincides with the external forces recognized by the university concerning a changing demographic, sustainability and burgeoning debt. With additional strategically allocated support we can improve both the overall quality of the department and its contribution to the university's vision. This type of support can be transformational with a sustainable, long-term impact.

Needs to accomplish the vision:

Initiatives to accomplish our goals include development of both an honor's undergraduate program and a master's program with a focus on our chosen areas to attract the best students and prepare them for a career in public policy.

The major needs to accomplish these goals include the addition of five faculty members, (two senior and three junior) with specific expertise in the public policy or macroeconomics which would increase the size of the faculty from 25 to 30. Additional support includes three additional doctoral students, three faculty chairs, three doctoral fellowships, new undergraduate scholarships and infrastructure support for student services for the two new programs. This support would allow us to pursue the level of distinction to match our aspiration.

Financial strategy:

Table 3.4 shows the needs of the department and the sources of revenue excluding, for simplicity, external grants. As the table indicates, the department needs an additional $1.65 million annually to accomplish the goals set out in its strategic plan. A calculation of the total net revenue generated by the department is shown in Chapter 4. The department anticipates being able to fund $825K annually from the tuition, fees and subsidy from the new program, which from the strategic plan has an emphasis on public policy.[44] It also plans to reallocate $150K annually from other uses of its own funds. The remaining amount of needed funds becomes the development goal, which is further explained in Chapter 7.

<u>Likely reactions to the above plan</u>: Given the stature and record of the department, reaching the desired level of quality and distinction is likely to be judged positively by others assessing the department plans. Still, to financially support the plan, the administration needs to provide start up funding before student tuition for the program materializes. It may be challenging for the administration to do so, especially since faculty hiring is not easily reversed if the program does not fare well. A reasonable approach is for the dean or provost to agree to provide temporary funding that is contingent on the future enrollment and overall success of the new Master's program.

TABLE 3.4 Financial Strategy for Five Year Plan: Hypothetical Department of Economics (all numbers in thousands)

Initiative	Cost	Additional Revenue: New MA program	Reallocation from Dep't funds	Fundraising goals
Increase faculty by 5	$ 800	$ 650	$ 100	$ 50
Increase chairs by 3	$ 300	---	---	$ 300
Increase scholarships	$ 75	$ 50	---	$ 25
Increase doctoral support	$ 200	---	---	$ 200
Increase staff	$ 100	$ 100	---	---
Honors fellowships and infrastructure	$ 125	---	$ 50	$ 75
New marketing/misc expenses	$ 50	$ 25	---	$ 25
TOTALS	$ 1,650	$ 825	$ 150	$ 675

ALIGNMENT AND COMMUNICATION

<u>Rewards and Incentives</u>: Success in implementing the mission and vision requires that rewards and incentives are aligned to achieved the desired outcomes. Too often a unit's reward for productivity and efficiency is that it is overly taxed by the administration. Areas that teach a heavy student load at relatively low cost or generate above average revenue through donations and entrepreneurial programs are often targets for the administration to extract funds that are used to subsidize other areas. Some

subsidization is appropriate but a role for any academic leader is to ensure that merit is rewarded while not imposing an unfairly heavy tax on high performing units. A great temptation is to continue to subsidize less efficient and lower quality areas in order to avoid difficult conversations about cutting their allocation. The reality is that with a permanent decline in the support for higher education, some areas must either downsize or reduce their aspirations in order to sustain the long-term quality of the university.

At a complex university, alignment of rewards and incentives can be difficult to achieve. The president and the provost may emphasize specific initiatives that may not be the priorities in every college or every department. For example, the president and provost might be focusing on initiatives to increase the quality of the undergraduate learning environment and they may have adjusted the budget model to provide incentives to do so. At the same time, it can be the case that a department or school is attempting to increase graduate rankings and the size of its doctoral program. In this case, the department could be at risk of losing resources if it lowers the number of undergraduate students in order to devote more resources to research. A prudent chair and dean should always study the incentives at each level and consult with the provost to avoid unintended consequences. An integrated set of strategies is the goal, but in a comprehensive, complex university this goal is often difficult to achieve. One way to foster clarity of the incentives and rewards, which will be discussed in Chapter 4, is to implement a responsibility centered management framework for the allocation of resources. If the provost and president are reluctant to move in this direction, at the very least they should distribute the current budget allocations and explain the rationale behind them.

Cross subsidies: The academic leader should identify the cross subsidies that are taking place and establish a process to decide which subsidies to continue and which to decrease or eliminate. Transparency is critical. In many cases, areas of the campus subsidize initiatives without ever being asked if they wish to do so and with no knowledge that the subsidization is taking place. Table 3.3 and the above discussion describe a process that is open to all constituents with clearly articulated decision rules for resource allocation. For example, departments that fall into the lower right hand quadrant exhibit low quality and are not generating sufficient revenue to cover their expenses. Currently, these areas receive a subsidy from more productive units that are judged to be of higher quality. But these subsidies are largely historical accidents that reflect the necessity of covering department deficits during budget shortfalls. A strategic plan should identify priorities and determine if and when it makes sense to take away resources from highly productive areas to subsidize lower quality, less productive areas.

A transparent process uncovers which areas are being subsidized and guides a reallocation of resources. Less productive or lower quality areas can be asked to become more efficient and to produce a less ambitious plan, with reduced scope and lower expectations of research prominence. Some subsidies make sense. The collective wisdom can be to subsidize areas that are judged to be important by society but are not attracting sufficient numbers of students or faculty. For example, individuals who pursue careers in the STEM areas are not rewarded as highly as the corresponding benefit that is provided to society as a whole. Their role in new discoveries that benefit areas like medicine, science and education are likely to have a greater impact on society than will be their own personal gain. In this situation, from society's perspective, an insufficient number of students will pursue these areas. A role for the leader is to identify those areas where a gap exists between social and individual returns. The leader can induce students and faculty to study and work in these areas by providing tuition scholarships, seed grants to help faculty prepare major grant proposals and other support packages. This subsidization should be made transparent; all units should understand that their resources are being taxed to support the university's vision in this way.

How often should a comprehensive planning exercise be undertaken? Any process that is performed too frequently can become less effective because individuals naturally perceive diminished value in a series of repetitive exercises. A five to seven year cycle for the development of an overall strategic plan can work well with annual updates and corresponding modifications of actions as necessary. A suggested format for providing a detailed update is shown as follows:

A Typical Annual Update

1. Vision, Mission, and Positioning Statements.
2. Current assessment relative to last five years.
3. Progress on previously prioritized actions.
4. Remaining gaps relative to vision.
5. New initiatives for consideration.

An annual retreat is a useful way to maintain momentum by reinforcing the plan, requesting input for possible modifications to the vision, mission and existing priorities and for identifying and discussing new initiatives. In most cases, a half-day or full day retreat is sufficient. Quarterly communications can also be helpful via an electronic newsletter, especially for the external constituency.

Relentless pursuit of the vision: The leader should expect constituents to constantly test the credibility of the vision. Students, faculty, alumni, donors and others frequently offer suggestions for initiatives that do not coincide with current priorities. How the leader reacts is crucial; every statement and every decision must be consistent with the vision. Does the suggested action add value? Does it help achieve the vision or is it inconsistent or irrelevant to the vision? Relentless reference to the vision and priorities fosters consistency in decision-making and builds credibility that leadership is serious about the stated goals, priorities and actions. The leader's role is to assess each opportunity based on its potential to help achieve established goals. Some flexibility should be included in the plan. When ideas arise that are likely to have a beneficial impact, the leader needs to have the flexibility to react. The financial strategy should include an allocation to support new initiatives that were not contemplated in the original plan. Transparency is especially important when operating "outside the plan." Each initiative should be carefully explained and regular communication should follow concerning progress being made. If this process is done well, constituents become increasingly convinced about the commitment to the vision. The ultimate result is that resource allocation decisions, efficiency and productivity improve because everyone understands what truly matters.

Summary and Conclusions

Academic leaders are increasingly recognizing that implementing an inclusive process to develop priorities and strategically position their unit is critical to achieving sustained competitiveness. At the same time, they also recognize that making tough allocation decisions and openly communicating priorities creates strife and controversy. Some worry that the most likely reward for "too much" innovation and transparency is a short tenure in office, which as pointed out by Fethke and Policano (2012a) has been the case recently for several university presidents. A more comfortable approach for some leaders is to adopt a strategy to support ideas emanating from the majority of constituents and then implement a policy of incremental change that upsets the fewest people. At the margin, little innovation takes place. This approach is understandable, especially for those academic leaders who view their role as "taking their turn" with a goal to create minimal anguish. The result is a slow plodding organization with bursts of innovation every five to ten years that occur during the honeymoon period of a new leader. While this strategy may be desirable for some leaders, the outcome is rarely good for the institution. An incremental approach is likely to cause significant financial and competitive decline for the university, especially in the current drastically changing paradigm for higher education.

Universities need to adopt distinctive strategies and efficient organizing processes that can effectively react to the disruptive forces currently affecting higher education. Developing a generic mission is easy; identifying distinction that leads to long run competitive advantage is a much more difficult task, one that has eluded many universities. Today's fiscal reality fuels arguments by legislators and others that higher education is inefficient, and the cost is too high. Faculty do not teach enough, they spend too much time doing esoteric research and they are protected by an archaic tenure system. The framework developed in this chapter can help the academic leader engage constituents in a credible, productive strategic planning exercise that results in a set of choices to position the university for long run competitive advantage. The result is financial self-reliance with transparent accountability. Those universities that do not strategically respond to these forces will eventually find themselves in declining competitive and financial positions. Indeed, the best universities in the future will be those that have developed a distinct competitive advantage within a financially sustainable strategic plan.

KEY TAKEAWAYS: CHAPTER 3

* A lack of strategic planning not only limits the potential that a university can attain, it puts the university's current support at risk.

* Universities need to demonstrate that they are part of the solution, not part of the problem.

* The financial paradigm has changed drastically; a university's vision should reflect both individual and societal priorities in a sufficiently compelling way to induce constituents to provide funding for its activities.

* With few agreed upon priorities, universities subsidize areas with low enrollment, high costs and often, marginal quality, thereby depriving resources from more highly valued areas. Over time, this misallocation of resources eats away at the excellence of the university.

* Sometimes a complacency or even a hostility to a market-based approach obstructs an area from building a supporting constituency. In this case, the eventuality of a declining resource base is a self-inflicted wound.

* One of the primary responsibilities of an academic leader is to define reality.

* Multidisciplinary research is often lacking because the benefit to each discipline is not as great as the collective benefit. Leaders should provide incentives to support prioritized interdisciplinary efforts that might otherwise not be undertaken.

* A mission statement that promises everything prioritizes nothing.

* With all the demands on their physical, human and financial resources, universities need to identify the intersection between the areas where they are most capable of adding significant value and those that are deemed most important by society.

* Without a financial plan, strategy is meaningless; without strategic priorities, budget allocations are meaningless.

- When university leaders fail to identify the metrics upon which priorities are established, the allocation of resources becomes largely a mystery. This environment leads to game playing, mistrust and frustration.
- Universities often employ a "build it and they will come" mentality, moving ahead with projects based on an unrealistic hope that funding will appear. When revenues fall short, the reality sets in that "hope" is not a strategy.
- Even if academic quality is high, the absence of an expression of value by students via tuition, taxpayers, donors, external agencies or other areas of the university via subsidy, indicates a low prioritization by society. Value must be externally validated by someone's willingness to pay for the activity.
- Relentless reference to the vision and priorities fosters consistency in decision-making and builds credibility that leadership is serious about the stated priorities and actions.
- With a permanent decline in the support for higher education, some areas must either downsize or reduce their aspirations in order to sustain the long-term quality of the university.

Financial Strategy and Budgeting Models

• • •

When we run out of money, we have to start thinking.

—Winston Churchill

INTRODUCTION

A SUCCESSFUL STRATEGIC PLANNING EXERCISE produces an integrated set of choices that position an organization to achieve superior outcomes relative to competitors over time.[45] Effective implementation requires alignment of the resulting initiatives with a financial model that facilitates achievement of the vision. Good budgeting reinforces effective strategy. Essential steps in building a credible financial strategy include determining the cost of initiatives identified in the strategic plan, matching these initiatives to constituents who are willing to pay for them, and then adopting a budget model that reinforces alignment of incentives and rewards. This chapter begins by examining the potential for the most common sources of funds to be significant contributors to financial needs. Once a financially feasible strategy is developed, its successful implementation requires utilization of an appropriate budget model. The discussion explains and contrasts the two most prominent models used by universities, *Central Administrative Management* (CAM) and *Responsibility Centered Management* (RCM).[46] Finally, an example is provided of how an academic department can compute the amount of net revenue it generates. This exercise allows a department chair or dean to be better informed when negotiating either for resources under CAM or for the assignment of allocation weights that underlie the rules in an RCM implementation.

POTENTIAL FUNDING SOURCES

As the strategic plan is being developed, a key role for an academic leader is to create a corresponding financial strategy that identifies credible sources of funding. While seeking new funds is critical, the basis of a well-devised financial strategy involves constant scrutiny over the current use and redeployment of funds. Turnover from retirements and departures combined with cost cutting and efficiency measures can yield sizeable savings. Reallocation of these funds should follow a process similar to the strategic planning exercise described in Chapter 3 where funds flow to their best use based on an assessment of quality and productivity in each area and a determination of which areas to subsidize. Here, the discussion focuses on the potential revenue flow from new sources.

With a permanent decline in taxpayer support, the strategies that are least likely to be successful in securing significant new funds include lobbying the financially strapped government or pleading to the already resource constrained higher level of university administration. Other strategies that have been commonly implemented to increase revenue include increasing external research grants, financial gains associated with technology transfer, donations, entrepreneurial activities and tuition and fees. The following discussion examines the viability of each of these funding sources to play a significant role in a realistic financial strategy.

External research grants: One defining feature of academic culture at research intense universities is a high regard for those disciplines that generate external research support. Accomplished faculty in areas like the medical school, the hard sciences and engineering can attract multi-million dollar federal grants for projects that include new laboratory facilities, equipment and in some cases, large research teams. These resources are critical in supporting the infrastructure necessary to maintain a highly productive research agenda. Universities often publicize their success by describing the impact and significance of the research and by emphasizing their usually impressive amount of external support. Less frequently are the financial consequences of the research program openly discussed.

A commonly held fallacy is that externally supported projects are financially self-reliant. The reality is that at many universities the cost of the contracted research exceeds the amount of the award. Overhead return, although often still referred to as "negotiated," is stipulated and only somewhat reflects actual costs. Federal agencies place limits on each category, for example as a fixed percent for administration, and they audit space usage as though people and functions could be moved around flexibly. Since increasing compliance and other obligations are mandated without overhead concessions, universities now pay substantially more for overhead costs that previously were funded. At public universities, these shortfalls are covered from a combination of the remnant of the state subsidy and a retained portion of tuition. Moreover, universities have mostly adopted the practice of "sharing" the overhead generated with principal investigators or the school, making external grants even more costly. The result is that principle investigators routinely believe they contribute positively to the general fund through the overhead they "earn," not understanding that every grant received generates an increase in cost.

The cost of contracted research creates significant financial stress, especially at research intense public universities. For example, indirect costs of conducting federally funded research at the University of California (UC) are estimated to exceed the funds provided by the granting agencies by 5 to 18%.[47] Moreover, research projects funded by other external agencies including state governments, corporations, foundations and donor gifts often provide support for indirect costs at levels significantly below those provided by federal agencies. Universities must subsidize the uncovered expenses from other revenues. Public universities especially are finding it increasingly difficult to do so because they have historically covered a good portion of these costs by using a now diminished taxpayer subsidy.

When asked about the above issues, one of the interviewees from a major public research intense university became silent and his main advisor, who also attended, became noticeably anxious. After some probing, they revealed that an area that has been very successful in attracting major grants is draining resources from several other areas. The university recently adopted elements of a transparent budgeting model that revealed the pattern of subsidization; the specific areas identified as providing a subsidy included the Humanities. Apparently, political tensions are very high. Still, the reality is that with a significant decrease in the state subsidy, tuition dollars are now a major source of subsidies for research. The areas generating these funds are pressuring the administration that they should be involved in the decision to subsidize research in other units.

Deep cuts in federal outlays caused by sequestration have posed even greater challenges. In the 2013 Fiscal Year, sequestration required that federal research agencies including NSF and NIH cut 5% of their budget, which led to a decrease in awards totaling several billion dollars. Federal discretionary funding stabilized in 2014 and 2015 as a result of the Bipartisan Budget Act of 2013. In 2016, there was a boost of $2 billion to the NIH budget, which is very much needed but still, sequestration will continue in 2017 through 2021 unless new legislation is enacted. Moreover, obtaining external research funding is challenging, at best. In 2003 NIH funded about 30% of proposals that were submitted; by 2012 the success rate of submissions had fallen to 18%. The impact of reduced research funding has especially harmed the development of junior faculty members who frequently lose competitions to more experienced senior faculty.

Looking ahead, given the prospect of only moderate economic growth combined with heavy demands on federal funds from an aging population, the outlook for significantly increased federal funding for research is not optimistic. Moreover, priorities for obtaining research funding are shifting. Universities are under constant pressure to improve their impact on growth, employment and overall well-being. Granting agencies often require and seriously evaluate a statement by the principle investigator explaining the practical applications of the proposed research. The implication is that general fund allocations for research should be based not only on faculty quality, but also on the impact of the research on the needs of society. One role for the leader is to incentivize faculty members, through seed grants and other awards, to seek an intersection between their research program and national priorities as established by granting agencies.

In sum, the vitality of research intense universities continues to depend on external research funding, but the playing field has shifted. Competition is intensifying as faculty members vie for a permanently reduced pool of funds. Even when successful, it is often the case that the amount of the award does not cover the cost of conducting the research. With insufficient funds to maintain historical support levels for all areas, leaders face the difficult task of prioritizing. A key role for the leader is to use seed grants and other mechanisms to incentivize those faculty who are most likely to succeed to apply for support in areas that external agencies are most likely to fund. These are the areas that society is prioritizing.[48] While doing so, the leader should recognize and communicate that the primary reasons for increasing external grant activity are to partially fund the research enterprise, attract top faculty and build recognition. The overall goal is to have a positive impact on society. But, attempting to increase the university's general fund by increasing external grants is not a credible strategy.

Technology Transfer: The liberalization of patent rules in the Bayh-Dole Act of 1980 provided an inducement for universities to develop technology transfer operations; today, over 200 universities have done so.[49] Technology transfer from the university to the community not only has the potential to generate revenue but it also satisfies a pressing need to demonstrate how the university promotes economic growth. There are good reasons why increased university corporate partnerships make sense. Industry seeks both talented graduates and ideas for innovative and relevant research. Faculty can gain from collaborations to enrich both research and teaching programs. Licensing agreements and new businesses can be spawned that might otherwise not occur. Still, while increased flow of information can help create useful partnerships, whether this activity can lead to a significant flow of revenue for the university is less clear.

Many faculty members focus on fundamental research, which often has little intersection with the profit-motivated priorities of a company. The decrease in government funding has raised faculty interest in working with industry in areas outside their main line of research. Still, faculty members primarily seek opportunities where the funding provided also benefits their core research program. As discussed by Valdivia (2013), the reality is that only a handful of universities create significant revenue from start up and license agreements. In fact, most university technology offices do not generate enough revenue to cover their own operating expenses. Valdivia's data also shows a dramatic uneven distribution of success across universities. In 2012, the top 5% of revenue producers included eight universities that generated 50% of the total licensing income; the top 10% (16 universities) generated almost 75%.

The main challenges associated with technology transfer involve a low probability of success of new ventures, lack of faculty incentives and rewards to engage industry, a large cost associated with a patent and technology transfer operation, and conflicts concerning who owns the intellectual property. Several interviewees including Joe Alutto and Gary Fethke indicated that while legislators, governors and external advisory board members often encourage universities to expand technology transfer activities, their rationale is usually based on an inflated notion of their potential rate of return. Even one of the most successful universities, Columbia, generates gross revenue from licenses (unadjusted for the cost of generating this activity) that in 2014 accounted for only about 4% of an annual university operating budget of over $3.8 billion. Most universities that have sizeable revenue from these activities have had one major success; for example, Columbia collected $790 million in licensing fees since receiving patent approval for the Axel patents that provided a method for insertion of DNA into certain types of cells.

In sum, investing in technology transfer can have many positive aspects for the university and community. Resulting innovations can lead to licensing opportunities and startups. Both activities can generate revenue that can help fund the continuing operations of the tech transfer operation and fund other research projects. A major research university needs this activity to actuate and validate its fundamental research platform. Still, the reality is that for most universities, this activity, even if an improbable major breakthrough occurs, is unlikely to provide significant flexible operating revenue.

Donations: Development operations have expanded dramatically at all universities over the last several decades and have played an increasingly critical role. Gifts can have a significant impact, especially in supporting new program initiatives and building campaigns. They are less likely to offer a realistic solution for the operating fund challenges faced by most universities. Donors generally restrict the use of funds to projects they are passionate about; they are not likely to support ongoing operations. As will be discussed in Chapter 7, donors who provide major gifts often support targeted new initiatives that result in adding new costs rather that covering existing needs. Moreover, while corporate foundations and companies that have public relations and marketing budgets can potentially be significant funding sources, they receive many funding requests. Foundations are becoming more diligent in granting awards and many companies have decreased discretionary outlays for marketing and sponsorships since the Great Recession.

In sum, every gift is important and every donor who is stewarded well can become an advocate for the university. Major donors can provide support that becomes the margin of difference between an excellent academic unit and a truly extraordinary one. Certainly, successful fundraising is critical to the vibrancy of the university, but for most universities it is unrealistic to rely on donations to be a major source of revenue for ongoing operations.[50] At current rates of expenditure for endowments, every $1 of a recurring expense requires an endowment of $20 to $25 to generate a sufficient annual flow of funds. Replacing a loss of state funding of $50 million requires an unrestricted endowment of $1 billion to $1.25 billion. While billion-dollar campaigns are becoming more common, receiving this level of funding for unrestricted use is beyond the reach of most universities.

New revenue producing programs and entrepreneurial activity: Universities continue to vigorously develop a host of entrepreneurial activities including health and sports clinics, food services, sports contracts, brand licensing agreements, and third party dormitories. Another creative avenue involves the monetization of some of the capital assets of the university. Joe Alutto provided several examples from Ohio State, including giving the right to control existing parking facilities to a third party, with university guidance. The agreement involves coordination with the university concerning changes in the facilities and setting of future fees with a cap on annual increases. The university received about $480 million up front for the leasing arrangement, which has a term of 75 years. This money was placed into the university's endowment and the income has been used to hire new faculty and accelerate the development of new research and teaching facilities. Similar arrangements can be developed with dormitories.

The goal for entrepreneurial activities is that they become financially self-reliant and in some cases, generate revenue that flows to the general fund. With the popularity and attention given to NCAA athletics, often the question arises as to whether athletics can spin off significant revenue for the general fund. The reality is that in 2012, only 23 of 228 athletics departments at NCAA Division I public schools generated enough revenue to cover expenses. Even in this group, 16 received some form of subsidy.[51]

While entrepreneurial activities can potentially provide a stream of funding, challenges arise in any organization that expands scope beyond its core activities. Non-traditional staff members need to be added to administer and lead these activities; many report to an academic leader, usually the chancellor, provost or dean. The leadership of the university can find itself spending an increasingly worrisome amount of time on details of these business arrangements. Donna Shalala indicated that the some of the most complex situations that a university president faces emanate from a university hospital or major football program. Each requires heavy involvement of the president and brings ample potential for financial stress, complex regulatory oversight, scandal and damaging public relations crises.[52] Effective leaders can manage both well; Shalala led both the University of Wisconsin and University of Miami and was successful even though both have major hospitals and large athletic programs. Michael Drake as Chancellor of the University of California Irvine inherited a medical center facing such severe financial challenges that the University was advised to sell the hospital. Still, with significant effort and astute financial strategies, the university was able to work through a turn around, making the hospital a profitable enterprise. After nine years at UC Irvine, Drake became President at Ohio State University where, after only one year, he has hired a new head for the Wexner Medical Center and has helped move the center to a significantly improved financial position.

In spite of the above success stories, the complex activities associated with major athletic programs, medical centers and other entrepreneurial initiatives involve difficult challenges that need to be addressed primarily by the leader. Entrepreneurial ventures can be a good strategy in some areas. Certain enterprises like the sports program and health complex should run as independent enterprises that are financially self-reliant. Unfortunately, at many universities these activities must be subsidized from the general fund. While the top administration can find it beneficial to engage in these activities, it is pragmatically a challenging distraction for individual units to wander too far from their academic core.

Tuition revenue and fees: The funding source that holds the greatest potential to generate flexible operating revenue is tuition. After the cuts following the Great Recession of 2008, virtually all universities reacted by increasing tuition revenue through a combination of fee increases for current programs and the development of new revenue producing programs.[53] Even though these activities lie within the core expertise of universities, the issues involved are complex. Increasing resident tuition at public universities raises heated opposition. Attempts to increase non-resident enrollment face political backlash over which students should receive top priority for admission.[54]

Creating new programs entails a slow, deliberate faculty governance process and is also a risky proposition. Market research can be difficult and the fixed costs of establishing a new program infrastructure are not insignificant.

In spite of these factors, tuition revenue provides the most realistic source of funds to fill the gap between costs and other revenue sources. Determining the efficient level of tuition for each program is a relatively straightforward exercise in microeconomic theory.[55] Issues related to equity and access need to be balanced with efficiency arguments; the extent to which fairness trades off with efficiency provides the context for public debate. Because the ability of public universities to increase resident tuition has been politically restrained, they now find themselves increasingly being moved from a high-subsidy, low-tuition model to a financially unsustainable low-subsidy, low-tuition model. Private universities are able to set tuition close to the actual cost of education and support access through a generous financial aid program. This high-tuition, high-financial aid, low-subsidy model has allowed private universities to excel relative to public universities as taxpayer support has fallen. As described in Chapter 3, private universities now dominate the list of top twenty universities in the country.

THE BOTTOM LINE IN A CREDIBLE FINANCIAL STRATEGY

The traditional method for a dean to seek additional funding is to lobby the provost for an increased allocation. In today's environment of permanently reduced funding, these attempts are likely to fall on deaf ears. The same holds true when a department chair seeks funds from the dean. Each unit needs to demonstrate increased efficiency, cost controls and feasible sources of revenue. Costs of delivering the curriculum are being restrained through increased use of adjuncts and expansion of distance education.[56] Controlling costs for research are more difficult; the natural inclination is for universities to react to the funding cuts caused by sequestration by increasing grant proposals. The challenge is that additional grant support can actually increase financial stress if a subsidy is needed from already stretched general fund. Alternative options of looking to donors, increasing entrepreneurial activities and technology transfer offer limited possibilities to permanently bolster flexible operating funds.

The best opportunity to generate increased revenues is to increase tuition revenue by increasing fees on existing programs and creating new financially self-reliant programs. For this approach to be successful, the leader needs the flexibility to both retain a reasonable percentage of the generated revenue and to use these funds without excessive constraints. Accordingly, a reasonable strategy for a department chair (dean) is to first develop a credible financial strategy and then present a plan to the dean (provost). The chair or dean has a considerably stronger bargaining position if the desired outcome is increased flexibility rather than increased funding. For example, a dean meeting with the provost is apt to receive a more supportive response if the conversation begins as follows:

I am not here to request an increased allocation from your resources; rather, I am here to request the flexibility to generate, retain and use a reasonable fraction of my own.

To be convincing, the leader should have a deep understanding of how the net revenue generated by the unit is determined. Also, given the growing movement by universities away from CAM to RCM, the leader should be well versed in the advantages and disadvantages of each approach. Which model serves the unit better? Which is best for the university? The following analysis examines these issues.

PRINCIPLES OF UNIVERSITY BUDGETING

The basic features of the budget process, as shown in Figure 4.1, are similar at most universities regardless of which budget model, CAM or RCM, is utilized. If there is a state subsidy, that appropriation along with tuition revenue, indirect cost recovery revenues, and other sources of income are collected centrally and are then distributed to colleges and shared-services providers. The distributions are determined either by the central administration or by predetermined formulae that are based on metrics aligned to performance in individual units. The budgeting process involves four decisions: the revenue to retain by the central administration for shared initiatives, the method used to allocate funds to the academic units, the tax to levy on both entrepreneurial programs and private donations; and the negotiated rate of indirect cost recovery.

Central Administrative Management (CAM) and Responsibility Centered Management (RCM)

Most public universities have traditionally employed a CAM budget model under which allocations are determined incrementally often with little relation to activities or performance. CAM is often referred to as an "opaque" system because allocations, flow of subsidies and shared service costs are neither widely shared nor easily identified. The administration decides on an amount to hold centrally for new or special initiatives and then distributes the remaining funds to cover overhead, shared service centers and academic units. Marginal adjustments are made to the previous year's budget for each area with the possibility of an additional increment for new initiatives. Subsidies flow from low cost, efficient units to high cost, low enrollment units in a way that is difficult to uncover.

The philosophy underlying RCM is to decentralize decisions by bringing them closer to their origin. A transparent incentive and reward system is aligned with the goals set out in the vision and mission. Key parameters can include enrollment of majors, student credit hours, cost per student full-time equivalent and the dollar amounts of research awards and donor gifts. An RCM process encourages decision-makers to respond to changes in enrollment patterns, program delivery methods, priorities established by research funding agencies, and the wishes of donors. RCM introduces both transparency and accountability to each unit in a way that is absent in CAM. The intent is that RCM brings enhanced focus on managing enrollments, program cost, and competitive quality. Private universities generally utilize some form of responsibility centered management and there is now a movement among public universities to also adopt some version of RCM.

Under RCM, rules assign tuition revenue, indirect cost recoveries, and a portion of the state appropriation to programs (typically to colleges) based on activities that can be attributed to each responsibility center. For example, revenues might be allocated to each college according to a weighted average of student credit hours generated by majors and student credit hours generated by all students who take courses in the college. University overhead and shared service costs are paid by individual units through explicit taxes on imputed expenditures. Hybrid examples of CAM and RCM models seem to be increasing, where the administration retains discretionary funds for university-wide innovations and the remaining funds follow an RCM approach.

FIGURE 4.1 The Flow of Funds

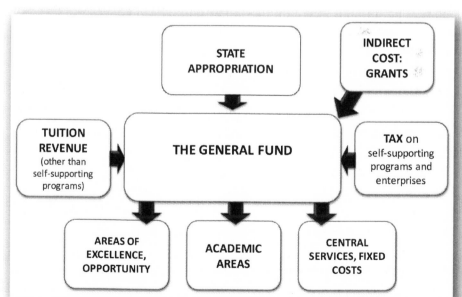

The components of an RCM approach include the following:

1. The central administration receives tuition revenue, indirect cost return and a taxpayer subsidy (if a state supported institution) and then determines an amount to be retained for innovations, special programs, rewards for quality and efficiency and strategic subsidies;

2. Overhead and shared service costs are assessed through a tax related to the amount of the service utilized by each unit;

3. A formula driven framework determines allocations according to the revenue generated by each unit;[57]
   a. Tuition revenue and in some cases, a portion of the state subsidy, are usually allocated based on a weighted average of enrollment by majors and total student credit hours;
   b. Indirect cost return allocation percentages are determined for the college generating the grants, with consideration for depreciation of current facilities and start up packages for new faculty members.

4. Cost adjustments are made according to comparison of cost per full-time equivalent in specific units with nationally published figures. If the unit is above the average, the allocations can be cut and if below the average, the unit can be rewarded;

5. The central administration may also wish to establish an insurance fund in the event of unforeseen budget shortfalls in particular units or for the university as a whole.

The fund retained centrally can be used to incentivize development of new areas, cross disciplinary work, faculty and student recruitment and other strategic initiatives. The fund can also be used to subsidize areas that do not generate sufficient revenue to cover costs.

Advantages and Disadvantages of CAM and RCM

Some believe that a major advantage of CAM is the predictability of its historical allocations of tuition revenue, taxpayer support, and indirect cost recovery. In addition, across the board adjustments suggest an element of fairness, which during downturns may be favored by administrators who wish to avoid difficult decisions and uncomfortable situations.

Universities often struggle with how to cover the cost of shared services. CAM allows the central administration more control over resources than in the formula driven RCM model. The provost can more easily allocate funds to invest in new initiatives, cover shared services and subsidize units that are not financially solvent. Shared services include at least some portion of activities provided by the main library, university student placement, advising, information technology, public relations, marketing and legal services. While faculty governance exerts pressure on the administration under either CAM or RCM, a CAM model allows the central administration more discretion over which areas to subsidize without the controversy that might develop under a more transparent RCM framework. Support for initiatives that are critical to the university but not as highly valued by some areas may be easier to generate under CAM than RCM. It is also reasonable to believe that if a transformational strategy is needed, CAM would be an easier framework for the central administration to be able to orchestrate the significant change required.

One disadvantage of CAM is that there is little pressure on departments to be accountable for covering their costs because allocations do not directly depend on enrollments or the revenue that a unit generates. The result is that poor resource allocation decisions are made. In a CAM system, areas often make proposals for new programs, arguing that these additions can be made without requiring new resources. The implication that should be drawn from this statement, but rarely is, is that the department has excess capacity. Unless the proposal is based on a reallocation of resources, the question that should be posed is whether the area can cover its current responsibilities with fewer resources. If so, what is the best possible use of these resources; should they be allocated elsewhere?

When the subsidy was ample, scope expansion could be financially accommodated even if the new courses brought low enrollments. As the subsidy declines, an expanded curriculum causes challenges; over time, a pattern of internal cross subsidies develops because some units spend more than the revenue they generate while others spend less. When revenue is plentiful, the existence of subsidies creates little conflict; when funding streams decline, the opaque transfer scheme causes conflict, as those units who are generating significant revenue beyond their allocation believe they are being treated unfairly.

Another challenge posed by CAM is that its opaque allocation mechanism can lead to misperceptions about relative allocations. With little data available, units have a tendency to believe that they are underfunded relative to others.[58] The result is a concerted lobbying effort on the part of chairs with their dean and deans with the provost to obtain additional resources. In this way, the allocation discretion that is provided to the provost under CAM can exert a heavy time cost on the university. A transparent rules-based model, such as that provided by RCM, makes these interactions less critical because the allocation rules and actual allocations are public knowledge. As one of the interviewees described, an RCM model is like a clock; once it is built, the handles move by themselves with predictable results that all can see.

By decentralizing decisions, RCM promotes innovation and entrepreneurship because the publicly available allocation rules allow units to understand the actions required to increase revenue. Rewards accrue by attracting students and research support and by improving operating efficiency. Units are allowed to manage their expenditures and determine the staffing and scope of their programs, guided by university-wide standards and the constraint to be financially self-reliant. For RCM to work effectively, the amount of funds to be allocated must cover the actual operating costs of the units receiving the funds. It is usually the case, especially at public universities, that tuition revenue is insufficient to do so. Taxpayer support and other funds are then necessary to cover the gaps and the central administration utilizes these funds to do so. In public universities, when the administration retains control of the allocation of the state appropriation, the result can be internal political conflict and renewed lobbying. Those units with ample tuition revenue seek more and those units with historical subsidies resist cuts.

One disadvantage with RCM is that too much focus on revenue generation can be harmful. Development of programs to generate revenue may increase enrollment in areas that are not consistent with the university's mission. Moreover, there is often a tradeoff between increasing enrollment for revenue generation and quality of the student body. Setting transparent quality standards through the strategic planning process and rewarding quality are key ingredients in a successful deployment of RCM.

WHICH MODEL SHOULD A DEPARTMENT CHAIR OR DEAN PREFER?

As is the case for any complex question, the answer to which model is preferable is "It depends." One way to envision the way in which CAM works in practice is captured in the following statement by President Ronald Reagan when he described his view of how Congress operates:

> *"If it moves, tax it. If it keeps moving, regulate it.*
> *If it stops moving subsidize it."*

For many years, central administrators avoided significant controversy by doling out incremental budgets each year. When units succeeded, the increase in revenue they generated could be used to support less productive units, thereby avoiding the political controversy of applying cuts to subsidized areas. Under CAM, most of this subsidization occurred with little knowledge by the units involved. If the administration believed that some areas became "too success-ful;" that is they were attracting too many majors or being too innovative, they could be slowed down by not providing adequate support or thrusting heavy faculty governance in their path. A less than transparent system allows significant leeway for the administration. This system worked well during periods of ample subsidy but fails to provide efficient solutions when budget constraints are binding. From the standpoint of the university, at least some use of an incentive based model can help improve quality and efficiency.

All universities display a wide distribution of demand and cost per full-time equivalent (FTE) across academic areas. Those units that have high costs and are least likely to attract students, donors or research funds re-sist RCM and argue to continue with a system of historical allocations. Alternatively, those areas that have abundant student demand and/or low de-livery cost recognize that they have been a "cash cow" providing subsidies for low-demand areas. These areas are likely to vigorously support a movement to RCM. From the perspective of the university, subsidizing high-cost, low-demand areas with revenues from efficient, high-demand areas will eventu-ally undermine incentives to improve in both the subsidized and the taxed programs. The end result is an erosion of the excellence of the university. Whether or not a particular unit benefits from a transition from CAM to RCM depends on the net revenue the unit generates. In either system it is critical to understand how to do this calculation, which is explained below.

Finally, when introducing RCM, to obtain buy-in from high cost-units that have modest revenue generating ability the administration of-ten promises that all units will initially be held harmless. Doing so usually involves dividing the current year allocation by full-time equivalent en-rollment to arrive at a "cost per FTE." These weights are used in subse-quent years to adjust RCM allocations. This methodology continues to at least temporarily support the previous subsidy-distorted CAM structure. While less than optimal at the start because inefficient units continue to be heavily subsidized, the hope is to adjust these weights over time in a movement toward a more beneficial outcome.

Computing the net revenue contribution for an academic department

Under CAM, the department chair (dean) negotiates with the dean (provost) to determine annual allocations. The leader's leverage can be improved by understanding the components and amount of the net revenue contribution of the academic unit. Obtaining the necessary information can be challenging at a large comprehensive university that uses CAM. Much of the information is hidden and can be difficult to extract. Moreover, the administration might be reluctant to offer data that reveals discretionary allocations than could generate controversy.

TABLE 4.1 Calculation of Revenue Net of Financial Aid and Overhead Costs: Hypothetical Department of Economics

Line	Item	Undergraduate Program	New Masters Program
1	Resident Enrollment	31,954 SCH	900 SCH
2	Resident Tuition	$249/SCH	$475/SCH
3	Total Resident Tuition	$7,956,546	$427,500
4	Non-Resident Enrollment	2,700 SCH	600 SCH
5	Non-Resident Tuition	$505/SCH	$950/SCH
6	Total Non-Resident Tuition	$1,363,500	$570,000
7	Set-Aside Financial Aid	($3,262,016)	($99,750)
8	Student Fees	$721,958	$31,250
9	Total Program Revenue	$6,779,998	$929,000
10	Share of State Subsidy	$5,325,667	0
11	Subtotal: Program Revenue and Subsidy	$12,105,251	$929,000
12	Charge for 35% overhead	($4,236,979)	($325,150)
13	Net Revenue	$7,868,676	$603,850
14	Indirect Cost Return	$75,000	
15	Combined Net Revenue	$8,547,526	(Includes MA program)

As shown in Table 4.1, the hypothetical department of economics described in Chapter 3 is used to provide an example to compute the net revenue generated by its degree programs. The purpose of the exercise is to determine how much of the revenue the department produces is returned to the unit through its annual allocation from the provost. The central administration receives the tuition generated by undergraduate and masters programs, indirect cost return and, if at a public university, a subsidy from the state. The tuition generated by a doctoral program, whose students usually receive tuition waivers, is assumed here to be zero. Allocations are made to the doctoral program from the graduate school for teaching and research assistants. These funds are typically included as part of the allocation to the department, which is not delineated here.

The bottom portion of the table includes an assessment for overhead and centrally shared services that can include (a) capital costs, lighting, heating and water; (b) student services, central administration, library and technology; (c) taxes on enterprise programs; and (d) benefits, if covered centrally. The amount of revenue net of financial aid and overhead costs be compared to the allocation provided by the administration. If the department's net revenue is greater than its allocation, it is providing a subsidy to other units. In the opposite case, the unit is receiving a subsidy.

Annotated explanation of Table 4.1: In Table 4.1, lines 1 – 6 are self-explanatory. Data should be readily available on student credit hour enrollment and tuition per Student Credit Hour (SCH). In line 7, the amount of set-aside financial aid is usually determined by the university or university system. Here, undergraduate and graduate financial aid are assumed respectively to be set at 35% and 10% of total tuition revenue. Most universities charge additional student fees. which are usually calculated based on Full-Time Equivalents (FTE). The FTE total is computed by dividing total SCH by an agreed upon number of SCH associated with a full-time load. Here, it is assumed that a full-time annual load is 24 SCH; the number of undergraduate and masters FTEs are respectively 1,443.91 and 62.5 and the fee per FTE is $500. These figures yield the total student fees shown in line 8. Adding total tuition and fees net of financial aid yields total program revenue on line 9.

For public universities, the state subsidy is typically allocated to the university based on a fixed dollar amount per resident enrollee. Here, the subsidy is assumed to be $4000/FTE for resident undergraduates. There is no subsidy included for the masters program, which is revenue producing and intended to be financially self-reliant. States do not provide subsidies for non-resident students. Line 10 shows the amount of the subsidy based on the 1331.4 FTE undergraduate residents who are served by the department. Line 11 totals program revenue, which is then taxed to cover the centrally borne costs described above. On line 12, the tax rate is assumed to be 35% but some universities can justify a significantly higher tax. A key feature of CAM is that the tax and underlying costs are hidden and can be difficult to uncover. Negotiations for resources with the provost are challenging for deans who are often informed that their overhead costs are higher than they assumed. An RCM approach reveals the cost structure.

Line 15 indicates that the department generates approximately $8.5 million in net revenue, including an assumed $75, 000 indirect cost return as shown on line 14 . If the department's total allocation from the provost (not shown) is less than the net revenue it generates, then it is providing a subsidy to other areas. Under CAM if the subsidy is large, the chair can use this information to negotiate for an increased allocation. If the allocation is greater that the funds generated, then the department is receiving a subsidy. In this case, the leader should identify inefficient activities, including under enrolled courses or activities that have an insufficient base of support.

SUMMARY AND CONCLUSIONS

Universities are facing a new financial paradigm, one that demands a distinct vision, strategic positioning and self-reliant financial planning. A key role for the leader is to develop a credible financial strategy by first estimating the cost of initiatives identified in the strategic plan and then identifying constituents who are willing to pay for them. The challenge is that universities have limited options for obtaining funds that can be used to cover operating expenses. While donations, technology transfer and entrepreneurial activities can be helpful, the most realistic source for significantly increasing operating funds is tuition revenue. Developing and implementing a financial strategy requires that the leader gain a working knowledge of how revenue is generated and calculated. A firm understanding of the university's budget model and the parameters of the CAM, RCM or hybrid model employed by the university are also essential.

A strategy without a credible financial plan is not meaningful. A budget model without a distinctive strategy is equally ineffective. Either model can damage the quality of the university. Allocating funds in the absence of setting priorities leads to distortions that transfer resources from highly productive areas to subsidize areas that either face lower demand or are inefficient. The success of all universities relies on their ability to adapt to the quickly changing funding environment. Those universities that adopt an activity-based budgetary framework and flexible tuition structure that appropriately values both private and public willingness to pay are pacing the way to succeed in a highly competitive, resource constrained environment. Those universities that resist the necessary changes and hope for a return to large public subsidies are likely to face a bleak future with an eroding resource base and eventual competitive decline.

Key Takeaways: Chapter 4

* A common fallacy is that externally supported research projects are financially self-reliant. At many universities, the cost of conducting contracted research exceeds the amount of the award.

* Granting agencies often require that principle investigator explain the practical applications of the proposed research. General fund allocations for research should be based not only on faculty quality, but also on the social impact of the research.

* A key role for the leader is to use seed grants and other mechanisms to incentivize faculty members to submit grant proposals in areas that external agencies are most likely to fund. These are the areas being prioritized by society.

* Under a Centrally Administered Management (CAM) budget model allocations are determined incrementally, often with little relation to activities or performance.

* CAM is often referred to as an "opaque" system because actual allocations, flow of subsidies and shared service costs are neither widely shared nor easily identified.

* Responsibility Centered Management (RCM) decentralizes decisions by bringing them closer to their origin. A transparent incentive and reward system is aligned with strategic goals.

* Subsidizing high-cost, low-demand areas with revenues generated by efficient, high-demand areas undermines incentives to improve in both areas. The end result is an erosion of the excellence of the university.

CHAPTER 5

Strategically Investing In Human Capital: Recruitment, Retention And Development

• • •

Take away my people but leave my factories and soon grass will grow on the factory floors. Take away my factories but leave my people and soon we will have a new and better factory.

—ANDREW CARNEGIE

INTRODUCTION

PEOPLE ARE THE LIFEBLOOD OF any organization. While this frequently used statement has become trite, understanding how to best motivate and support individuals can prove to be elusive, especially for faculty who have had sparse experience doing so. Focused primarily on educating and advising students, most faculty members have given little thought to the broader concept of strategically investing in human capital. Building and retaining a productive, collegial faculty and staff involves levels of complexity and time commitment that is often underestimated. This chapter provides some perspective on how to successfully recruit, motivate and develop faculty and staff in a way that propels both an individual's professional aspirations as well as the success of the unit. The intent is not to develop a comprehensive treatment of human resource strategy but rather to focus on issues that are most pertinent in an academic environment. The key ingredients involve effective strategic planning, carefully implemented recruitment and development plans and most of all, a leader who takes a genuine interest in the success of others.[59]

A newly appointed department chair or dean often perceives that a major indicator of their success is the extent to which they increase the size of the faculty. But retention of existing top faculty is just as important, if not more so, than attracting new faculty. The discussion examines faculty retention strategies for responding to both external offers and requests from current faculty members for additional compensation. The analysis also includes an overview of various aspects of faculty recruitment and development, as well as management of troublesome faculty issues. Finally, the chapter provides a discussion of the critical nature of the staff.

BUILDING THE FACULTY

The hallmark of a highly regarded university is the excellence of its faculty. A carefully selected student body and a high performing, dedicated staff are also critical, but building quality starts with the faculty. The desired size, mix of specializations and overall quality of the faculty are determined through a strategic planning exercise like that described in Chapter 3. The plan provides a roadmap that identifies the department's research and teaching areas and the level of quality that the department can financially sustain. The plan delineates the long run or steady state number of faculty at each level (tenure, tenure-track and non-tenure track). If appropriate, it can also include the same analysis for each sub-discipline in the area. Finally, the plan also describes a timetable for achieving specified goals.

RECRUITMENT AND RETENTION

Logistics: Recruiting processes and policies are well documented at every university. The university's legal version, commonly contained in a "faculty policy and procedures" or "academic planning" manual, is complemented by the traditions of each department concerning how a recruiting committee is selected, how department votes occur, who makes the offer and who is the primary representative of the unit in negotiations. The discussion here does not delve into these mechanics; rather the focus is on key components in implementing a successful recruiting strategy.

At most universities, a call for department and college-wide recruiting requests occurs annually and all colleges submit their proposals simultaneously to the provost. Department recruitment plans begin with the faculty and then require approval by the dean and provost. The process can also require input and recommendations from an academic senate committee and other university-wide groups. Typically, approvals are granted for one year, but it is reasonable for the chair and dean to request support for a longer-term vision. For a multi-year recruiting effort, the provost should consider allowing the department to reach the steady state over a three to five year period, subject to funding availability.

The ability to recruit and retain faculty is influenced by a myriad of both internal and external factors, all of which should be considered when developing the area's strategic plan. Too often plans fail to more broadly consider the constraints imposed and opportunities afforded by the external environment. As explained in Chapter 3, one part in doing so is to recognize budget constraints and market factors and pose a plan that is financially sustainable and realistic. In addition, a recruiting proposal should explain how additional faculty would help the department respond to campus, community and societal needs. The requested resources can then be positioned as reaping university-wide benefits rather than primarily filling the needs of one department.

Retention: Recruit your existing faculty first. While most departments focus on expanding the size of the faculty, a critical component of a successful recruitment strategy is to recruit your own faculty first. Retaining highly recognized faculty members can be a high stake game with formidable challenge. If retention efforts are not successful, the negative effect on faculty morale can cause others to follow a similar path. The effect on the academic leader can also be demoralizing. A department chair can find it disconcerting when faculty receive "outside offers." It is not unusual for leaders to become upset and perhaps depressed that colleagues can be so disloyal and in some cases leave for another institution. But the extent to which other universities attempt to woo the faculty is a signal of quality. From the perspective of a department chair or dean, if competitors are not trying to "raid" the faculty of a department that portends to be highly recognized, then there probably should be cause for concern. The chair and dean have the responsibility to monitor market conditions and appropriately reward highly marketable faculty. Top universities remain at the top by finding a way to recognize and compensate those faculty members they choose to retain.

Reacting to requests for additional compensation: Even if the department chair and dean are diligent about keeping pace with the market, they should expect that some faculty members will receive external offers each year. There should be a general understanding between the dean and chair concerning how to react to these offers before they occur. Some suggestions for doing so are offered below. Moreover, there are always faculty members who, even without an external offer, believe they are undervalued and request a salary increase. Many universities attempt to deter game playing by requiring a written offer before they will consider adjusting compensation at times other than during the normal salary review cycle. The faculty member's counter argument typically begins by posing the question "Are you really going to make me go out and generate an offer in order to increase my salary?" This line of thought is generally followed with the logical conclusion that if someone starts salivating about an actual new opportunity they are more apt to leave.

Before reacting to these situations, it is useful to first review the department's compensation structure and strategy. Compensation ranges should be determined primarily by examining comparative salary and support packages at the peer and aspirational departments delineated in the strategic plan. The plan describes both the level of quality that currently identifiable resources can support and an enhanced level of quality that is possible if additional resources become available. Each faculty member is compensated and supported based on both individual performance and a comparison to the peer group to determine the value they add to the mission of the department and university. While this approach is theoretically plausible, in practice it can be difficult to reach agreement among the relevant parties as to what that value actually is and how it translates into a specific level of compensation. Whatever support package is decided upon, market forces usually work to determine its validity.

When a productive faculty member receives an offer from another highly respected department, it can be difficult to generate a sufficient retention package. In addition to financial constraints, rewarding one individual beyond the existing compensation scheme can be politically daunting. Internal department anguish can be minimized if the faculty participates in the development and approval of the vision and they accept the rationale for compensating highly productive individuals. A not widely understood benefit of providing a significant retention package for someone at the top of the range is that all faculty can benefit if, as is often the case, department salary allocations are made annually as a percent of the existing base. Moreover, if others in the department are equally meritorious, then the updated market information provides leverage for the chair to request support from the dean for additional salary adjustments.

While retaining a highly valued colleague can be difficult, it can be even more stressful to appropriately react to someone who makes compensation demands that are not merited by performance. Caving in to requests for undeserved salary increments would create pressure to provide a comparable package for others with similar levels of performance. Ultimately, the department could find itself in a financially unsustainable state because it is over compensating faculty. A difference of opinion concerning an individual's value can occur in a number of ways. Two of the most common circumstances are:

1. An equity review reveals that the individual's compensation is below that of others who have the same longevity.
2. The individual receives a higher offer from an institution that is regarded as being of lower quality.

Equity: Compensation discrepancies can unfortunately occur due to purposeful unfair treatment. This scenario usually results from allowing too much salary discretion in the hands of one individual with too little oversight. While these cases tend to be rare, when they do occur it is critical to carefully justify an appropriate adjustment based on merit. The better solution is to change the salary determination process to allow greater participation from relevant parties.

Alternatively, the vast majority of unwarranted salary differentials occur due to the nature of allocations for salary increments. Annual salary pool allocations are driven to a great extent by external factors, which tend to produce randomly larger increments for individuals whose performance is best in years when the pool is greater. Through unintended consequences, individuals can fall behind when they should not because their productive years occurred when the pool was relatively small.

One way to avoid or correct unintended differentials is to annually examine a rolling five-year account of past salary adjustments for each faculty member. By comparing the five-year percentage adjustments across the faculty, the chair or dean can determine whether the accumulated salary changes have accurately reflected relative performance and whether each individual's total compensation appropriately reflects merit and is equitable. Adjustments can then be made annually before any discrepancy grows to the point to cause unnecessary turmoil.

A more challenging scenario can develop in an environment that is unionized or where there is an established tradition to provide equal rewards rather than increments based on merit. Even in this case, the decision concerning how to react to a discrepancy for individuals of equal longevity can be relatively straightforward if the university has clearly articulated performance standards and metrics and if there are identifiable differences in the records of relevant faculty. More typically, performance standards are only loosely defined with phrases like "we seek excellence in research, teaching and service" and the metrics are either vague or absent all together. The battles that can ensue in this case can be messy and very distasteful. It is often wise for a department chair to consult with the dean, provost and university legal staff and allow a more experienced central administration to intercede in these muddy cases.

Offers from lower quality institutions: As fundraising successes at universities have become more prevalent, departments receiving endowed chairs often attempt to lure faculty members from more highly recognized universities. What should the reaction be when a faculty member receives an offer from a lower quality department? As with all critical decisions, the answer lies in the mission, vision and strategic plan. Compensation is determined based on individual performance and comparison to the peer group identified in the strategic plan; abnormally high offers from lower quality departments should not be matched. There is value to having colleagues who are more productive and more highly recognized. This value should be weighed against a greater compensation package from a lower quality department.

Why do faculty members leave? Recruiting and retention success depends on a deep understanding of the specific issues that motivate each individual. Whatever the issues may be, the leader should not interpret departures as a signal of personal failure. Although there are exceptions, like or dislike of the department chair or dean and loyalty to the institution have little to do with retention. Individuals are motivated by many variables, some of which are not in the control of the university. Voluntary departures can derive from factors like family decisions, geographic preferences and better professional opportunities. Whether or not compensation is a major factor varies across individuals. For many, when the compensation packages are within say five to ten percent, non-monetary factors become more important. For others, any sense of attachment to the institution ends at the price of a cup of coffee. In most cases, universities can find a way to retain the best people and support the best areas. If money is the main reason that causes someone to leave then very likely the department, dean and/or provost have decided the additional compensation is greater than the cost associated with the loss of the individual's productivity and any resulting damage to the area.

Some voluntary departures are natural events. In the case of junior faculty who are underperforming, it is not uncommon for an individual to recognize and/or be told that there is little chance for advancement at which point the faculty member chooses to withdraw from the tenure process. Universities usually can accommodate the request by allowing a grace period for the individual to remain on the faculty over the next academic year while securing a position elsewhere. The best-case scenario is that the department helps the individual find a different opportunity that is both a better fit and provides an extended clock to reach tenure.

Another scenario that could result in a faculty departure can occur when an individual brings higher value to one institution over another. In some cases, the recruiting department may have decided to prioritize and add significant resources to expand the size of the faculty in this individual's area. As described in the example below, the current department may not value the individual's area as highly and after considering alternative use of the funds, may decide not to offer commensurate remuneration.

EXAMPLE: WHEN ANOTHER DEPARTMENT OFFERS A BETTER FIT

An associate professor who was being considered for promotion received a full professor offer with a compensation package that was well above the department's compensation scheme. The promotion case was strong and a quick process was viewed to be a key component of a retention package. Subsequently, the promotion was approved in a shortened time frame. Colleagues contacted at the competing department revealed that they were building this individual's area and that there would be excellent support. It became clear that since this individual's area was not a priority in the current department's mission, the value to the competing department was greater than to the current department. The decision was made that matching the offer would not be consistent with current priorities. The retention offer was set at the high end of the scale but about a ten percent difference still remained. The perspective was that the department had reached a point of indifference; they would have been delighted if the faculty member were to accept their counteroffer but they would not respond to any further requests.

In the end, the faculty member decided to accept the outside offer. After the decision, rather than being resentful, the current department offered congratulations and actually provided a bottle of champagne. As much as they did not want to lose this individual, they recognized that the new department offered opportunities that they could not provide.

EXTERNAL RECRUITING

What area and what level? How should a department decide on the sub-discipline and the level of a position it is about to recruit? Most departments simply examine who left most recently and immediately approve recruiting someone in the same area. This approach provides a good portion of the explanation behind the lack of response by universities to changing environmental factors. A more effective response would be to focus on the areas prioritized in the strategic plan, which take into account changing societal needs, current demands in each area, the current demographic composition (age and diversity) of the faculty and budgetary constraints.[60] It is often the case that the university's budgetary considerations limit hiring to the junior level. When senior faculty leave, the intent of the central administration is to capture the difference in salaries for the purpose of financing either priorities in other areas or university wide initiatives.

When confronted with a mandate to hire only at the junior level, the department chair and dean can pose several counter arguments to the provost. While the administration's policy seems plausible, in practice salary compression in many academic areas hinders the central administration's ability to capture significant funding from salary differentials. Moreover, there are a number of tradeoffs associated with hiring junior rather than senior faculty that are often overlooked. Hiring junior faculty is a risky proposition; in some areas the rate of success in attaining tenure is as low as ten to twenty percent.[61] Significant start up and development costs weighed against the probability of success should cause some hesitation to hire an untested individual rather than a tenured faculty member. The counter argument, as detailed below, is that hiring tenured faculty increases fixed costs and decreases the department's flexibility to quickly react to changing patterns of demand.

At any level, recruiting the "right" faculty can be a frustrating activity, especially if the goal is to hire highly recognized individuals. Based on the accumulated experiences of the interviewees, the key factors that influence a prospective candidate's choice between alternative opportunities include:

1. Quality of colleagues;
2. Quality of local schools for their children;
3. Professional opportunities for a spouse or partner;
4. Location;
5. Research support (travel, research and summer funds and if relevant, equipment and space);
6. Unhappiness in the current position;
7. Family preferences;
8. Prestige of the department and university;
9. Workload and sabbatical policy; and
10. Financial remuneration, benefits including health and retirement, and cost of living.

The order of importance of these factors often depends on the life stage of the individual. Geographic location, for example, is generally less critical to younger faculty. Retirement packages can often be a major concern for senior appointments, especially if some portion of the former institution's support is forfeited upon departure.

Recruiting at the senior level: Senior faculty members can be very difficult to move. Unhappiness due to the financial situation at the current university or conflicts with the administration or colleagues are strong motivations for faculty to seek outside offers. Still, one has to assume that most highly recognized faculty are well supported and appreciated at their current institution. It is also often the case that spouses have a professional career or that children are in critical stages of their education and it would not be prudent for parents to disrupt them. So what would influence a senior faculty member to consider an alternative possibility? A necessary condition is that the new academic atmosphere is at least equivalent to their current situation. But even a more highly recognized, more supportive academic environment is usually not a sufficient reason to trigger a move.

Frequently, the most important factor for senior faculty is location; if the candidate is truly interested, discussions will reveal that family live near the area or that there is a geographic preference for the ocean, mountains, weather or either an urban or small city environment. For example, attempting to attract senior faculty to Iowa City, Iowa or Newport Beach, California can lead to a non-intersecting set of candidates. Both can be done successfully but a careful screening of candidates based on locational preference can save substantial time and avoid wasted effort. At the junior level, candidates are understandably more concerned about academic colleagues and prestige, research support, teaching and service loads and initial financial support.

Senior recruiting demands patience and diligence. Family and professional decisions are not made easily at this level and the process can involve a long time horizon. If the individual is a key match for the department then it is critical for the recruiting department to be persistent. A senior faculty member may agree to a recruiting visit even if they have little initial interest in entertaining an offer. By maintaining personal contact, over a period of time it may be possible for the chair or dean to sway the individual to more carefully consider both the personal and professional possibilities. It can be helpful to invite the individual to return with family for a casual visit without placing expectations on next steps. If all goes well, a visiting appointment, say for a year, can provide a trial period for the candidate, and for that matter, for the department as well. There are countless examples of senior recruiting that spans several years before being finalized.

Junior level recruiting: Different academic disciplines at any university and the same discipline across universities can have varying philosophies concerning junior faculty deployment and development. Some believe that the junior faculty should do the heavy lifting in teaching and service to free up ample time for productive senior faculty to conduct research. There is a high degree of turnover of the junior faculty in these departments and the tenured faculty is built through senior hiring. This philosophy is rare at public universities but has been a long-standing tradition at a number of prestigious private universities. A more common strategy regarding junior faculty is to hire high quality individuals with a goal to develop and support them to not only achieve tenure but also spend their entire career at the university. This strategy involves significant development costs during at least a five or six year probationary period that include reduced teaching loads, equipment, space, matching funds for grants, research assistants, summer support, travel and professional expenses. When considering these issues, especially if the probability of tenure is low, it raises the question whether junior recruiting is too costly and perhaps should be avoided.

One advantage of hiring junior faculty is that probationary positions provide flexibility. Every promotion with tenure converts a variable cost into a fixed cost and lessens a department's ability to react to budgetary shortfalls and fluctuations in demand. Tenure-track appointments provide an opportunity to observe and assess performance with a possibility of non-renewal based on either a sub-par record or changing market conditions. In this sense hiring at the junior level is similar to buying an option, but this option can be expensive when considering the high cost of development and in some cases, the low probability of success. One alternative to a newly minted hire is to recruit an advanced assistant professor whose accomplishments provide some degree of certainty about future performance. This strategy is especially attractive if there is extensive salary compression in the area since there may be little difference between new and advanced assistant professor salaries. Still, newly trained, younger faculty members are vital to bring new ideas, innovative techniques and flexibility to help shape the academic unit optimally over time.

Strategic recruiting involves an active research seminar series when not recruiting combined with a policy of allowing several additional candidate visits beyond the norm when recruiting. Candidates, especially at the junior level, should include campus visits by individuals who are "long-shots." The goal is not realistically for hiring in the present, but rather for planting seeds for the future. Several years later it may be the case that the individual is unhappy or that the individual's department rarely tenures junior faculty. A strategy to maintain contact with top junior faculty who have successful recruiting visits but accept offers elsewhere can reap solid returns.

MAKING AN OFFER AND NEGOTIATIONS

Logistics: After a department faculty votes to make an offer, the department chair forwards the recommendation to the dean. For non-tenured faculty offers, the dean usually has final say on the approval, subject to perfunctory approval by the university. For tenured offers, the process is the normal review process for tenure, which will be described later on in this chapter. The department chair has the responsibility to negotiate the terms of an offer in concert with the dean and in some cases, the provost. For a tenured appointment, before embarking on the onerous tenure review process the recruiting chair should seek a contingent acceptance letter from the candidate, where the terms are agreed upon subject to the granting of tenure. The chair's role in negotiating the offer is critical. As is the case for retention of existing faculty, recruiting a higher quality faculty member leads to tensions over equity if there is a need to offer compensation outside the current range. To avoid undue stress, before the recruiting season begins, the faculty should discuss and agree to a strategy to make competitive offers that may be above the current salaries of most faculty. Again, the underlying rationale is that adding faculty at top salaries not only enhances recognition but also ultimately lifts the scale for all faculty who deserve additional rewards.

Responding to unreasonable requests: Even if the faculty agrees to an aggressive compensation strategy when recruiting, the department chair should establish an upper boundary beyond which further demands become unreasonable. The main goal is to achieve a fair market package. But what is fair is debatable and what is reasonable to some is unreasonable to others. The negotiation process itself can present a significant challenge. Reacting to unreasonable demands can be difficult for a chair who is trying to simultaneously represent the candidate's needs and the welfare of the department. The candidate could soon become a colleague and the chair has no interest in creating a long time enemy by being non-supportive during the negotiation process.

The chair or dean should expect that most negotiations entail some unreasonable requests. A line has to be drawn. Over extending the budget has a multiplier effect on both morale and finances, especially if the individual does not perform to expectations. An effective negotiation strategy is a willingness to walk away. Negotiations can work well, especially for senior faculty, if the chair, dean and in some cases, the provost are working closely together and agree to their roles before the process begins. With a pre-arranged strategy, the chair can respond to demands outside the norm by indicating that "I will have to check with the dean," with the option of eventually saying, "I checked with the dean and I tried my best but we simply cannot do that." This "good cop, bad cop" routine helps to keep packages in line with less chance of creating local animosity. In some cases, the faculty member being recruited may not be seriously interested but rather is seeking a bona-fide external offer to use in salary negotiations at the home institution. Department chairs can attempt to uncover this behavior by probing the seriousness of the individual's intent. The chair can gauge the reaction to an invitation for the candidate's family to visit or to an offer of a tour of the community with a real estate agent. The department chair can also contact known colleagues at the individual's current department.

Example: Getting the Facts

As a department chair I was attempting to convince a top faculty member to seriously entertain an offer. Not surprisingly, he was being considered by some of the best departments in the country. Throughout our discussions he frequently e-mailed me to let me know which schools he had just visited and how excited they were about the prospect that he might join them. As far as I could tell, none of them had actually made him an offer. During his campus visit, we reviewed the specifics of the offer that we were contemplating extending to him. When discussing the teaching load, he indicated that at MIT the load was two courses per year and that our load was twice that amount. I asked him if MIT had made him an offer and he indicated that they had not. My response to him was the following:

> *"Since MIT has not made you an offer, if we don't make you an offer, you can teach two courses for us, too."*

He found this humorous but he also understood the message; two weeks later he accepted our offer and has been a highly valued member ever since.

<u>Understanding negotiation styles</u>: It is helpful to understand the individual's personality before entering into a negotiation. Once a reasonable compensation package in on the table, the process by which you obtain closure can be just as important as the package itself.

EXAMPLE: UNDERSTANDING THE CANDIDATE'S NEGOTIATION STYLE

A top candidate, whom we can call Joe, had given an excellent recruiting seminar and the faculty was excited about moving quickly to make him an offer. As chair of the recruiting committee, I met with department chair to discuss the terms of the offer. Based on the market analysis, the appropriate salary at that time, which was the early 1980's, was around $85K. We then discussed Joe's personality and recognized that he loved to negotiate. In fact, he took great delight in retelling stories of how adept he had been at negotiating both his most recent car and house purchases. We decided that the chair should offer $10K below the final salary and allow the candidate to bid up the price. The chair turned around to the blackboard behind his desk and wrote "offer Joe $75K and eventually settle at $85K."

The chair and I did not have any further conversations about the offer but shortly thereafter Joe accepted and joined the faculty. A few years later, over lunch Joe and I were discussing an individual we were trying to recruit when the topic of negotiation strategies arose. I asked Joe how the negotiation went when he was contemplating our offer a few years earlier. He replied that it was very straightforward. He was sitting in the chair's office discussing his offer when he noticed that written on the board behind the chair was the statement "offer Joe $75K and eventually settle at $85K." It made the negotiation very simple.

FACULTY SUPPORT AND DEVELOPMENT

The composition of faculties in the U.S. is changing rapidly. Thirty years ago, the vast majority of the faculty at research universities were tenured or tenure track. Since then, as pointed out by Mason (2012) and others, a substantial increase in the use of part-time faculty at universities has reduced the share of the tenure-track and tenured faculty by over forty percent. One obvious reason for this significant shift is that permanently reduced taxpayer support has induced universities to decrease the cost of delivering the curriculum. In addition, universities have expanded efforts to increase alternative revenue sources. Recent activities include expanded revenue producing programs, enhanced fundraising efforts and increased partnerships with the community. The research faculty has little time or inclination to take on this type of activity. Recognizing the need for a more diverse faculty, universities have recruited adjunct faculty members who possess a wide range of talents including effective teaching and student advising and a willingness to provide service. Moreover, part-time faculty can perform these activities at a much lower cost than the research faculty. The research faculty has resisted this movement, pointing to the large opportunity cost associated with the loss in research productivity.

The challenge for the department chair or dean is to oversee this increasingly diverse faculty by appropriately rewarding and incentivizing both tenure-track/tenured and adjunct faculty. A critical role of the leader is to intervene if there are overt signs of disrespect of one group toward the other. The long-standing tradition in academia is that the research professor is at the top of the faculty food chain while the part-time lecturer is at the bottom. How does the academic leader affect cultural change so that each group works in harmony with the other?

Non-tenure track faculty: While the opposition of the tenured faculty to replacing faculty research positions with adjunct faculty is understandable, recent declines in state support and the effects of sequestration on funding from agencies like NIH and NSF has severely curtailed funds available for research. Universities are scrambling to find alternative funding sources while also attempting to identify significant cost savings. A critical role for the chair and dean is to demonstrate how hiring adjunct faculty who teach heavier loads at lower cost can subsidize faculty research. At the same time, the leader should create a welcoming atmosphere for the adjunct faculty, inviting them to serve on committees, providing support for professional expenses and ingraining them into the social fabric of the department. The growing importance of adjunct members has been recognized by accreditation societies like AACSB International for business schools, which has modified its standards to include the development and support of adjunct faculty as a key requirement in the accreditation process.

Many universities have career paths for lecturers that can lead to more permanent employment. These individuals teach heavy loads and provide service as student advisors and committee members. They also attend community events and provide support for activities that research faculty have little time to accommodate. In many ways, the hybrid faculty model is a straightforward example of allocating resources to their best use. The leader can facilitate acceptance of this model by explaining that adjunct faculty provide positive externalities to the research faculty by freeing up their time from these types of activities.

Developing tenure-track faculty: Low tenure success rates found in the study by Conley and Onder (2014) suggest that in some disciplines the academic profession is failing in its goal to educate and develop the next generation of researchers. Why do so few doctorate faculty in some disciplines fail to produce high quality research on a consistent basis? Individuals accepted into the best doctoral programs are in the top cohort of the population in terms of basic intelligence and academic performance. Their eventual lack of success as researchers is alarming when considering the substantial cost of educating a doctoral student followed by the recruiting and development costs associated with a newly minted junior faculty member. The issues are complex but some possible reasons include:

1. Poor training;
2. Lack of creativity;
3. Lack of motivation;
4. Lack of sufficient research support;
5. Personal issues;
6. Parenting time pressures;
7. Poor time management;
8. Lengthy review cycles and low acceptance rates at top journals; and
9. Poor communication, assessment and mentoring,

While it is not clear whether the individual, the doctoral program, the hiring department or some combination of all three is at fault, the focus here is on the factors that impede the development of junior faculty in their first position. How should a department prepare for and react to the above factors? First, the due diligence during the recruiting process should uncover attributes like poor training and lack of creativity or motivation. Unfortunately, these issues are sometimes revealed only after the individual is hired. At that point, the ultimate outcome is likely to be contract non-renewal; in this case, the sooner the individual is informed the better for both the individual and the university.

Next, top research departments provide ample aid for junior faculty to obtain the support necessary to conduct their research program. The layers of support can include internal grants, assistance in applying for external funding, equipment, space, research assistance, travel, summer funding and reduced teaching. Given this support and the fact that most new doctorates are highly intelligent and well trained, why do so many assistant professors produce so little? While lengthy journal and book review processes and low journal acceptance rates play a role, the following discussion argues that the senior faculty can make a significant difference in the success of junior faculty through improved communication, assessment and mentoring.

<u>Communication, assessment and mentoring</u>: Methods of communication include:

1. An orientation for new faculty that communicates the vision, mission and quality standards and an explanation of the faculty review process;
2. An annual faculty and staff retreat;
3. An annual meeting for all assistant professors with the promotion review committee(s) to clarify the process and standards;
4. Assignment of a mentor during the probationary years;

5. A formal written assessment of each assistant professor's progress relative to the tenure path several times throughout the probationary period; and

6. A follow-up in-person meeting to discuss the written assessment and to clarify statements and offer advice and support if needed.

Universities require formal written assessment of a junior faculty member's performance and progress toward tenure several times throughout the probationary period. In addition to the tenure review, typical scenarios in a seven-year cycle include reviews annually, biannually, or in years three and five. Perhaps the most effective and most welcomed model by assistant professors is to provide annual feedback. Junior faculty can become isolated with little reaction to their work other than infrequent reviewer reports on articles and grant proposals or intermittent comments from discussants at seminars and conferences. Careful, honest assessment of performance annually with constructive criticism can provide much needed guidance along the path to tenure.

In addition to written assessment, a formal one-on-one meeting with the department chair and, if the size of the faculty is not too large, the dean can help to avoid miscommunication about what is expected. If performance is below what is expected, recommendations for improvement are provided; the sooner the better. Later on in the cycle, if performance remains below the path expected to reach tenure, non-renewal of the individual's contract may be warranted before the tenure review process begins. No one gains from a long review process that has no hope of success.

The mentoring role of senior faculty and the chair or dean: In addition to reviewing progress toward tenure, an important objective of mentoring is to coach the individual on time management. Appropriately valuing the opportunity cost of time can be a challenge for a new assistant professor. At five or more years away, the tenure decision can seem to be far off into the future. Establishing shorter-term goals through, for example, requirement of an annual research seminar combined with an annual performance review can create a sense of urgency.

Mentoring can help the individual prioritize research, teaching and service activities in accordance with the mission and vision of the unit. Junior faculty can sometimes become enamored with teaching, which is wise only if the mission is primarily focused on the learning environment. It is also important to protect junior faculty from too much service. They may perceive that they are not in a strong enough position to say no when senior faculty members approach them to take on service activities. One of the responsibilities of the department chair or dean is to assess the service load of each faculty member and intervene if needed to ensure equity and efficient use of time.

EXAMPLE: MEETINGS WITH JUNIOR FACULTY

As dean of a smaller school (about 50 tenured/tenure-track faculty at the Paul Merage School of Business) I was able to meet with each assistant professor every fall. One objective was to explain the school's strategy concerning the development of junior faculty. The philosophy of the senior faculty is that it is their responsibility to support the junior faculty with a goal that every assistant professor should achieve tenure. In turn, a key responsibility of the junior faculty is to work diligently to develop the strongest case possible. Each assistant professor was asked to envision the composition of their desired performance portfolio at the time of the tenure decision, with a focus on the accomplishments that would leave no doubt about their case for tenure.

Once the desired portfolio was developed, the individual was asked to perform an exercise where they worked backward from the time of the tenure decision to the present to develop a timeline that showed when specific goals should be met. For example, if the goal was "x" additional "A" publications five years from now, then how many papers would be need to be (a) accepted for publication; (b) in a revise and resubmit stage:

(c) under review; and (d) in working paper form four years from now, three years from now and so on back to the present. One could then devise what research was necessary to be working on today. Each year the plan was updated and progress was assessed. A record was maintained of their oral description of their plan, goals and progress.

The annual discussions were very revealing. After the first year, some of the assistant professors created and shared a formal plan and timeline. Others envisioned the plan less formally but readily discussed the details. These two groups usually relished the opportunity to present their work at the annual research seminar and they enjoyed discussing their work and seeking advice. Still others appeared not to remember the previous discussion. They seemed to be unaffected by the pressure of the timeline and had a more random approach to their schedule and their work. This group worried about the requirement to present their work annually. The reaction of each assistant professor to the strategic thinking, time allocation and implementation of the plan turned out to be a reliable indicator of who needed additional support and advice. The reaction also was a fairly accurate predictor of their ultimate success. Those that were methodical tended to carry through on their plan; those that were more haphazard tended to lack focus, work on too many projects simultaneously and failed to complete specific projects.

The above process is one way to identify problematic issues. Whenever there was an over commitment to service or teaching, actions were taken to correct the imbalance. If there was a lack of a consistent research program and strategy, the department chair and other senior faculty were informed and they reacted by engaging in joint work, more frequent review of working papers and closer mentoring. In some cases, the tenure clock could be extended for parental or maternity leave or by taking an unpaid leave from the university. Overall, setting individual assistant professor development plans with clear priorities for research, teaching and service proved to be very helpful in providing appropriate direction during the probationary period. The plan combined with an annual assessment of the quality of the work helped to clarify expectations and provide serious evaluation of progress toward tenure.

<u>Formal mentoring programs</u>: A growing number of departments provide formal mentoring programs for junior faculty members. A typical scenario for the development of these programs is described in the example below.

EXAMPLE: A MENTORING PROGRAM

One of the interviewees described a situation that occurred earlier in his career when he was a dean. Several women who were tenure-track faculty indicated to him that they felt they were not being mentored well. One issue was that there were very few senior women on the faculty at that time and the women perceived that the male faculty had better mentoring opportunities. The dean then decided to conduct an anonymous survey of all junior faculty members to explore a number of environmental factors including how well they felt they were being mentored. The results were clear; it was not just the women who felt they were not being mentored well. Almost all the faculty who responded felt the same way.

When the results accompanied by a proposal to establish a mentoring program were presented to the tenured faculty, some faculty expressed opposition. They believed that smart people don't need mentoring; academia operates in a Darwinian model where the best succeed on their own and the weak are weeded out. Still, the dean felt that he had sufficient alignment, if not full consensus and a formal mentoring program was developed. Senior faculty volunteered and junior faculty anonymously requested mentors through a neutral party. The dean's office and chairs did not know who requested mentors nor did they know the pairings. Admirably, the senior faculty who expressed interest in being mentors requested information on how to be an effective mentor. A training session led by experts was provided and it was widely attended. Interestingly, after the session, two senior faculty members opted out, recognizing that they felt they did not have the combination of empathy, skill and patience required to be an effective mentor. Participants were asked to anonymously evaluate the program each year. While not perfect, the junior faculty felt that the mentoring they were receiving had improved in terms of both the time they spent with a mentor and the quality of the advice provided. Over time, additional faculty participated and the program became part of normal discourse of the department.

Reduced teaching and time management: Although rarely discussed, is it possible that a newly hired assistant professor can be given too much free time in the first year and that lack of a more rigid schedule can impede progress? Especially at research-intense universities, the norm is to award a reduced teaching load in the first year of a junior faculty member's appointment. Most faculty members support this policy based on the perceived benefit of allowing time for both adjustment to a new environment and initiation of a substantive research program. But immediately reducing the teaching load has the negative impact of not immediately establishing a normal workload in the mind of new assistant professors. Moreover, with the tenure decision in the distant future, the value of a reduced load in year one can easily be underestimated. The result is that the gain in productivity from a first year teaching reduction can be below what would be expected. Alternatively, a reduced teaching load is likely to be more beneficial later on, say in year four or five. At that time, the individual is likely to have several projects at various stages of completion and under review. With the tenure decision that much closer, substantial uninterrupted time should be more productive.

TENURE DECISIONS

The decision concerning whether or not to grant tenure in one of the most critical decisions an academic leader makes. Every promotion provides a signal to other faculty members, to the university and to the profession about the quality of the academic department. Moreover, tenure decisions have significant budgetary consequences. Promotion with tenure turns a variable into a fixed cost, with enormous financial obligation for the university. Mistakes are costly. Tenure cases and difficult personnel decisions can also exert a significant toll on the leader in terms of both time and stress. All academic leaders should study every tenure case with extreme care, if possible first developing an independent decision and then taking into account the votes of the faculty and other relevant individuals or promotion review committees.

Logistics: The typical promotion review process is initiated within the department. An ad-hoc faculty committee is usually appointed to perform an in-depth review, present the case and make a recommendation to the voting faculty (usually the tenured faculty) at a formal meeting. The department chair then summarizes the case and forwards the faculty's vote and a personal recommendation to the dean. The dean also reviews the file and then makes a recommendation to the provost. The process may also entail reviews by both college-wide and university committees. The individual's file with the recommendations from all the reviewers is submitted to the provost who has the final say, subject to perfunctory approval by the president and possibly the overseeing body of the university. In this structure, the department chair has primary responsibility to ensure the quality of hires across the areas in the discipline; the dean ensures quality across all departments in the college, and the provost plays the same role across all the colleges in the university.

In practice rarely does a dean or provost reject recommendations; the political cost is too high and there is little benefit. When positive recommendations are overturned, there is usually good reason. Sometimes, the provost needs to take on the role of "bad cop" because either the department chair or dean finds it too difficult to say no. In these situations, the layered structure allows the correct decision to be made without creating angst among colleagues who need to continue to interact frequently. In rare instances, the provost may overturn a negative decision by the dean, approving a promotion that was denied at a lower level. In any case, whenever the provost's decision does not accord with that of the dean, there should be ample consultation between them before the final decision is made. Rational individuals can disagree but they should ensure that all information has been considered and both parties should understand the reason for the decision.

<u>Dealing with difficult cases</u>: At the level of the department, it is usually the case that the decision by the chair aligns with the vote of the faculty. Still, there are a number of reasons why there may be disagreement. First, some cases are very difficult to read. Questions may arise concerning the individual's potential, how much of the work is independent if there are co-authors, or whether the individual is sufficiently passionate and serious to continue on a productive path after tenure. Sometimes, faculty votes on tenure cases are skewed by human nature. Faculty tend to vote yes on close call cases; some may have developed friendships; others may not devote the time necessary to build a defendable rationale for a negative vote. Another possibility is that a clique of faculty vote no for reasons other than academic quality. When a department chair faces such tensions, the dean should be consulted. The dean's support and/or the vote of a college-wide committee enables the chair to "do the right thing" with the support of a higher order of authority. A layered decision-making process allows for difficult personnel decisions to be made at a more distant level from the individual.

Similar pressures arise at the level of the dean. Again, the vast majority of decisions have uniform outcomes at various layers of the process. But if the dean feels strongly that a decision should be overturned then the provost can play a critical role in supporting the decision. In some cases the provost can be called upon to make the final negative decision. The bottom line is that it is the responsibility of the academic leader to ensure quality; if it is clear that the outcome should be to deny tenure, then in spite of political tensions, emotions and differing opinions of other layers in the process, the leader's role is to make the right decision. Tenure decisions have become even more critical in the current environment of uncertain budgets and declining public support. Each positive tenure decision commits resources for 30 to 40 years, a period over which funding availability is uncertain. Every decision weighs heavily on the university and should be made with great scrutiny.

A familiar scenario is one in which the individual is an excellent teacher and colleague but the research record is too sparse or does not meet the quality standards of the unit or the university. Years of observation suggests that, if an assistant professor has not produced sufficient research in the first five to seven years, it is highly unlikely that productivity will significantly improve thereafter. An individual who is promoted based primarily on potential rarely fulfills that potential. Over time, both colleagues and the individual become frustrated because promotion to full professor is problematic and every merit decision is likely to result in below average raises. Granting lifetime employment to faculty members in an environment in which they have little hope to excel is almost never a good decision for the institution or the individual.

Some environments need an enhancement of quality. In this case, it is inevitable that the leader constantly battles with an embedded tenured faculty whose best interest lies in maintaining lower standards. To handle this situation effectively requires that the leader possess a tough skin with ample ability to accept criticism. This scenario is challenging at best and leaves little room for the leader to be more than a short run change agent. More typically, negative decisions are made infrequently. Most tenure track faculty are guided before the "up or out" decision to move on to a more suitable university. Still, if the decision to deny needs to be made, it falls to the leader to do so.

Example: Making a tough tenure decision

A very close, but negative tenure vote for a candidate resulted in the dean's decision to deny tenure. Essentially, the faculty member was a solid colleague and excellent teacher but the research did not satisfy the university's standards. The faculty member became incensed and publicly berated the dean and the university. Subsequently, the faculty member attempted to sue the university, but an attorney examining the case found no legal basis on which to do so. During the usual one-year grace period, the faculty member found a position at another university, but left with a hostile attitude toward the dean and university.

Almost two decades later, by happenstance, the dean and faculty member crossed paths at a meeting where the dean was making a presentation. Their interaction was cordial; the faculty member complimented the dean on his presentation and then described what had transpired after the negative decision occurred. It became obvious that the faculty member had thrived in a different environment at a teaching focused college, with a reduced emphasis on research. The faculty member was satisfied with the career that had evolved after tenure had been denied. Whatever tensions might have existed were now gone. The faculty and dean had made the right decision, both for the university and the individual.

POOR PERFORMANCE OR BAD BEHAVIOR

Regardless of the incentive system, culture, recognition and rewards, in any organization there are always some employees who severely underperform. A department suffering from non-productive or poorly behaving faculty naturally seeks ways to either dismiss these individuals or induce them to leave. While actions can be taken for revoking tenure, the process entails endless meetings, distasteful confrontations and an overall major distraction for the leader and the unit. As illustrated in the example below one alternative is to use salary increments through the normal process to reflect the individual's underperformance. If the individual remains on the faculty, over time the compensation relative to other faculty will decline and eventually the salary will approach the true value added.

EXAMPLE: UNDERPERFORMING FACULTY

This scenario took place within a college of about 100 faculty members. It was commonly recognized that five faculty members were chronic underperformers. Over a period of 10 to 15 years, these individuals had received minimal salary increases. In at least two cases, even newly minted assistant professors were paid above these senior faculty members. Still, some faculty members were irked that these individuals were not meeting current standards and they requested that the college begin the process to revoke their tenure and remove them from the faculty. In a subsequent meeting with the department chairs and dean the issue of dismissal was discussed. After a vigorous forty-five minute debate, the fervor to terminate these faculty members abated after one of the department chairs presented the following argument (paraphrased):

> *Five percent of the employees in every organization are dead wood. It is a long process to dismiss anyone; if we fire these five, then another five will take their place. We know these five well and have dealt with their compensation. So, why don't we just keep the five we have now?*

His argument made a lot of sense. Removing these individuals would come at great expense. At that time, these individuals were being paid appropriately for the activities they were performing for the school. With that logic, the five continued and the chairs felt less concerned about their productivity relative to the cost of their compensation and the alternative cost of moving to dismiss them.

Reacting to poor behavior: Sometimes the behavior of a highly productive faculty member can be so destructive that other faculty express a desire for the individual to leave the department. Several of the interviewees revealed situations where an otherwise productive faculty member lacks collegiality and takes advantage of faculty relationships, mistreats staff members, acts as the "know it all" on committees and insults other faculty and staff. The result is that faculty members refuse to work with the person, either in research or on committees. Staff members fear and try to avoid interacting with the individual. How should an academic leader react to these situations? First, doing nothing is always an option but letting the issues persist is likely to allow the situation to become even more problematic. Second, talking with the individual and explaining reality is a possibility, but this option is unlikely to yield desired results and can be very distasteful. Third, as suggested above the leader can use the salary adjustment mechanism to provide a signal to the individual. Finally, since the person is productive and marketable, the leader can urge the individual to leave.

In these situations the leader needs to recognize legal realities and constraints. Meetings with the individual should never be one-on-one. Always include a second-in-command. Involvement from university legal counsel is prudent if a consequential option is being discussed. It is also wise to consult with the next higher level of leadership. It is never a good idea to make an impactful decision without checking to see if the administration will support your position. A more detailed examination of how to react to difficult personnel issues is provided in Chapter 8. Sometimes a faculty member is reasonably productive through tenure but later on publishes less frequently, if at all, in the outlets most highly valued by the department. The individual's research support is subsequently reduced or the teaching load is increased. In this scenario, university legal counsel and the provost should be informed and arrive at an agreement before any action is taken. The likelihood is that if support is removed, the individual will file a grievance. It is critical for the leader to pursue such cases to show the faculty that the unit is serious about the standards it has identified in its vision and mission. At a major research university, the individual's grievances are likely to fall on deaf ears. The best outcome is that the individual recognizes the deficiency in performance and begins to contribute by engaging in activities that fill needs in the unit. At that time, appropriate support can be given to do so.

HELPING FACULTY MOVE ON

Anyone who is nearing the end of their career naturally draws a significant part of their identity from their current position and title. For many it can be difficult to contemplate a life without the sense of purpose and professional connection. But the institution rarely is served well by individuals who continue in a full time capacity beyond their productive years. The inevitable tensions that arise are confounded by the fact that few universities have mandatory retirement policies. The following provides some insights and hopefully helpful examples.

EXAMPLE: THE IMPORTANCE OF CLOSURE.

People want and need closure. A new dean became aware that a faculty member who retired in the previous year was attempting to continue to run a program he had created years earlier even though someone else had been appointed to do so. After consulting with the associate deans, the dean decided to meet with the faculty member and explain that the program was in good hands and he no longer needed to be involved.

During the subsequent meeting, the faculty member passionately described how he developed the program and made it successful. He indicated that he will always think of the program as a major contribution to the school that would not have happened without him. It became clear that he felt that this contribution had not been adequately acknowledged. The dean agreed and then searched for an appropriate vehicle to provide the missing recognition. A tradition of the school was to hold a fall banquet for faculty, staff, spouses and major donors that was attended by 250 to 300 people. It was decided to provide a special invitation for this individual and to honor him for the major role he had played in this program. A plaque commemorating his contributions was designed and a gift was purchased. At the event in addition to honoring him for his many contributions and especially for all he had done for the program, the dean said something similar to the following:

And now that he has retired we will greatly miss him because he will no longer be leading the program that he founded.

The dean then called him to the podium, congratulated him, presented the plaque and sincerely expressed the school's appreciation. The faculty member had tears in his eyes as he addressed the audience, thanked everyone for this recognition and explained why he had dedicated himself to the success of the program. After that evening, while he continued to show interest about the status and progress of the program, he no longer looked for an active role in its administration.

While this example indicates how important it is to provide recognition and closure, there was one other related impact. As the evening was winding down one of the assistant deans thanked the dean for a wonderful evening but then expressed his strong desire that the dean never give him a plaque.

THE CRITICAL ROLE OF THE STAFF

No academic unit can operate effectively and efficiently without a highly skilled, dedicated staff. The staff represents the face of the university to the public through frequent interactions with current and prospective students, parents, alumni, donors and other units on the campus. The reputation of the unit depends critically on the quality of these interactions. Academic leaders come and go but staff members generally remain in positions beyond the tenure of any one individual. The university depends on the staff to maintain continuity of local knowledge, university rules, policies and procedures. The leader should recognize and play a role in forming strategies to recruit, develop and support the staff, especially for those positions that oversee key priorities. Every staff member should understand the vision and mission of the unit and the role they play as an individual in achieving the goals set out in the strategic plan.

The leader should make a serious effort to become acquainted with key staff members, to understand their background and the role they play. Meeting formally with the staff to obtain their ideas and to discuss implementation of strategic initiatives should be part of the leader's normal routine. Lunches with groups of staff members, town hall meetings and special celebrations of staff accomplishments are all steps in a process of building a solid open communication network. Handwritten notes to recognize special achievements or contributions are an especially effective way to express appreciation.

Create career paths: One shortfall at many universities is the lack of a mentoring system to help employees pursue successful career paths. As a leader, you should encourage staff to seek both opportunities for personal development and possibilities for career enhancement. For direct reports, it is useful to work with each individual to create a career path with a five-year plan. The staff member will appreciate your interest; your show of support can motivate the individual to excel in the current position while building credentials to seek additional responsibility. If appropriate, you can indicate that you would like the individual to continue to work for you over the long term. At the same time, because it is not always possible to satisfy career aspirations within your unit, you should also express your support even if the individual eventually seeks employment elsewhere. In this way, you are unlikely to be surprised by an unexpected departure. Better yet, if retention is not possible, then you will be able to support the transition and celebrate the individual's success. One of the most satisfying aspects of the interviewee's careers was the extent to which they had mentored and helped develop the people they worked with, even if it meant that the ultimate personal success of their mentee lied elsewhere.

One challenging aspect in grooming talent concerns how to react when an individual underperforms. There is a natural tendency to invest in the individual's weaknesses through additional training and mentoring. While there is a minimal degree of skill that everyone should possess, as shown in an extensive employee survey by Gallup, an organization is likely to develop more engaged employees by honing the best talents of individuals rather than by devoting significant resources to improve weaknesses.[62] Exceptional performance is more likely to result from the transformation of already excellent skills into extraordinary ones rather than from improving below average skill levels to average.

Most universities conduct employee surveys to assess satisfaction and solicit comments and suggestions. One of the most informative questions is "Do you have sufficient time everyday to work on what you do best?" It may be the case that poor performance results from an assignment of tasks that don't utilize the individual's best skills. If so, it may be possible to shift tasks between individuals to allow a more productive and enjoyable day for each. In this way, essentially costless adjustments can be made that pave the way for increased productivity and a more satisfied staff.

Summary and Conclusions

Taking on the role of a department chair can prove to be challenging for the average faculty member. Few universities provide more than perfunctory training for new chairs. Sustaining a productive and collegial faculty takes considerable effort and emotional stability. Many departments employ a rotating chair; usually for a two to four year term, with opportunity for renewal. The concept of a rotating chair, rather than a permanent head, has the advantage of allowing a cross section of the faculty to experience the challenges faced by the chair. Hopefully, this understanding provides the basis for a more sympathetic and empathetic faculty for the individual who happens to be chair at any given moment. Another advantage is that additional faculty members have an opportunity to view the department as a whole and better understand tradeoffs that need to be made at a higher level than most individuals experience. The disadvantage of a term that is too short, say two years, is that the responsibility is not taken seriously. The cost of investing in policy and procedure and developing a strategic plan is formidable relative to the benefit for someone who will soon return to the faculty.

A primary responsibility of chairs and deans is to recruit, develop and retain the best faculty and staff at the level of quality identified in the strategic plan. Comparison to peer and aspirational departments, subject to financial constraints provides guidelines for faculty recruiting, support and compensation. A role for the leader is to intervene when the system fails to act in accordance with the vision of the university. For example, valuable faculty and staff are sometimes overlooked due to quirks in the reward system. Bureaucratic quagmires can slow down innovations that are clearly advantageous. Effective leaders take on these challenges and find ways to both develop and reward performance and affect meaningful outcomes.

Key Takeaways: Chapter 5

- Recruiting proposals should explain how the department responds to campus, community and societal needs. The requested resources can then be positioned as reaping university-wide benefits as well as filling department needs.

- While most departments focus on expanding the size of the faculty, a critical component of a successful recruitment strategy is to recruit your own faculty first.

- A not widely understood benefit of providing a generous retention package for someone at the top of the range is that all faculty can benefit from a larger salary pool and updated market information.

- Unintended salary differentials can be avoided by annually examining a rolling five-year account of salary adjustments to determine whether they capture relative performance accurately.

- Abnormally high offers from lower quality departments should not be matched. There is value to having colleagues who are more highly productive and recognized.

- Recruiting and retention success depend on the issues that motivate each individual. Loyalty to the chair, dean or university is rarely a critical factor.

- Junior level recruiting is similar to buying an option, but this option can be expensive when considering the high cost of development and in some cases, the low probability of success.

- The tenure decision can seem to be far off into the future for a new junior faculty member. Establishing annual hurdles combined with a performance review can create a sense of urgency.

- It is the leader's responsibility to ensure quality; in spite of political tensions, emotions and differing opinions of other layers in the process, the leader 's role is to make the right decision.

- An individual who is promoted based primarily on potential rarely fulfills that potential.

CHAPTER 6

External Relations

• • •

The CEO is the link between the inside, that is, 'the organization'
and the outside of society, economy, technology, markets and outcomes.
Inside there are only costs. Outside is where the results are.

—Peter Drucker

Introduction

The essence of the transition from ivory tower to glass house is a university leadership that strategically and systematically engages the external constituency. Establishing closer community ties allows universities to more directly respond to societal priorities, while building a deeper network of potential funding sources. To facilitate this activity, universities are increasing the number of external advisory boards and the involvement of influential community members who serve on them. At the same time, the general public is being encouraged to attend an expanding set of programs that showcase university leaders and faculty. This external dynamic poses several challenges for the traditionally isolated ivory tower university. Most academic leaders have little experience either working with a board or addressing the broader external constituency, while new external advisory board members are often unfamiliar with academic culture and faculty governance. The purpose of this chapter is to provide a framework to help academic leaders successfully navigate board inter-actions while enhancing their ability to strategically communicate both internally and with the public.

Many of the skills required to address the challenges in the current environment, including strategic thinking, political savvy and public rela-tions, are essential for successfully connecting with both internal and ex-ternal constituents. This chapter provides a guide for honing these skills with a focus on techniques to identify, recruit and work with members of an advisory board. While many academic leaders eventually enjoy these activities, it can be difficult initially to make the adjustment from interact-ing primarily with academic colleagues to engaging a more general audi-ence. Effective communication requires an ability to deliver a substantive message in a succinct manner. The discussion examines elements of public speaking and provides suggestions for the development of informative and impactful presentations.

EXTERNAL UNIVERSITY BOARDS

University-wide external boards have a long tradition in academia. Essentially all universities have a board of regents, board of trustees or oth-er official body that oversees its activities. University boards have varying levels of fiduciary responsibility. Public universities are usually governed by a board of regents that has the authority to set a variety of strategic goals including tuition, enrollment targets, admissions requirements and aca-demic policy and standards. Regents also oversee the university's financial strategy and recommend budget allocations to the legislature and governor. Private universities typically have a board of trustees that has similar but sometimes more expansive responsibilities than their public counterparts.

External advisory boards for individual academic units first became prevalent in professional schools such as business and law. Pressures placed by both accreditation societies and media rankings to engage employ-ers and alumni induced these schools to create formal opportunities to receive external input. Today, almost every school, college and many other academic units have formed external boards. The benefits of an effectively engaged board can include input on curriculum, cooperative research projects, student mentoring and placement, advice on overall strategy, and political clout with university administration and external constituents. If done well, board interactions can lead to in-kind and financial support. Board members can also provide valued personal advice for the leader. But working with a board also poses some risk; a poorly structured or poorly run board can do more damage than good. An approach is described below that can maximize the benefits of board interactions while avoiding some common pitfalls.

Developing and Working with an External Advisory Board

New academic leaders often have little experience overseeing a board or in many cases, even serving on a board. The steps involved in developing and working with an external advisory board are summarized in Table 6.1 and explained below.

Define the purpose of the board: Prominent members of the community are likely to have experience serving on a board of directors for a company or a governing board for other types of organizations. In these situations, board members have decision-making authority and direct accountability The leader should clarify that this board is advisory only, with no fiduciary responsibility. Members offer suggestions and advice, which may or may not be followed. Next, is the purpose of the board to provide fundraising support or is the goal primarily to obtain advice? Academic units are increasingly establishing "Leadership Councils" that are focused on raising funds within the context of a university-wide capital campaign. Many of these councils require a financial commitment. Alternatively, the primary purpose of the board can be advisory with the hope that eventually some members become so passionate about the unit's initiatives that they offer to financially support them. Advisory boards may also require a financial commitment, usually in the form of an annual fee. Whatever the board's purpose, potential members expect and deserve clarity. Individuals who believe they are being recruited for their wisdom and advice are likely to lose interest if immediately approached for a donation. To avoid an awkward situation, early in the recruitment process, the leader should explain the board's purpose and whether or not a financial commitment is required. Some potential members will have no difficulty with a fundraising emphasis or financial obligation, while others will decline the invitation.

• • •

TABLE 6.1 Steps in Developing and Working with an External Advisory Board

1. Define the purpose of the board.
2. Staff the board.
3. Develop the board's structure and by-laws.
4. Identify and recruit members;
    a. Develop a value proposition for a board member,
    b. Provide an orientation for new members.
5. Develop an understanding of board member expectations.
6. Carefully plan each board meeting;
    a. Develop a board calendar,
    b. Develop the meeting agenda with the board chair,
    c. Send out materials at least one week in advance,
    d. Provide a role for as many board members as possible,
    e. Provide minutes for each meeting.
7. Develop a stewardship strategy for each board member.
8. Provide progress reports on actions in between meetings.

• • •

There appears to be little research on which primary role of a board, advisory or fundraising, provides the most benefit for the university. From personal experience, when an annual fee is required, board members sometimes view this payment as fulfilling their financial obligation to the unit. In this case, the annual payment creates a barrier blocking the path to a more significant donation. Still, a membership fee model can work, especially if a "give or get" strategy is utilized where the obligation is to either to donate personally or secure donations from others to fulfill the annual commitment. For an academic center or an institute, a fee-based model can provide much needed operating funds. Center board members may not be as senior as the members of a college or university advisory board and their giving potential may be limited. In some cases the companies represented on the board may be able to support a small annual donation but a large gift may not be feasible. Here, the primary emphasis of the board is advisory and annual fees provide funds that approximate the income flow from an endowment.

One perspective on whether the primary focus of a board should be advisory or fundraising is captured in the following well-known statement:

"If your goal is to raise money, ask for advice.
If you want advice, ask for money."

Requiring a financial payment can work well in the right situation but if the goal is to develop a lasting commitment from the board, it is likely that engaging its members in the vision, mission and strategy of the unit with no explicit upfront monetary obligation is a better alternative. With this approach, members often become passionate partners who are deeply involved in the unit's initiatives, directly providing financial support and engaging others to help the unit in a significant way.

Examples: Is a required fee a help or hindrance?

In 2004, the Dean's Advisory Board at the School of Business at the University of California Irvine had for several years been requiring a

$5,000 annual donation but only a fraction of the board was up to date on payments. Development officers in the school had essentially become a collection agency trying to induce board members to make good on over-due fees. Giving from all donors during the previous nine years averaged about $1.1 million per year including board member fees. It was decided to abolish the annual requirement and reaffirm the primary focus of the board as advisory to the School. The board became integrally involved in recasting the school's vision, mission and financial strategy. New board members were recruited, committees were expanded and the board took on a major role in several key initiatives. A strategic plan like the one de-scribed in Chapter 3 was developed with a financial strategy that provided the development priorities with specific needs. Over the next 9 years, board members collectively pledged over $45 million to the School. The previously viewed obligation for a small annual donation evolved into a passion for the vision, mission and initiatives of the school that members were willing to support in a significant way.

Another example involves a common structure at many universities where a university-wide group invites leaders of the major companies and organizations in the community to join as members for an annual fee. The group usually serves largely as a social and networking organization. Membership fees can range from $15K to $25K annually. The concept of establishing such a group is usually to provide an entrée to the campus for key individuals who are then directed to also interact in areas of their interest at the university. Many times this strategy works well. The chal-lenge is that sometimes members of this group decline requests to par-ticipate and provide funding for other campus units explaining that their time is limited and their company donation is already being provided to the university-wide groups.

Staff the board: choosing a board liaison. Developing and nurturing a board requires ample time and skill. An experienced staff member should be assigned the role of board liaison with the primary responsibility of board interactions. The skills and characteristics required for this posi-tion depend on the purpose of the board. If fundraising is the primary purpose, then a senior development officer is appropriate. If advice is the primary purpose, then assigning a development officer can be counterproductive, sending an off-putting message to individuals who are not interested in joining a fundraising board. Possible candidates for the primary contact in this case include a non-faculty assistant dean for external relations or if the unit is small, the dean's executive assistant.

The board liaison plays a key role in enhancing communication between board members and the leader. Some board members may be reluctant to express doubts or disagreements directly to the leader, especially in a large meeting. If board members trust and confide in the liaison the leader gains from another avenue to obtain feedback. The individual chosen as liaison should possess a level of sophistication and nuance to carefully navigate these sensitive interactions. The leader needs to place sufficient trust in the liaison, maintaining an open mind and accepting criticism willingly. In some cases, if there is sufficient value, the leader can address the issues at the next board meeting without openly identifying the originator of the comments. In other cases, the leader may wish to schedule a private meeting with the board member to clarify and address the concerns.

Another role for the liaison is to ensure scrupulous attention to detail. The level of professionalism for board members is higher than the typical level for internal university activities. All materials and all interactions with the board should be error free. Board members are particularly sensitive to misspelled names, incorrect information, typographical errors and other missteps that suggest a less than professional organization. They are extremely busy and the danger is that mistakes or a perception of lack of respect can cause a decrease in participation and loss of interest. The liaison has primary responsibility for all communications with the board and needs to possess sufficient humility to apologize and accept blame when mistakes are made.

Define the board's by-laws and structure: To operate effectively, boards need governance principles and structure. Before a new leader begins soliciting members, a set of by-laws should be either updated or developed that describe the board's mission and organizational structure, and the role and responsibilities of board officers and members. Appendix A provides an example of a set of by-laws for a advisory board for a college that can readily be adapted for a department or center. A sample outline for the by-laws is as follows:

1. The mission, purpose and role of the board;
2. The nomination process, selection process, term and term limits for board members;
3. The size and structure of the board including standing committees;
4. The role of the chair, vice chair and other officers of the board;
5. The selection process and term of the chair and vice chair of the board;
6. The role and expectations of a board member including:
   a. any fiduciary responsibilities or lack thereof;
   b. expected time commitment and meeting attendance;
   c. expected in-kind support; and
   d. financial support if required for board membership.
7. The role of the chair, vice chair and other officers of the board;
8. The charge for each committee;
9. The intended board composition in terms of desired industry or organization, specific skills, potential for giving and diversity; and
10. The frequency of meetings.

Term limits: For most boards, members should be appointed for a renewable term in the range of three to five years. Doing so allows the leader to retain productive, contributing board members while graciously thanking others who are not participating as their term ends. By-laws typically include a term limit whereby no member can serve more than two contiguous terms but can be nominated again for a board position after a hiatus period. There are exceptions: some boards can involve senior, highly recognized individuals whose extended service on the board is beneficial to the unit and the leader. In this case, term limits can be counterproductive.

Board seats can also be awarded based on the position rather than the person; for example, the chairs of other external advisory boards in the unit or emeritus board members may be given an automatic board seat.

Board size: Too large a board is burdensome for the leader who needs to maintain contact and provide an active role for most of the members. Too small a board can hinder effective meetings because schedule conflicts can result in low attendance. Beyond these pragmatic considerations, the size of the board depends on the complexity, size and diversity of the unit. For complex units like a college of social sciences, which may have seven to ten departments, a larger board with committees for each discipline can be appropriate. Department chairs can interact with the relevant committee or they may choose to create their own board. If departments have their own boards, then a useful coordination technique is to provide an automatic seat on the dean's college-wide board for each chair of the department boards.

Chair of the Board: The chair of the board plays a critical role in advising the leader on the overall strategy of the unit and the priorities for each board meeting. The chair also helps to attract new board members and often accompanies the leader on meetings with prospective candidates. The chair should be a prominent, well-respected individual who has a deep understanding of the academic environment and ideally has several years of experience serving either on this board or as a member of a similar type of university board. Over time, the chair and leader can develop a special bond, where the chair becomes a mentor and valued source of advice.

Vice chair of the Board: To maintain continuity in leadership it is useful to appoint a vice chair who assumes the chair position at the end of the current chair's term. The vice chair also serves to oversee any meetings that the chair is not able to attend. Establishing an overlap of board leadership preserves history, allows easier transition and maintains momentum between regimes. The term for the chair and vice chair should be at least two years. A three-year term is often preferred because it allows time for the officers to fully understand the issues, plan actions and carry through an agenda that they personally have established.

Executive Committee: If the board size is larger than around fifteen members, an Executive Committee can play a valuable role, providing strategic direction and opportunities for more intimate discussion with the leader. This committee provides a sounding board for advice on major initiatives in the unit, strategic use of the board, and the agenda for board meetings. The size of the Executive Committee should be scaled to the size of the board and generally ranges from three or four members to as many as ten to twelve for a board with thirty or more members. The Executive Committee can play a significant role in advising the leader about controversial issues in a more comfortable setting than would occur at a meeting of the full board.

Other Board Committees: Larger boards work best when committees are formed. In addition to the Executive Committee, other common committees include Undergraduate Programs and Curriculum; Masters Programs and Curriculum; New Program Development (usually a subcommittee of the above two committees); Alumni Relations; Nominating and Membership; Marketing; and Development. The committee structure should be strategic. Every committee involves a cost; each needs to be staffed, the members need to be stewarded and the committee's charge and meetings need to be well designed. If there is real work to be done then the cost is usually worth the time commitment. If the committee's charge does not clearly indicate how its deliberations can add sufficient value, then its formation should be put on hold and re-evaluated in the future. The board organizational structure should reflect the interactions between committees and the board, and should identify the board and committee chairs and other key players. An example of an organizational chart for an advisory board is shown in Figure 6.1. Not every board needs every committee shown and some boards may require different types of committees.

Identify and recruit board members: The leader should expect to expend considerable time and effort to identify and recruit the "right" set of individuals. Nominees are identified primarily by other board members, alumni and the development staff. Typically, nominees are first vetted by the Nominating and Membership Committee and then are presented to the board. The leader should oversee the recruitment process to select individuals that have the greatest potential to address the mission and objectives of the unit. The goal should be to attract a diverse set of individuals who offer different attributes, experiences and perspectives. The ideal person for an academic advisory board is a well-respected, highly successful individual who has a significant network, collegial personality and giving potential. Better yet, if the individual is also an alumnus, the passion and attention is that much greater. After a board member has been recruited, ongoing stewardship is required to maintain interest and maximize the value of the individual's participation.

FIGURE 6.1 External Advisory Board and Committee Structure

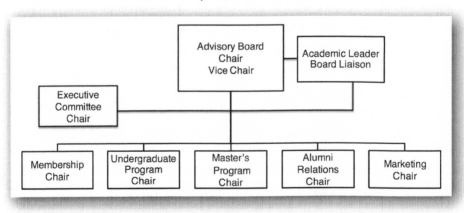

Value Proposition: Prospective board members have many opportunities and they naturally weigh the merits of various alternatives before making

a commitment. It is critical to provide a value proposition that explains the potential benefits of serving on the board. This statement can include the prestige of serving on a university board, engaging with and advising an educational institution, networking with other prominent individuals at board meetings and university functions, fulfilling a social responsibility to provide community service and in the case of alumni, giving back to their alma mater. Many board members appreciate when their role is publicized through an ad in the local paper or a listing of board members in publications, the unit's web site, letterhead and perhaps on digital media in the department or college. Also, some members view the board as providing an opportunity to learn and keep abreast of issues in their field or educational issues more generally. A sample value proposition is included in Appendix B. One important caution is that if part of the value proposition is to provide indirect monetary benefits to board members through free or reduced fee programs or other benefits, then the taxable portion of any donation needs to be adjusted accordingly.

Orient new board members: Individuals who are unfamiliar with academic culture are often surprised by the resistant governance structure and the challenges associated with attempting rapid innovation at universities. The leader should meet with new board members to provide an introduction to several key issues including: the external environment facing universities; the vision, mission, strategic plan and financial strategy of the unit; and the decision-making and approval processes that are necessary to implement change. A standard package containing this information should be distributed to each board member and should be readily available on-line.

Expectations of the board member and the academic leader: Board members should include prominent individuals who have experience with complex organizations and are connected through a deep network to potential supporters. The leader should make a concerted effort to understand what board members expect in their role as advisors to the unit. At the same time, the leader should have realistic expectations of what board members can provide. Board members should be expected to share their perspective on the unit's mission, vision and strategy with specific input on such topics as curriculum assessment and development, employer needs, marketing efforts and financial planning. Members can also provide internship and placement opportunities, student mentoring, guest lectures, in-kind and financial corporate support and personal contributions. Board members also have the ability to generate ample support in the community; their advocacy can provide significant momentum for the unit.

Board members expect to engage in meaningful discussions, providing feedback that is valued by the leader and others. To do so effectively, they expect to receive informative but not voluminous material far enough in advance of meetings to allow sufficient time to study and develop reactions to the issues. Importantly, board members expect to be informed about the results of their efforts. The leader should systematically communicate to the board that their input is needed and that their suggestions matter. Major outcomes and a progress report on resulting initiatives from previous meetings should be presented at each subsequent meeting.

Planning a board meeting is serious business: Effective board meetings require careful planning, scrupulous attention to detail and an intimate understanding of the board member's perspective. Board members are extremely busy; they should be given ample advance notification and reminders of each board meeting. Establishing a board calendar at least six months to a year in advance of meetings is greatly appreciated and needed. Distributing materials at least one week in advance helps to increase interaction at the meeting. Prior to each meeting, the leader or liaison should call each board member to encourage attendance, discuss the agenda and explain how much their participation is valued. Several board members should be asked to take on a formal role at the meeting.

The agenda for the meeting should emphasize three to five priorities from the unit's strategic plan and should first be reviewed internally with key faculty and staff. The leader should then invite comments and suggestions from the board chair. Next, about two weeks before the board meeting, the agenda and issues should be discussed at a formal meeting of the Executive Committee. The leader can gain valuable insight on how the board can best provide input to the issues by engaging first with the Executive Committee.

Once the agenda is finalized, the board meeting should be designed around one theme: how can the unit maximize the benefit from the talent and experience in the room? All too often, members arrive at a meeting eager to offer ideas only to be drowned in a one-way fire hose of information. Academic leaders are accustomed to providing extensive detail in their teaching and research; they have been educated to examine every issue from every angle. But busy board members expect their time to be used wisely; they want to add value. Forcing them into primarily a listening mode is not a productive way to engage highly talented board members. These individuals have many opportunities to serve; they choose activities where their input can provide the greatest value. The likely result of one-way communication is a loss of interest and a decrease in involvement.

The agenda should allow a role for seven to nine board members. For a small board, say fewer than a dozen members, discussions with the whole group are feasible rather than breakouts. Smaller groups foster interaction and participation if the board is large. The leader benefits most by not joining any one group but rather by circulating between them, listening for an appropriate amount of time and then moving to the next group. It is useful to designate a staff and/or faculty member to join each breakout group to take notes and offer clarifications, but not to engage in substantive discussion. The breakouts are intended to allow board members, not faculty and staff, to offer opinions. The leader should ensure that the faculty and staff understand their role: they should never become defensive. Informational, non-emotional responses with expressions of gratitude promote healthy dialogue; emotional, defensive responses close the door to productive interaction. As an indication to the board members that their input is valued and has impact, at each subsequent meeting the leader should provide a report on the actions and progress on the advice given by the board at previous meetings. A sample board meeting agenda is as follows:

I.   Welcome by the Chair of the Board
II.   Self-introductions by attendees
III.   Opening comments (Chair of the Board)
IV.   Brief review of the Vision, Mission and Strategy (Academic Leader)
V.   Update on Actions deriving from Board input (Academic Leader)
VI.   Committee reports (Committee Chairs)
VII.   Overview of Issues for Board Input in Breakouts (Academic Leader or appropriate designee.)
VIII. Break out into groups on the above issues (All)
IX.   Reports from groups (assigned Board members)
X.   Closing comments (Academic Leader and/or) Chair
XI.   Optional reception including spouses and/or significant others

Who should attend the board meeting from the academic unit? As with any board, the "officers" of the organization should attend board meetings. In the case of a school or college, the associate deans, select assistant deans, the budget officer, the board liaison and the senior development officer would normally attend. Additional faculty and/or staff can be invited depending on the specific agenda items for a particular meeting. The main concern is to avoid a meeting where the majority of the attendees are from the university. Be careful not to "over invite" individuals from the unit before a sufficient number of board members have replied that they can attend. It can be very awkward and perhaps insulting to "disinvite" faculty or staff members the day before a meeting when it is recognized that there is light attendance from board members. Finally, after each meeting, the leader, associate deans and other staff who attended should conduct a post-mortem to uncover the strengths and weaknesses of the proceedings.

<u>Develop a stewardship strategy for each board member</u>: Meaningful engagement with each board member creates an environment conducive to fostering serious input and eventual financial support. At least one interaction with each member should be planned between board meetings. The leader depends on the liaison and development officer to monitor interactions with each board member and develop a strategy for when to meet, what to discuss and at the right time, how to approach for a gift.

<u>Provide progress reports on actions</u>: Providing brief, regular progress reports helps to facilitate discussion and maintain enthusiasm. Busy board members are more likely to read an executive summary rather than a ten page document. The intent is to indicate that the leader received and documented the board's input, the ideas presented are valued; and they are being considered seriously. Details can follow in an appendix. An easily accessible web page can provide archived materials. At each meeting, the leader should clarify the process for reacting to board input. Not all ideas presented by the board can or should be implemented. To manage board member expectations the leader should explain how board input is processed. An example is as follows:

1. Some suggestions made by the board can be immediately assessed and if viewed positively, can be acted upon by the leader;
2. Some suggestions require more detailed analysis and governance and will be added to the agenda of the appropriate committee, with progress reports provided to the board for additional input;
3. Finally, there are some ideas that the unit simply cannot or will not do, but an explanation will be provided.

In some cases, an annual retreat can be a useful way to engage the board in an extended discussion of the vision, mission and strategy. This meeting can provide a more detailed analysis of committee charges, activities and results, especially on items suggested by the board. A longer meeting can focus the board on helping to prioritize activities. One way to obtain this information is to conduct an anonymous survey of the board at the end of the retreat after all major initiatives have been discussed. Which activities would they prioritize more highly? Which do they perceive to be of lower value? This type of input allows the leader to obtain a reality check on current activities; actions should follow definitive results from the survey.

Challenges: Boards that make a difference offer a diversity of perspectives from a collection of impressive, often colorful individuals. Effective board members provide critical opinion and are comfortable disagreeing with one another, but they are always collegial and respectful. While boards can be very helpful, assembling and working with a board can be fraught with challenges. Even when new board members are vetted through a nomination process, some individuals may not fit well with the board's culture. Members not well familiar with how universities operate and the impediments presented by faculty governance can sometimes dominate discussions with comments on what should be and how things should be done. Others who are accustomed to being in control may frequently make forceful comments expecting others to agree and the academic unit to act.

Some members may view the board as an opportunity for personal gain through networking and social engagements. One interviewee described a situation where a married board member flew in for every meeting with a different woman. Another interviewee mentioned difficulties at social events with board members, faculty, staff and community guests where a board member engaged in excessive drinking and inappropriate behavior. Hopefully, these scenarios are infrequent and not too serious; still, the leader should be prepared to address any that do occur.

How should the leader respond to any of the above problematic scenarios? First, the board liaison should have sufficient savvy to identify some of the issues before they become more difficult to control. For example, the liaison can observe the behavior of board members during pre-meeting conversations and at receptions or events. Once an issue is identified, the chair of the board plays a critical role in helping to communicate the issue to the board member. In some cases, the issue may simply be one of miscommunication. In several instances in my own experience, board members who were dominating discussions needed only to be informed by the board chair that they were doing so. Once they realized how their behavior was being perceived they became more respectful. In other cases, for example with inappropriate social behavior, it may not be possible to affect meaningful behavioral change. The only solution may be non-renewal of the board seat at the end of the member's term.

The "special sauce": Ed Fuller, retired President of Marriott International Lodging has served on numerous university boards. He has observed that the effectiveness of boards is determined primarily by the "special sauce" that the leader possesses to capture the board's support and make board interactions impactful, meaningful and enjoyable. The special sauce, which includes a compelling vision and a passion to make a difference based on data, substance and action, induces board members to become first intrigued and then committed. The leader's ability to mobilize a board and utilize the talents of its members productively not only encourages current members to devote meaningful time but also attracts other community leaders to seek a seat at the table. A leader builds trust by bringing controversial issues to the board, openly providing information and seeking advice. Reacting to suggestions from the board, either by taking action or explaining why some ideas will not be adopted, conveys that board member input is valued. All of these attributes of the leader contribute to a well functioning board that adds significant value.

In sum, board members expect to be given a meaningful charge and to be allotted ample opportunity to provide input. They also expect to receive systematic feedback concerning how the board's input is used and how it can make a difference. A leader with vision, who intelligently listens and strategically implements a collective mission gains a valuable wealth of wisdom from the board. Over time, the board develops trust in the leader and a commitment to the university, so much so that they are willing to provide significant financial support.

The Art of Public Speaking

A key component of an effective communications strategy is a carefully chosen set of speaking engagements at which the leader addresses students, other units on campus, alumni and the broader community. How frequent should these interactions be? Steve Sample described his experience as President at the University of Southern California as one filled with over 150 presentations each year; several of the interviewees indicated about the same degree of activity in their positions.[63] Moreover, in addition to scheduled external and internal events, unplanned interactions can be just as critical. Whether it is a passing comment in the hallway, a brief greeting to a group, or a major keynote presentation, people take the leader seriously. Every interaction provides an opportunity to communicate a consistent message; the leader should be the most well prepared person in the unit to do so. Effective communication requires considerable effort; first in developing a vision and mission that is both captivating and realistic, and then in succinctly delivering a compelling message that inspires others to contribute passionately to the unit's goals.

Internal communication: Systematic communication that conveys a consistent, relentless adhesion to the vision and mission is essential within the organization. While the leader may tire from delivering the same message, constituents need to be convinced that the mission matters and that decisions are based on the priorities it identifies. Frequent communication and repetition promotes consistency and builds a sense of trust in the leader.

A fundamental commandment of strategic communication is "do no damage." Saying nothing is better than sending a negative message. Even an off-the-cuff short quip can create incorrect perceptions that stir controversy. Inevitably, the demands associated with constantly 'being on" can sometimes lead to an unfortunate faux pas. To avoid unintended outcomes, the leader should develop and practice a set of messages that are designed for a variety of uses. Some should be appropriate for brief random encounters with students, faculty and staff. Others should carry a more substantive core message that can be modified for different venues and audiences. Being prepared is essential for a successful communication strategy in every context, no matter how seemingly inconsequential.

External communication: With declining public support universities are looking increasingly to their local community for desperately needed funding. Convincing constituents to provide support requires academia to create a value statement that clearly and succinctly defines the benefits the university brings to individuals in the community. Universities are creating ample opportunity to engage the community by offering frequent presentations about specific areas, programs and research. One of the leader's responsibilities is to take part in these programs and to explain the value of the university's activities in a vernacular that can easily be understood by a general audience.

Communicating effectively outside the academic environment can be challenging. Most faculty have little, if any, formal training concerning presentation skills. Doctoral programs are notorious for thrusting candidates into teaching situations with scant little background on the fundamentals of either creating an effective learning environment or delivering an impactful message. Many faculty members feel that they have acquired the necessary skills over time through their extensive teaching experience and that they should be able to clearly communicate with any group. Perhaps, but the skills required for teaching a course over a semester are very different from those needed to deliver an impactful, concise message to a lay audience in ten to twenty minutes. This type of presentation can be difficult for almost anyone, but it can be especially challenging for faculty who are accustomed to providing ample detail utilizing technical language.

Faculty who are adept in communicating to their students and colleagues have typically honed the following skills:

* Scrupulous attention to detail;
* Consideration of numerous alternatives to the main approach;
* Speaking and writing in professional syntax;

* Depth of knowledge and passion about their specialization; and
* Answering questions in great detail, offering comprehensive perspectives under alternative assumptions.

While the above skills are valued in an academic environment, they are less effective when attempting to deliver a compelling talk to a general audience. If the leader depends primarily on these skills, the result is likely to be a confused, disengaged audience that is mystified about the purpose of the speech and becomes disinclined to engage further with the university.

DESIGNING AN IMPACTFUL PUBLIC PRESENTATION

Substance: For any subject, it is critical to understand the perspective of the audience. Why should they care about this topic? If the main message pertains to the academic unit, members of the audience need to be convinced that there is a tangible benefit from the unit's activities that is relevant for them. If increased involvement with the unit is a goal of the presentation, the speaker needs to explain how the attendees can derive value from being associated with the area. Few people are willing to provide funding simply because the area expresses a need. While these comments appear to be straightforward, all too often presentations by university officials follow the scenario depicted below.

Leader: *Our department has top faculty who conduct highly regarded research.*

Audience perception: *How does that benefit me?*

Leader: *The competition is ever increasing and funding for our programs and research is dwindling. Our long-standing high level of recognition is in jeopardy and we would greatly appreciate your support.*

Audience perception: *Why would I give money to help you maintain faculty research that means little to me?*

At this point, most of the audience has likely lost interest. One way to create a presentation that is meaningful to the audience is to begin by outlining the major points and then describing why the attendees should care about each one. The example below illustrates a presentation that is more likely to peak audience interest.

EXAMPLE: EXPLAINING WHY THE AUDIENCE SHOULD CARE

Donna Shalala, currently President and CEO of the Clinton Foundation and former Chancellor of the University of Wisconsin Madison, Secretary of Human and Health Services and President of the University of Miami is a masterful presenter. She studies and understands her audience and knows how to educate, entertain, and entrance the attendees. Her presentations immediately create a bond with the audience, explaining why they should care about the university. Below is a paraphrased example of her opening statement in a speech from the early 1990's to a large audience from the local community in Madison, Wisconsin.

Good evening! Thank you all for attending this evening. I have some wonderful news from the University of Wisconsin. But before I share this news with you, I am sure some of you are wondering, "Why should I care?" Let me explain why. How many of you have family members who drink milk? Did you know that Vitamin D was discovered right here at the University of Wisconsin-Madison? And how many of you watch the weather report every night on TV? Do you know where the technology was developed that allows you to view weather radar? You guessed it; right here at the University of Wisconsin. And how many of you have heard of the Hubble telescope? Well, the parts that actually work on the Hubble telescope were developed right here at your University. Now let me describe other research taking place here that directly affects your life.

This type of opening captivates the audience, inspiring them to be associated with and support the university. While the above example relates to a presentation given by a university president, a dean can modify the approach by again beginning with exciting developments at the level of the university and then continuing with examples from the college or school.

Style: The speaker should expect that most audience participants are passive listeners who process comments superficially and are likely to remember only a few main points. The data and details behind the main points are necessary to establish the validity of the arguments, but too much detail during the presentation causes the audience to lose interest. Audiences demand and deserve substance and brevity. Points can be made succinctly; as Muriel Humphrey was famous for saying to her husband Hubert, "A speech doesn't have to be eternal to be immortal."

After researching the key topics and assessing the interests of the audience, the next step involves presenting each point in the simplest, most compelling way with the least amount of detail. Additional key points to creating an effective style are summarized in Table 6.2. The ability to captivate the audience with a story is a defining characteristic of renowned public speakers.[64] Anyone who has ample speaking experience recognizes that often what attendees remember most is a humorous story or provocative anecdote. Even after considerable time has passed, memorable stories can spark reflections on the purpose of the event, the organization and the speaker. Many speakers open with a humorous tale but a more effective approach is to wind humorous stories, surprising facts and audience participation throughout the presentation. Appendix C contains quotes and vignettes that can be adapted for use in specific settings.[65] Key concepts can also be embedded in short videos and summarized in PowerPoint bullets. One method for maintaining interest is to pose questions and ask for audience feedback, either by a show of hands or by using technology that captures anonymous responses. Inviting participation minimizes daydreaming by creating a sense of anticipation. These techniques provide a way to make critical points without resorting to endless detail and dry arguments. Members of the audience listen more intently, not wanting to miss the next amusing anecdote or provocative question.

• • •

TABLE 6.2 Key Factors for Effective Presentations

What can go wrong? Poor presentations result when:

1. The audience is confused about why they should care and how they can benefit from the presentation.
2. There is no clear point.
3. The points are too technical and/or too detailed.
4. The sequence of the presentation is hard to follow.
5. The presentation is poorly delivered.
6. Slides are not readable.
7. The presentation is too long.

Key steps for developing an effective presentation are as follows:

1. Understand what the audience wants to learn.
2. Be brief.
3. Emphasize no more than one to three key takeaways.
4. Make it easy to understand your key points.
5. Use facts but don't become embroiled in details.
6. Use meaningful, relevant stories.
7. Use intelligent humor; be entertaining with substance.
8. Build to a memorable conclusion.

• • •

Making a substantive presentation that is both succinct and entertaining requires significant preparation. It is wise to practice several times, modifying the commentary and perfecting the timing, especially when telling stories. A critical goal for the speaker is to gain a rapport with the audience. A confident, comfortable presence with constant visual contact that spans the room puts attendees in a welcoming frame of mind. The most gifted presenters make each member of the audience feel like the speaker is talking directly to them. A dose of creativity combined with preparation can pave the way for the speaker to be simultaneously entertaining and substantive, making points that are memorable due in large measure to the passionate, compelling way in which they were presented.

SUMMARY AND CONCLUSIONS

Throughout most of the history of academia, the role of university leaders was focused internally on ensuring academic excellence. Today's environment requires leaders who are externally focused; their skills include not only a keen sense of academic culture but also the ability to relate the value of higher education to a broad constituency. As academia opens its doors through increased interaction with the community, it is naturally subjected to increased scrutiny. Frequent demands for accountability and relevancy need to be responded to with clarity and substance in a succinct and non-defensive manner. Doing so effectively can be challenging for faculty that have had isolated careers within the traditional ivory tower existence of universities. This chapter lays the foundation for effective public engagements and especially for productive interaction with external advisory boards. Boards can provide valuable input, advocacy and support. They provide opportunities for higher education to more directly address societal needs; the end result can be more responsive universities.

The leader should strive to be the best-prepared and most effective communicator in the organization. Poor presentations can do damage. Speakers who are difficult to understand can frustrate an audience and create a negative atmosphere about the program and university. Warren Buffett said it well when he described one of his main philosophies for choosing where to place his money—invest only in what you can understand. If the leader cannot effectively communicate the message, no matter how strong a vision, potential supporters will find other places to contribute their time and resources. With appropriate preparation and practice, the leader can become a polished presenter, delivering substance with a passion that is so compelling that audience members contemplate increased interaction with the university and consider providing financial support for its efforts.

KEY TAKEAWAYS: CHAPTER 6

- Board members can view a mandatory annual fee as fulfilling their financial obligation to the unit. In this case, the required payment creates a barrier blocking the path to a more significant donation.
- If your goal is to raise money, ask for advice. If you want advice, ask for money.
- Board meetings should be designed to benefit most from the experience and talent in the room. Forcing prominent board members into a listening mode is likely to result in a loss of interest and decrease in involvement.
- The leader should ensure that the faculty and staff understand their role at board meetings. Informational responses and expressions of gratitude promote healthy dialogue; defensive responses close the door to productive interaction.
- Board members expect to be given a meaningful charge and ample opportunity to provide input. They also expect to receive systematic feedback concerning how the board's input is used and how it can make a difference.
- The leader should be the most effective communicator in the unit. Whether a passing comment in the hallway, a brief greeting to a group or a major keynote presentation, people take the leader seriously.
- Constituents need to be convinced that the mission matters and decisions are based on the priorities it identifies. Frequent communication and repetition promotes consistency, commitment and a sense of trust in the leader.
- Audiences demand and deserve substance and brevity.
- Most audience participants are passive listeners who process comments superficially and are likely to remember only a few main points.

Appendix A:
Dean's Advisory Board Membership
Criteria (Sample)

• • •

Board Mission

The mission of Dean's Advisory Board is to:

* serve as a senior advisory group to the Dean, faculty members and staff in strategic planning efforts;
* act as advocates for the college and promote the interests of the college in regional and national business communities;
* assist in recruiting additional members to the college's support organizations;
* assist in fundraising campaigns to help increase the financial resources of the college.

Membership Expectations

Members of Dean's Advisory Board are nominated by the Board Membership Committee or other key supporters of the School, and are invited to join by invitation of the Dean. By accepting nomination and membership, board members are expected to:

- actively participate in meetings of the Board, actively serve on one committee and participate in quarterly committee meetings;
- support and actively participate in specific initiatives undertaken by the Board;
- provide expertise and evaluate strategic directions pursued by the college's leadership as it implements initiatives designed to fulfill the vision;
- actively represent the college to the broader community and encourage significant participation and support.

Membership Benefits

The Dean's Advisory Board members are an important component of strategic planning and growth of the college. Members will be invited to contribute expertise and advice and participate in events and meetings featuring world-class lecturers, academic leaders and strategic thinkers. Members of the Dean's Advisory Board are considered a vital source of wisdom and leadership whose select participation will be incorporated into important college events.

Board Size and Composition

The Board consists of thirty-six external members and the Dean. Every attempt will be made to have a diversified Board without regard to age, gender, race or religion. Further, it is desired to have appropriate representatives from a diverse set of organizations and professions, with individuals who collectively possess a variety of relevant skills.

Membership Term and Term Limit

The term for members of the Dean's Advisory Board members is four years. Membership is renewable by consensus of the Membership Committee for a maximum of two contiguous terms. Members who have served two terms can be nominated again after a hiatus period of two years. Every effort should be made to stagger board terms to ensure continuity of board membership. Ideally one fourth of the board should be reaching the end of a four-year term of service each year. Officers of the Dean's Advisory Board shall rotate offices after a maximum three-year term.

Membership Criteria and Considerations

The college desires to recruit board members who are willing and able to work to support and further its mission and vision. Accordingly, candidates should have strengths in one or more of the following areas:

- *Strategy Development.* Individuals who can advise the Dean on the development of or improvement of the college's strategic plan. Such assistance could come from any number of candidates including those whose expertise is in the area of strategic consulting;
- *Curriculum Assessment and Development.* Individuals who, based on their own educational and professional experiences can advise the college on the substance of the curriculum and its relevance and timeliness;
- *Marketing.* Candidates with the skills to advise the dean to develop and execute marketing strategies to recruit the best and brightest students, raise funds, enhance the reputation of the School, and attract high caliber educators to the faculty will add significant value;

- *Local Outreach.* Business executives and other prominent or persuasive individuals who can assist in attracting the interest, expertise and assistance of local businesses, organizations and individuals to be involved with the college on an ongoing basis;
- *Partnering.* Individuals are desired who can provide access through their organization to student internships, who will partner with the college's students on projects specific to their company's market, and who are willing to consider graduates for positions in their companies;
- *Fundraising.* Individuals who can personally contribute, or influence the contributions of other parties, are desired.

In addition, Board members may be asked to participate with the college in the following activities:

- Attend board meetings and provide input on strategic discussions;
- Provide advice to the dean;
- Introduce the dean to community members;
- Participate as a speaker, mentor or panelist;
- Provide a project in your organization for students;
- Hire a student intern;
- Recruit students for permanent positions;
- Host a board meeting or event at your organization;
- Provide financial support for the college.

Appendix B:
Value Proposition for Board Membership:
Dean's Advisory Board (Sample)

• • •

SUPPORT HIGHER EDUCATION

* Enrich and enhance programming and opportunities for our students.

LEAVE A LEGACY

* Leave a positive and lasting 'foot-print' in the community.

STAY ON THE LEADING EDGE

* Attend School and University programs and events.
* Priority access, and discounts to programs and workshops.
* Access to research and white papers.

Lend Your Expertise to the Next Generation

- Serve as a student mentor.
- Become a guest lecturer.
- Participate in Career Panel discussions.
- Receive priority in meeting with and recruiting highly talented students.

Expand your Network

- Participate in Research Salons hosted at board member's homes.
- Attend strategic, industry specific conferences.
- Network with influential community leaders.
- Gain access to university leaders.
- Gain access to the faculty.
- Receive special invitations for private breakfast/luncheon events hosted by the dean.

Enhance your Recognition

- Prominent name recognition on digital signage within school.
- Name recognition on program materials.
- Exposure on website and marketing materials related to the school.
- Leadership opportunities on the Advisory Board.

Appendix C:
Quotations

• • •

ADVICE

If you can't convince them, confuse them.
-- *HARRY TRUMAN*

You miss 100% of the shots you don't take.
-- *WAYNE GRETZKY*

I never did give them hell; I just told them the
truth, and they thought it was hell.
-- *HARRY TRUMAN*

When your work speaks for itself, don't interrupt.
-- *HENRY KAISER*

Many a man would rather you hear his
story than grant his request.
-- *PHILLIP STANHOPE, 4TH EARL OF CHESTERFIELD*

If you think everything is going well, you don't
know everything that is happening.
-- *(UNATTRIBUTED)*

If everything seems to be in control, you're not going fast enough.
-- *MARIO ANDRETTI*

The only way to do great work is to love what you do.
-- *STEVE JOBS*

Don't be so humble – you are not that great.
-- *GOLDA MEIR*

BUREAUCRACY IN ACADEMIA

If the world ever comes to an end I want to be at a
university because it will happen there two years later.
-- *(ADAPTED FROM A QUOTE BY MARK TWAIN,
SUBSTITUTING "UNIVERSITY" FOR "CINCINNATI.")*

The real reason God was able to create the earth in 6 days is
that he didn't have to get approval from the Academic Senate.
-- *(ADAPTED FROM WILLIAM SIMON)*

CHALLENGES

If you are going through hell, keep going.
-- *WINSTON CHURCHILL*

CHANGE

In business, the best way to predict the future is to invent it.
-- *(ADAPTED FROM ALAN KAY)*

In the academic senate, the best way to
predict the future is to prevent it.
-- *(UNATTRIBUTED)*

The world is too big for us. Too much going on—it's an incessant
strain to keep pace. Science empties its discoveries so fast
that you struggle beneath them in hopeless bewilderment.
-- *(EDITORIAL IN THE ATLANTIC JOURNAL, JUNE 16, 1883.)*

COMMENCEMENT COMMENTS

It is never too late to be what you might have been.
-- *GEORGE ELLIOT*

I've imagined great races and I've imagined great victories.
The races are better.
-- *MARK HELPRIN REFERRING TO THE WINTER'S
TALE BY WILLIAM SHAKESPEARE*

CREATIVITY

Discovery is looking at the same data as everyone
else and seeing something completely different.
-- *ALBERT SZENT-GYORGYI*

DEANS

Being dean is like being quarterback of a football team but there are three differences: first, you don't get to call the plays; next, no one listens to you in the huddle; and third, your own team can tackle you.

-- *(UNATTRIBUTED)*

DEVELOPMENT/FUNDRAISING

A rich man's joke is always funny.

-- *THOMAS EDWARD BROWN*

Money is the best deodorizer.

-- *(UNATTRIBUTED)*

ECONOMY

In the long run, we are all dead.

-- *JOHN MAYNARD KEYNES*

There is nothing more permanent than a temporary government program.

-- *MILTON FRIEDMAN*

We have two classes of forecasters. Those who don't know...and those who don't know they don't know.

-- *JOHN KENNETH GALBRAITH*

EDUCATION

If you plan for a year, plant some seed.
If for ten years, plant a tree.
If for 100 years, teach the people.
-- *KUAN CHUNG*

I can't give you a brain but I can give you a diploma.
-- *THE WIZARD TO THE SCARECROW IN THE WIZARD OF OZ*

Years ago, when I was a student sitting in the
back of a six-hundred-person auditorium, now
that is what I call distance education.
-- *(UNATTRIBUTED)*

FACULTY

The faculty: a group that chooses to think otherwise.
-- *(UNATTRIBUTED)*

A professor is someone who talks in someone else's sleep.
-- *W.H. AUDEN*

GOVERNMENT AND POLITICS

A government big enough to give you everything you want
is also strong enough to take everything you have.
-- *THOMAS JEFFERSON*

It is a mistake to think that businessmen are
more immoral than politicians.
-- *John Maynard Keynes*

Republicans believe things that are not true.
Democrats want things that cannot be.
-- *(unattributed)*

Washington DC is the only place in the world
where sound travels faster than light.
-- *(remark at the annual convention of the Congressional*
Medal of Honor Society in New York; December 12, 1983.)

If it moves, tax it. If it keeps moving, regulate
it. If it stops moving subsidize it.
-- *Ronald Reagan*

Inspiration

A man is not finished when he is defeated.
He is finished when he quits.
-- *Richard Nixon*

A brilliant light may flash only once in a lifetime.
Make sure your eyes are open when it does.
-- *(unattributed)*

Investing

It ain't what you don't know that gets you into trouble.
It's what you know for sure that ain't so.
-- *Mark Twain*

There are two times in a man's life when he should not
speculate: when he can't afford it, and when he can.
-- *MARK TWAIN*

There is nothing so disastrous as a rational
investment in an irrational world.
-- *JOHN MAYNARD KEYNES*

LEADERSHIP

To lead the people, walk behind them.
-- *LAO TZU*

When Cicero speaks, people marvel.
When Caesar speaks, people march.
-- *IN TICHY AND BENNIS (2007) AND HEPPELL (2004)*

The secret of managing in baseball is to keep the four guys who
hate you away from the five who haven't made up their minds yet.
-- *CASEY STENGEL*

A real executive goes around with a worried look on his assistant.
-- *VINCE LOMBARDI*

MEASUREMENT

Not everything that counts can be counted and
not everything that can be counted counts.
-- *ALBERT EINSTEIN*

Personal Comments (to be used at roasts, retirements, individual celebrations)

(Name) is so fast on his feet, that he is the only person I know who can watch 60 minutes in a half an hour.
-- *(UNATTRIBUTED)*

Sometimes right, often wrong, never in doubt.
-- *Justice Antonin Scalia*

He is like a breath of fresh air, with gusts up to 90 mph.
(UNATTRIBUTED)

I asked (name) why it is that he did not retire sooner; after all he could have retired ten years ago. Well, he told me; "I gave this university 30 of the best years of my life. I decided that I wanted to give them some bad ones."
-- *(UNATTRIBUTED)*

When you retire, you go from who's who to who's that? (Name) will always be on our who's who list.
-- *Walter Wriston*

Strategic Planning

By failing to prepare, you are preparing to fail.
-- *Benjamin Franklin*

Vision without implementation is hallucination.
-- *Benjamin Franklin*

SPEECHES (OPENING STATEMENTS)

Two of the best cures for depression are a good laugh and a long nap. Hopefully you will get both of those here tonight.
-- *(ADAPTED FROM AN IRISH PROVERB)*

As I call your name I would like you to stand and keep standing. Thankfully, I got that right this time; last time I asked the audience to rise and keep rising.
-- *(UNATTRIBUTED)*

STRESS

A CEO recently told me that he had put his workers through a stress reduction program. When I asked how it worked he replied: "Well, it did have an impact. Productivity is down but now, nobody cares."
-- *(UNATTRIBUTED)*

TEAMWORK

None of us is as good as all of us.
-- *RAY KROC*

Spending time together seeking consensus is not the same thing as real work.
-- *JOHN KATZENBACH, MCKINSEY & CO.*

UNIVERSITIES

A major university is one huge global complex with lousy parking.
-- (ATTRIBUTED TO CLARK KERR)

CHAPTER 7

The Art and Science of Development: The Leader's Role

• • •

If you think donor relations are all about talking,
you haven't been listening.

—(ATTRIBUTED BROADLY)

INTRODUCTION

DURING A RECENT MEETING OF the academic council at a large public university the provost announced to the deans that from this point on, fifty percent of the dean's time would be spent off campus developing relationships with the community. The reaction, as described by one of the interviewees, was predictably mixed. Some deans, including those from engineering, law and business indicated that they were already spending at least this much time in the community. Others, from the physical and biological sciences, felt that their time was better spent working with external granting agencies in Washington DC and elsewhere. For them, the prospect of donors providing the vast sums of money necessary to conduct research seemed implausible. Still others felt that their main role was that of an internal academic officer and that their presence externally would cause undue personal stress and force them outside their comfort zone.

The provost's declaration, which is not atypical across public universities, reflects the reality of permanently reduced funding from two primary sources: state appropriations and federal research support. While development activities have historically been a defining feature of the best private universities, a focus on development at public universities has evolved more slowly, gaining momentum over the last few decades, primarily out of necessity. Through the 1970's the majority of public university expenses were funded by state budget allocations. Federal agency research funding was also relatively abundant and there was little need to seek other revenue sources. Today, facing growing pressures to become financially more self-reliant, public universities have created a significant development infrastructure and have increased their efforts to seek funding from philanthropic individuals and foundations.

Public universities naturally seek to learn from their private counterparts whose ability to build significant endowments is highly recognized and envied. But the success of private universities is no accident. Through well-designed strategies and techniques, private universities attempt to develop a "cradle to endowment" relationship with potential donors. Starting at the first interaction with a potential student during the admissions process, they begin to nurture a relationship between the parents, student and university. They provide a highly engaged learning environment followed by frequent interactions with alumni. As relations with alumni and other potential donors mature, private universities are well positioned to initiate opportunities for meaningful university involvement. The ultimate goal is to create a grateful friend of the university who provides a significant gift that funds a key priority. This strategy has been extremely successful at the top privates; for example, Harvard's endowment in 2013 exceeded $32 billion, Stanford's was around $18 billion and Chicago's was almost $7 billion.

The increasing focus on "friend" and fund raising has had a profound impact on the role and responsibilities of all academic leaders. Deans, center directors, department chairs, program directors and others need to be part of and add to this effort, much of which involves expanding relationships with the community. The chief development officer on every campus is the president whose responsibilities include leading the campaign, being involved directly with major gifts and guiding donors to the highest priorities for the university. For some academic leaders, the need to work with donors can appear to be a daunting task. In reality, for most, meeting and working with donors can be enjoyable and fulfilling, and in some cases, can become some of the most satisfying activity associated with an academic leadership role. But, development is not easy, nor is it inexpensive. There is a science behind successful philanthropy but there is also an art to becoming a publicly admired individual who people trust and have faith in, so much so that they are willing to provide financial support for the individual's cause. Moreover, a successful fundraising operation involves research, friend development, stewardship and meticulous attention to detail. Skilled individuals are needed to implement a well-devised strategy; if not carefully orchestrated the development operation can become a cost center rather than a vehicle for investment that reaps a beneficial return.

This chapter focuses on the leader's role in creating and implementing a successful development initiative. A first principle is that designing a fundraising strategy is not an independent exercise that generates a stand-alone list of needs. Rather, the priorities for development evolve naturally from the mission, vision, strategy and financial plan of the unit. A methodology is provided for systematically determining and explaining strategic needs in ways that donors find compelling, relevant and supportable. Creating a positive atmosphere for philanthropic support requires strategic communication through a variety of media. The discussion identifies several options including social media, web sites and traditional published materials.

Achieving development goals entails a mix of endowed and annual gifts. The importance of an annual fund campaign is explained, with some examples of fruitful approaches. Major gifts involve sustained coordinated efforts between academic leaders, development officers, potential donors and in some cases, faculty members. The cycle of successful development is described along with examples of the process by which several gifts were secured. Finally, some of the challenges associated with development are discussed; it is especially helpful to anticipate what can go wrong and what paths should be avoided before they become thorny and problematic. Importantly, not every gift should be accepted.

THE ROLE OF THE ACADEMIC LEADER IN DEVELOPMENT

The leader of the unit, whether a department chair, head of an institute or center, dean, provost or president, is the coordinator and director of the development team. The leader oversees the creation of the vision, mission and financial strategy for the unit and is responsible for working with all constituencies to set priorities, communicate effectively and manage internal expectations. The leader maintains overall morale, giving credit to others for successes, gratefully and publicly acknowledging donors, and accepting blame when something goes wrong. When a potential donor requests information about development needs, all too often the response is "We need faculty chairs, student scholarships and discretionary funds." The donor's reaction is almost always negative to this type of generic statement. Every academic unit needs this type of support—why is the request by this unit different? With today's inundation of requests for funds from a variety of worthy causes, why would a donor be compelled to respond to this one?

A critical lesson for anyone requesting funds is that "It is not about you." It is always about the donor first and finding a match between the donor's passions and the needs of the unit. The ultimate goal is to create a "joyful" donor who feels that providing support for your initiative fulfills a personal desire to make a difference. Donors respond to a compelling vision, a well thought out, realistic strategy and a passionate individual who is attempting to accomplish goals about which the donor cares deeply. Consider the difference between the above request for funds and the following:

Our department has made significant advances in stem cell research. We have developed methods used in emergency rooms that can prevent a type of spinal paralysis that results from injury if the treatment is performed quickly after an injury. We are on the verge of discoveries that can potentially cure liver and other types of cancers and can help Alzheimer's and diabetes patients. Support for three endowed chairs and a similar number of post-docs can allow us to better equip and staff an already productive laboratory and speed the discovery process.

Certainly, not all academic areas can purport to cure cancer but every area has the potential to develop a distinctive vision, prioritize its activities and present a development strategy that will be compelling to a select group of philanthropic individuals. To illustrate, the discussion below creates a case for development for the hypothetical department of economics that was introduced in Chapter 3.

CREATING AND IMPLEMENTING A DEVELOPMENT STRATEGY

If the unit has performed a comprehensive strategic planning process, it has already identified its development priorities. As discussed in Chapter 3, the strategic plan delineates the area's current status and its key initiatives. The vision is aspirational, indicating what the unit feels it can become if it were able to access additional support. In this way, a development strategy is not a stand-alone list of needs. Rather, development priorities derive directly from the vision, mission and financial strategy. The example below provides a brief overview of how a typical department can describe its strategy for an external audience.

Example: The Hypothetical Department of Economics

As developed in Chapter 3, the department's mission and vision prioritize public policy with an aspiration to enhance overall wellbeing through breakthrough research and public policy solutions emanating from distinguished faculty, students and alumni. The priorities of the department coincide with those of the university in the areas of a changing demographic, sustainability and growing public debt. Table 3.4 indicates the additional funding needed to attain the vision, which totals to $1.65 million annually. The table also identifies the intended sources of revenue. After accounting for new program revenue, additional allocations from the central administration and reallocation within the department, the remaining amount, $675K annually, becomes the development goal.

Next, the feasibility of the development plan should be assessed. Does the department have a support base that has the potential to donate $675K beyond the current annual level of gifts? If this amount were to be endowed the necessary target, assuming a payout of 4.5% to 5%, would be an additional endowment of around $13.5 to $15 million.[66] This goal might be beyond the reach of the unit, especially if the area is small or relatively new with young alumni. In that case, rather than attempting to endow the entire amount, one alternative is to increase annual donations to provide a portion of the funds needed. For example, if the annual campaign can yield an additional $300K, then assuming a payout of 5%, the required endowment falls from $13.5 million to $7.5 million. One scenario is to seek endowments for an honors program at $1.5 million and three chairs at $2 million each. Then unrestricted gifts that derive from the annual campaign can be used to fund initiatives like doctoral fellowships and marketing, which are areas where donors willing to fund endowments are more difficult to find. This development plan is illustrated in Table 7.1.

The potential for raising funds can be researched and assessed by the staff in the university's advancement operation. While setting high goals can sometimes work to inspire constituents, if research indicates that the fundraising target is not feasible, the plan should be revised. A commonly used strategy is to announce a slightly lower than achievable fundraising target and then outperform expectations. The alternative of not reaching a publicized goal casts a negative stigma that can be difficult to dissipate. The department should prepare a marketing document that summarizes the vision, mission, financial plan and development strategy with a rationale for each goal and an explanation of the intended impact of each gift. A perspective donor can then easily identify the value of a specific gift to the institution. This material can be accompanied by a proposal for a gift that matches the donor's interests and fills one of the needs described.

STAFFING A DEVELOPMENT OPERATION

<u>Logistics:</u> Many universities have a central foundation, which oversees the majority of development or advancement operations. Development officers (DOs) are hired by and report to the foundation and are assigned to each unit. Salaries are generally paid by the central operation using funds collected from the units via an overhead tax on either their funds raised or their endowment.[67] The overhead tax also covers the expense of services provided by the foundation which include research, legal and estate planning guidance and coordination of the donor base across the units. Depending on the size of the campaign and the potential donor base, units usually have the latitude to hire and pay for additional staff. An alternative is a decentralized model where each DO is hired by and reports to the college or specific unit. Salaries are mostly paid by the units and funds raised continue to be taxed to cover services provided centrally. Many universities use a hybrid model that allows discretion in oversight and staffing by each unit. Later in this chapter, the discussion examines the size and cost of the development operation.

The DO is trained on the development process and ideally has some breadth of knowledge and experience about how gifts can be made to best take advantage of tax considerations. The central development office also employs individuals with expertise concerning estate planning, how to identify and approach foundations for support, legal aspects of gift arrangements and how to perform background research to identify and qualify donors. This expertise is valuable and should be sought as needed by anyone who is involved with a significant development campaign.

TABLE 7.1 Development Plan: Hypothetical Department of Economics (all entries in thousands)

Initiative	Fundraising goals	Endowed Equivalent	Annual income from endowment	Annual Fund
Increase faculty by 5	$ 50	Annual fund	$ 0	$ 50
Increase chairs by 3	$ 300	$6,000	$ 300	$ 0
Increase scholarships	$ 25	Annual fund	$ 0	$ 25
Increase doctoral support	$ 200	Annual fund	$ 0	$ 200
Add 15 Honors scholarships and infrastructure	$ 75	$1,500	$ 75	$ 0
New marketing/misc expenses	$ 25	Annual fund	$ 0	$ 25
TOTALS	$ 675	$7,500	$ 375	$ 300

CREATING A POSITIVE ATMOSPHERE FOR PHILANTHROPIC SUPPORT

A key principle in successful development is to focus on "internal before external." External advice and involvement is important but an already busy faculty and staff are unlikely to be enthused about a new initiative if they have not been meaningfully involved in its development. One danger is that an academic leader creates a relationship with a potential donor and then adopts the donor's vision to structure initiatives without sufficient internal engagement. Who will pursue the initiative? Who will develop it and carry out the day-to-day activities? If the vision, mission and specific initiatives are developed with sufficient internal input, the academic leader has a specific plan with agreed upon goals. After the unit's strategy is defined and supported internally, the leader can build a meaningful relationship with the external community.

Involving the faculty: Donors enjoy interacting with and learning from gifted faculty members. Developing these relationships can be an important part of successful development initiatives. Still, asking faculty members to engage with donors can be a challenging and risky activity. Some have little interest or affinity to do so and will have difficulty relaying what they do to a lay audience. Asking reluctant faculty members to move outside their comfort zone can actually do more harm than good. Donors are quickly turned off by jargon that is primarily earmarked for other academics.

One way to initiate faculty interaction with the external constituency is to develop a speaker series on topics that are both current areas of interest in the community and priorities in the unit's mission. Participating faculty should be carefully chosen but it may be difficult to convince a faculty member that taking the time to develop a suitable presentation is in their best interest. The dean or department chair should have a mechanism to reward this activity, either through additional support for professional expenses or salary consideration in recognition of service. A "research salon" for a smaller audience may be more appropriate for some faculty rather than an open public lecture. Although some faculty may object, the leader should review the slides or written presentation. Brevity with substance at a suitable level for a lay audience is the goal.

Marketing strategy and development: Developing a positive atmosphere involves considerable effort through personal interaction, publications and digital media. Before multiple faculty and staff initiate a set of unrelated marketing activities it is critical to articulate the goals of the planned activity, coordinate the brand and set standards for materials intended for an external audience. While every unit has its own idiosyncratic objectives, there are three principles that all materials should satisfy: (a) adhesion to a set of published quality standards and guidelines including a coordinated logo; (b) assurance that all materials are user friendly, especially, in making it easy to donate; and (c) an unwavering commitment to do no damage. Factual errors, misspelling donor's names, accidental omissions and other incorrect details can cause undue stress and turmoil. The goal should always be a five-star product.

Printed and digital media: Printed materials, while expensive are still important, especially with the older demographic who represent potential major donors. Social media is critical for interaction with current students and younger alumni but if poorly constructed and infrequently monitored, social media can frustrate users and create a negative aura. An up-to-date and easy to navigate web site that is designed to maximize the quality and efficiency of the user's interface is essential. First and foremost, the mechanics of how to make a donation should be obvious to anyone who opens the web page. Ease of use is especially important toward the end of the calendar year, when many potential donors make decisions about charitable contributions. Most donors consider a small number of preciously selected charities. If potential donors search the unit's web site and cannot easily determine a path to make a donation, they quickly find another option. Printed material can also serve this purpose well. Including a gift envelope with pre-paid postage in an issue of the unit's newsletter or magazine that is distributed close to the holidays can reap valued returns.

Most donors, especially major gift donors, research organizations carefully before making a donation to determine where their funds can have the greatest impact. Stories on the progress of the unit should be posted on the web site and distributed through social media. Public relations efforts with the media should be developed to allow a positive connection between the expertise of the faculty, students and staff and the interests of the community. Accomplishments of faculty, staff, students and alumni should be prominently available. Key donors should be acknowledged with repeated statements of gratitude and impact.

Common zones of interest: Another method for creating a positive atmosphere for support is to identify intersections between important sectors in the community and the areas of expertise in the department, college or university. These "common zones of interest" define areas around which the unit can create an external advisory board for a program, department or center, and attract philanthropic support. For example, the faculty in theater, drama, dance and music can create a rapport with specific areas of the arts community; in high tech areas, information sciences, engineering and business can be involved with many external partners. The social sciences have ample opportunity to interact on public policy issues and economic forecasting and policy. There are countless examples where community interaction can enhance research, academic curriculum and community programming. Centers of excellence can be established in several of these areas and over time these interactions can increase the pool of friends of the university and lead to substantial support.

Alumni relations: Alumni involvement is crucial in creating a positive atmosphere in the community. The ways to do so are well known and are not repeated here. The main idea is that the best way to build a strong alumni base is to provide an excellent atmosphere for current students and to encourage a loyal ongoing attachment to the university. Faculty play a critical role. If not rewarded and recognized for activities like excellence in teaching, advising and alumni events, there is little hope that the faculty will contribute in a sufficiently meaningful way to help develop a positive, lasting relationship with alumni. Today's leading universities begin alumni relations with the first contact with a potential student. They provide excellent advising, extra curricular activities and faculty involvement.

One common challenge is a tension between alumni relations and donor relations. Alumni leaders view their main goal as friend raising, not fundraising. Separating these activities, at least with younger alumni, does make sense if the main goal is to foster a life-long relationship, whether or not the individual becomes a significant donor. Still, given the ever growing needs of public universities, there is mounting pressure to make alumni relations change their focus from relationships that are from "cradle to grave" to those that are, as discussed earlier, from "cradle to endowment."

THE IMPORTANCE OF THE ANNUAL FUND

There is a natural intersection between alumni relations and development in the annual fund. The importance of the annual fund is sometimes underestimated because it can be perceived as yielding a relatively small amount of money for a large effort. Experience shows otherwise. Interviewees indicated that frequently, donors who made a major gift, say of $25,000 or more, initiated their giving by contributing a small amount to the annual fund. Also, most made annual fund donations for at least 5 years before moving to a higher gift level. Every dollar in the annual fund is the equivalent of $20 - $25 in an endowment; in this sense the annual fund is a *living endowment*. The annual inflow of funds provides discretionary funding but more importantly it is a vehicle for creating relationships with a constituency that has potential for future large gifts. In the pyramid of development, the annual fund provides the base of the pyramid.

EXAMPLES: ANNUAL CAMPAIGNS

Annual mail and/or e-mail campaign: As the end of the calendar year approaches, many donors look for easy ways to make gifts to causes they value. As mentioned above, a hard mail or e-mail campaign that includes a publication with either a return envelope or link to a well-devised web site to make a donation can enhance an annual campaign.

<u>Annual telethon:</u> As much as individuals detest being bothered at home for a gift solicitation, an annual telethon continues to be both a good way to stay in touch with alumni and to begin a pattern of giving. Alumni enjoy interacting with current students. A typical model is to educate current students on how to effectively conduct the phone calls. Many universities employ highly skilled professionals or they engage outside consultants to oversee and conduct the telethon. The academic leader should be involved to set the message and ensure that students have correct information. In addition to providing prepared responses to questions frequently asked by alumni, the leader should meet with the group of callers to describe the major initiatives of the unit.

<u>Leadership Groups or Clubs:</u> One method for obtaining ongoing support from the community is to create a special interest group, either Dean's Leadership Circle or a President's or Chancellor's Club that provides benefits for members who contribute a set fee each year. The benefits can include free or discounted events, exclusive meetings with the academic leader and participation in an advisory board or social networking opportunities. As mentioned earlier, any monetary benefit of membership needs to be subtracted from the size of the overall payment and not included as part of the charitable donation.

The mathematics of major gifts

Each unit can determine their own definition of what level constitutes a major gift. Research shows that to generate a gift of $25,000 or more requires identification of between three and five prospective major donors. On average, securing a major gift requires nine meaningful contacts over a period of 6 months to two years.[68] Contacts include personal meetings, attendance at events, and interactions for student mentoring, advisory boards or class presentations.

A rule of thumb is that each development officer can accommodate between 70 and 100 potential donors. These parameters help to establish reasonable limits for a development campaign. If the financial strategy requires 50 gifts per year of at least $25,000, then at least 150 prospects should be identified and the unit should employ one and a half to two development offices.

THE DEVELOPMENT CYCLE

Figure 7.1 illustrates the cycle for successful development, which begins with the initial identification of the donor, followed by the request for and receipt of a gift and then proceeding to showing gratitude and stewardship.[69] There are a variety of interpretations of the cycle; the one offered here focuses on the underlying principle that the ultimate goal of successful development is to create a joyful donor.

Identification: The first step in the process is to identify and then qualify potential donors. In addition to alumni, the campus foundation should identify prospects from the community, foundations, and corporations. Foundation staff can perform an analysis of an individual's net worth and philanthropic tendencies and also provide connections to relevant corporate and other foundations. The initial contact with an individual prospect is usually a phone call from the development officer, the academic leader or a supporter from the community.

The Donor's Perspective: Philanthropy results when there is an intersection between the means to give and the passion for a cause. Passion relates to values, personal interests and vision to make a difference. The means to give relates not only to direct financial wealth but also to connections, the state of the economy and intellectual capacity. For any perspective donor, the giving ability for a cause remains inactive until the individual feels a deep connection to a purpose. Major philanthropists are constantly considering and choosing between a multitude of worthy organizations. They tend to make strategic choices based on where they perceive the gift will have its greatest impact in a way that fulfills a personal passion. The donor may also wish to create a family legacy, although this is not always a necessary condition. If the donor does have a legacy in mind, the driving force could reflect a number of different motives including

* Stipulating that the donor's children also become involved to encourage their interest in philanthropy;
* Naming a building, classroom or program;
* Honoring parents or spouse by supporting something that reflects their passion;
* Honoring a faculty or staff member who made a significant difference in the donor's life; or
* Establishing a scholarship to "pay back" the institution for scholarship support the donor received as a student.

Several interviewees indicated that in their experience, in addition to a legacy motivation, a major gift prospect is usually passionate about making a difference in an area that is critical to society. Major donors want to affect change—not just put out fires. The interviewees found that seeking a gift for operating funds rarely is successful unless the request is couched in a larger proposal for a greater vision that fulfills the passion of the donor.

The First Meeting: The leader should gain an understanding of the prospect's personal interests, ties to the university, common friends, giving history and the ability and willingness to give. In practice, it is often difficult to obtain all of these details prior to the first visit. Over time, interactions with the donor reveal additional background information and provide a sense of what level of giving, if any, may be possible. For a major gift prospect, the first visit should include the academic leader, the development officer and, in some cases, a highly recognized current donor who can add to the credibility of the case being made.

Next, the leader and development officer should plan how the meeting will be orchestrated. Perspective donors have many demands on their resources. Do not waste their time. When preparing for a donor meeting, imagine that the donor is thinking "I will give you two minutes to convince me that I should spend another three minutes with you." In some cases, it is useful for the academic leader and the development officer to rehearse various scenarios in order to anticipate the flow of the discussion, determine the role each should play, and prepare succinct strategic statements.

FIGURE 7.1 The Cycle of Successful Development

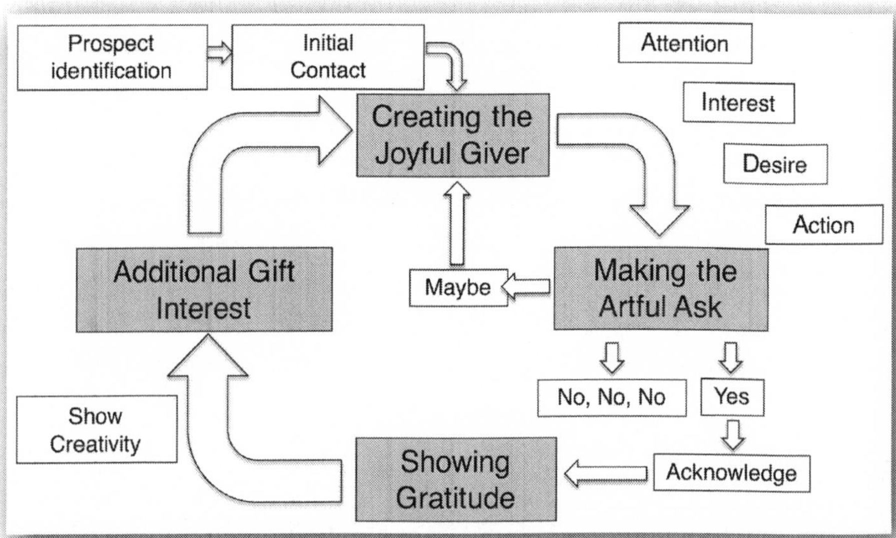

The first few minutes of interaction can set the tone, not only for the initial meeting but also for the ongoing relationship. Always open with a sincere expression of gratitude to the donor for taking time from a busy schedule to meet with you. Next, the university personnel should engage in active listening by adopting what has sometimes been referred to as a "Triple 'L' Strategy:" listen, listen again, and then listen some more. Listening first and then engaging the prospective donor by posing polite, but unobtrusive questions can assure the donor that the primary purpose of the visit is to hear their story and understand their passions.

The main goal of active listening is to seek a connection between the donor's passion and the top priorities and needs of the institution. The leader and DO should be ready to provide a concise view of the institution's mission and financial position but with a focus on the donor's interests and how they relate to the academic unit. It is also useful to provide examples of how previous gifts have helped the institution and how a number of highly respected donors have supported the university. Active listening is critical; it is important to be engaged but excessive talk on the part of the university rarely results in successful development. Usually, the first meeting is not the time to make an ask, especially if the ultimate goal is a major gift. Rather, the main goal of the first visit is to establish the underpinnings for a lasting relationship. Still, there are exceptions; as shown in the example below, on rare occasions even the first visit can be fruitful.

EXAMPLE: THE IMPORTANCE OF ACTIVE LISTENING

As Dean of the Business School at the University of Wisconsin, I was meeting for the first time with a retired alumnus who I will refer to as Bernie. My development officer, Don Gray, had contacted him and he invited us to his home for breakfast with him and his wife. We prepared beforehand; we knew several passions of the donor but decided that we would adopt a "Triple L" strategy; we would do very little talking, be gracious and ask questions that showed our interest. Our host welcomed us and immediately offered a tour of his beautiful home. At one point he led us into his office, which he referred to as his computer lab. He proudly showed us his technology and how he had adopted what was at the time the latest software, Quicken, to track his personal finances. He demonstrated how he now handled his monthly mortgage payment—after an initial set up, he indicated that he "memorized it" (saved it) and the program reproduced the check every month.

We then sat down at breakfast with his wife. Don and I asked questions about their family and current life and their experiences at the university. About an hour into the conversation, during which I had barely spoken, Bernie turned to me and said "So Andy, tell me about what is new at the School." Given that we had learned about his fascination with technology, I described the technology we were developing in our new building that would house the School. He was intrigued by the discussion, posed several questions and then asked what we needed. I explained that we lacked funds for several servers that would make the facility truly unique. He then asked, how much we needed. I responded around $30,000. He told us to follow him back to his computer room where he sat at his desk, pulled up Quicken and printed out and signed a $30,000 check. I was truly surprised and expressed my deepest gratitude. As he handed me the check I said; "Bernie, can you do me one favor...can you "memorize" this one?" And he actually did. Each year for the next several years, we received an annual gift from Bernie.

The first visit described in the example resulted in a gift, but this scenario is not typical. Generally, for larger gifts as many as nine to ten interactions may be necessary. A key element underlying the success of the visit was how the triple L strategy was applied, allowing the donor to reveal his preferences and passions and then allowing him the joy of asking how he could help. In this scenario, there was no mention of a donation until the donor offered. Too frequently, the university dominates the discussion with the donor. It is rare that this one-sided interaction results in the development of a meaningful relationship.

For the more usual case where the first visit does not result in an immediate gift, how should the relationship continue to be developed? If the prospective donor shows interest, then it is natural to lead the discussion toward how he or she would like to be involved. There are many activities that the DO can offer; if the individual has not been to the campus for some time, a visit and tour can be offered along with an invitation to events that may be of interest. Many individuals enjoy mentoring students or talking to student groups. Individuals who are accustomed to public speaking usually appreciate an invitation to speak in a class. For someone of stature who could bring significant value to the unit, an invitation to join an advisory board might be warranted. The purpose of these activities is to increase the individual's involvement. The danger is that the follow up is lax; too often after the visit, the system does not move quickly and the prospective donor loses interest. Before embarking on a first visit, the infrastructure in the unit has to be sufficiently deep to absorb and react to the individual's requests for future involvement. As part of the preparation for the first visit, the next potential steps with a prospect should be well understood and a plan for continued interaction should be laid out. Someone needs to be assigned as the lead person to follow up; if not, the potential donor will soon be lost.

For major donor prospects, an excellent way to increase involvement and interest is to ask the individual to join an advisory board for a program, center, school or for the university. After a few meetings, if the interaction has been positive, the intent is that the prospective donor begins to feel respected by the university as a meaningful advisor and friend. The individual then becomes more passionate about the unit's initiatives and more knowledgeable about its financial needs. If the strategy of the unit matches the donor's passions, then the best result is that the individual takes pride in asking how he or she can help. At that time, a proposal is presented as an opportunity to explain to the donor how their philanthropy can make a difference.

Example: The Center for Real Estate, The Paul Merage School of Business, University of California Irvine

For several years, the business school had worked on the initial steps to form a center that focused on academic and practical research and a specialization in real estate. But over this time, the center had generated very little funding. The dean and DO decided to work with a core group of six individuals in the community who were passionate about establishing a strong real estate presence at the university. Over the course of a year, the external group evolved into an advisory board and became integrally involved in working with the school to develop a strategic plan and subsequently a financial strategy. Out of the financial plan evolved the development strategy that identified exact needs for funding, how the funding would be used and what impact it would have. The dean presented the full plan to the group at its fourth meeting.

The excitement of the group was evident. Excellent questions were raised and the interaction was serious, well intended and constructive. The development strategy including specific giving opportunities was included as part of the presentation. Sensing the success of the discussion, the DO, sitting next to the dean, quietly handed him a note that read "Aren't you going to ask them for money?" Without attracting the attention of the group, the dean wrote back "No."

At the end of the meeting, five of the six attendees indicated to the dean that they wanted to help and pledged major gifts. Each expressed how proud and honored they were to be allowed the opportunity to be part of such an exciting initiative. Each had seen the funding needs, a well-developed strategy and financial plan. But each felt great satisfaction and joy in offering to help rather than being asked to help.

There is an important lesson in the example above. Never take away the donor's joy of giving. Asking too quickly robs the donor of the sense of pride that derives from offering rather than being asked to help. Still, it is critical to determine how and when to create an environment where the donor understands that an ask is being presented. When is the right time? *For major gifts, you must earn the right to ask.* After the relationship has matured and the individual has been involved in an integral way, once again, the best possible outcome is that the donor asks you how they can help. At that point, a formal proposal can be written.

How to respond to a negative reaction: Why might a prospective donor express little or no interest? First, the initial meeting may not have sparked the donor's passion. Perhaps the DO or academic leader was too verbose and the donor did not sense a personal interest in him or her. There are many reasons why a potential donor may decline the opportunity; the budget is tight, the request is too large, or there are many competing charities and contributing to all of them is not feasible. When reacting to a prospective donor's lack of interest, the leader should acknowledge the donor's perspective and react appropriately. One possibility is to offer alternative ways to structure the gift via multi-year payments or planned deferred giving. Another approach would be to explain different initiatives at lower funding levels or alternative ways to use the gift. Every experience is a learning opportunity; the comments raised can be used as valuable input for future interactions with others. Standard answers can be prepared for the most frequent types of comments and changes can be made to avoid these objections in the future.

Showing Gratitude: The gift is in! So you are done. Far from it. No matter how small or large the gift, every donor deserves to be gratefully acknowledged. Every gift is significant to the donor and the recipient should communicate to the donor why the gift is important to the university. For major donors a personalized, handwritten note of appreciation has significant meaning. Donors recognize and appreciate the leader's effort to express gratitude; a handwritten note, especially in a high tech society, transmits a level of sincerity that can be very meaningful. The letter should express gratitude, not only for the donor's financial support but also for the individual's advice, expertise and above all, friendship. Over time, the foundation should prepare an annual report for each major donor that provides a progress report on the activities and accomplishments made possible by the gift. The value of the endowment, the income payout and details on how the funds have been utilized are documented. For student scholarships, it is meaningful to the donor to receive a letter directly from the scholarship recipient.

For major gifts, the leader should offer a recognition event, ongoing meetings and some level of involvement in the activities of the initiative being funded. The amount of recognition that major donors desire differs across individuals; the key is knowing your donor. Some donors have little ego and prefer a low-key level of recognition. For these individuals, too much recognition can be uncomfortable and unwelcome. Others take pride in sharing their recognition with family, friends and the community. In this case, too little recognition can sour a relationship. For larger gifts, a dinner with a formal program might be warranted along with repeated expressions of appreciation and an offer for continued involvement with the unit. If done well, the outcome of excellent stewardship is a joyful donor who continues to contribute and also brings other donors to the unit.

EXAMPLE: A TRULY JOYFUL DONOR

Over a period of three or four years, my development officer at the University of Wisconsin, Don Gray and I had built a relationship with a very successful professional couple, "Janet and Ron," who were alumni of the School. We had worked with them to fulfill their desire to become more closely involved with the university and Janet had become a valued member of the School's Dean's Advisory Board. After a board meeting where we had described the campaign for a new building, Janet approached me and asked how she could help. A few weeks later Don and I met with them to discuss some possibilities. They described their desire to recognize Janet's parents through a naming gift for a room in the new building. Eventually, we decided on naming the auditorium with a plaque inside the room describing the family history and legacy that Janet and Ron wanted to share.

As we contemplated how to thank them, we recognized that they were very humble and that full-scale public recognition would not be appropriate. Rather, we suggested to them that we would like to hold a small dinner to express our appreciation; the attendees would include their family members and some of our most significant supporters and potential donors to the building. They were comfortable with this approach because they felt it would help the School, but they did not want long tributes to them, nor did they want to make anything but brief comments.

The event was attended by a small group and to keep the evening informal, after dinner, I welcomed and thanked everyone for joining us. I made a few remarks on the importance of the building and described that one of the key features that will have a significant impact on the life of the School is the auditorium. I then turned to Janet and Ron and began to thank them. But before I could finish the next sentence, Ron stood up, put his hand on my shoulder and motioned for me to sit down. He then said, (paraphrased)

> *No Andy, it is we who want to thank you for this opportunity. Janet and I feel very fortunate to be able to support the School in this way, while preserving the memory of individuals who have meant so much to us and to many others.*

He then very briefly described why it was so meaningful for them to participate in the success of the School through supporting the building. To this day, I remain humbled and in awe of this marvelous couple. They set an example that evening that others followed to help ensure a successful building campaign. Creating the opportunity for a donor to fulfill a passion can be one of the most satisfying experiences for an academic leader.

Ongoing stewardship: Successful development requires ongoing expressions of gratitude with annual reports showing that the donated funds are being used according to the gift agreement and they are having the intended impact. Above all, the leader should monitor quarterly foundation accounts to ensure that the income from endowed funds is being spent. Donors are understandably confused and upset when they receive an annual report that indicates the funds that the leader claimed were so desperately needed are now lying idle. Donors also deserve and expect to receive reports that explain the impact of their gift.

The faculty plays a critical role in carrying out the vision of the donor. Whether the faculty member is a center director, chaired professor or recipient of other types of support, the role of the leader to ensure that the faculty member's reward is appropriate for the level of activity expected. The role of the faculty member is both to conduct the required activity and report annually on the activities that have been accomplished with the support provided. To ease the reporting process, a standardized reporting format should be available. The development officer facilitates this process and ensures that all donors understand how their funds are being utilized and how grateful the individual and the university are for their support.

CHALLENGES

Covering the cost of a development operation: Effective development requires coordinated effort by skilled individuals. The desired combination of intelligence, warm mature personality, dedication, humility, and humor is rare. Talented development officers and staff are critical and the cost is not immaterial. Any charitable organization should openly share their cost structure. Donors need to be assured that the vast majority of funds raised flow to the cause and not to the operation. What is a reasonable cost? The answer depends on factors such as the stage of a campaign, the size of the majority of gifts received, the method used to generate the funds. Table 7.2, originally developed by Greenfield (1999), provides some useful guidelines.

TABLE 7.2 Fundraising Costs

Activity	Cost to raise one dollar
Capital Campaign/Major Gifts	$ .05 to $ .10
Corporations and Foundations (Grant Writing)	$ .20
Direct Mail Renewal	$ .20
Planned Giving	$ .25
Benefit/Special Events	$ .50 of gross proceeds
Direct Mail Acquisition	$ 1.00 to $ 1.25
National Average	$.20

Using once again the hypothetical economics department and assuming that the unit is just beginning its development operation, a cost of 20 cents to raise each dollar should be acceptable to most donors. One cost consideration is the tax levied by the foundation to cover centralized activities. Two common models are (a) a one-time fee, say 5%, that is collected when the gift is received; and (b) an annual fee, usually set in the range between .95% and 1.9% of the value of the endowment.[70] The example below assumes option (a) with a one-time fee of 5%. The time horizon for completing the development goals established earlier for the department of economics is assumed to be five years. Over this period, $9 million would be raised with $7.5 million in endowment and $300K per year in annual gifts. The average annual level of donations of $1.8 million then implies that with a 20% overhead, the cost of the development operation should be $360K per year.

Table 7.3 provides an example showing how the $360K annual cost can be allocated across a reasonable set of uses. The example assumes that the cost of marketing personnel is a shared expense in which the college centralizes some of the marketing but each department has some discretion or specific marketing initiatives in their own budget. If the development activity is successful, the department can plan to add additional development staff and grow the operation commensurate with the expected level of donations.

TABLE 7.3 Allocation of Development Costs Hypothetical Department of Economics

Expense to raise $1.8 million/year	Amount
Development Officer	$150,000
Assistant	$ 75,000
Clerical support	$ 12,000
Marketing director (% of salary shared)	$ 50,000
Publications, social media and web site	$ 30,000
Events and meetings with donors	$ 25,000
Foundation fee at 5%	$ 18,000
Total	$360,000

Beware of the gift that eats: A great temptation, especially at the beginning of a campaign is to accept every gift that is offered. But there are a number of reasons why some gifts should be declined. Donors are passionate, creative individuals who have a plethora of ideas, some of which do not mesh well with the vision and mission of the unit. A gift that has little internal support will leave the academic leader in a quandary concerning how to actualize the intent of the donor and then how to address the issue of faculty governance. Even if the gift fits with the mission, the amount, structure and intent of the gift need to be realistic. Is the donor's intended outcome feasible given the amount of support he or she is providing? A commonly shared example concerns the gift of a racehorse to a university. While valued in six figures, maintaining the horse was more expensive than the eventual return. From this example comes a well-known proverb of development; "never accept a gift that eats." Clearly, the saying applies to more gifts than racehorses; when the amount donated does not provide sufficient funding for the intended initiative, the gift creates a financial burden rather than addressing an existing need. Before accepting a gift, it is always useful to ask the following question: "Does this gift fill an existing hole or does it create a new one?"

Another factor that is especially relevant for naming gifts concerns whether the donor's ethics, background, experience and public persona fit well with the university. Attaching a name in perpetuity to a program, room, building or college creates a responsibility for the academic leader to ensure the individual is worthy of this recognition.

Example: Ethics should always prevail

One of the interviewees described a situation that occurred when he was a dean. He and his DO had been introduced to a wealthy individual who they were told was a potential major donor. The individual was not an alumnus but he had deep roots in the state in which the university is located and he enjoyed interacting with friends who were heavily involved with the campus. He was also engaged in an advisory group for a center at the university. After several visits with the dean and DO, the individual expressed an interest in a naming opportunity for the dean's school. Within the next few weeks, the dean and DO prepared and sent a complete proposal to the individual and then arranged a meeting to continue the discussion. At that meeting, the individual indicated that he and his wife had agreed to name the school. He estimated that a gift of about $60 million would be possible with the upcoming sale of one of his businesses.

At this point, the dean and DO were ecstatic but they quickly recognized that because the individual was recommended by a board member and also was a public figure, the foundation had obtained only superficial information about his background and activities. Subsequent research revealed that the individual had been involved with a number of questionable ethical practices; although he was never indicted, these activities were of sufficient concern that the dean and the DO felt strongly that the gift should not be accepted. The school and university have high ethical standards that would not be served well by having this individual's name on the school. They contacted the chancellor of the university, the head of the foundation and various members of his dean's advisory board and provided the background on the situation. All agreed that the gift should not be accepted. Regardless of the size of a gift, all believed that the university's reputation and ethical standards should not be compromised.

Competing for donors across the campus: A major function of the foundation is to coordinate development initiatives across the many units of the university. Few activities put the university in a poorer light than when a donor is bombarded by uncoordinated requests for support from different arms of the campus. It is also embarrassing for an academic leader to visit a donor without knowing that another university leader has also recently visited. To avoid these awkward and potentially damaging situations, the foundation assigns a primary contact for at least every major donor and in many cases for all donors. The primary contact serves as a clearinghouse, approving all requests by university personnel for meetings with their assigned donors. In addition, through a web-based contact report system that is accessible only to academic leaders and development staff, the proceedings of each donor visit are recorded confidentially.

Before meeting with a new prospect, the development officer checks with the primary contact to ensure that the donor is not already considering a major proposal and is willing to accept additional university visitors. In addition, the DO accesses the contact history in order to reflect a coordinated effort on the part of the university. It is not uncommon for several units to claim "ownership" of high potential major gift prospects. When this occurs, it is critical to recognize that the donor's wishes come first. The donor decides, based on personal passions and interests which parts of the university to support. Still, the donor seeks an understanding of the priorities of the university and wants to understand where a gift will have the greatest impact. Here, the president, provost and head of the foundation should guide the donor to ensure that the gift matches both the passion of the donor and the highest needs of the university.

Portals: Some disciplines, like business, medicine and engineering, have a natural connection to individuals in the community who have higher giving potential. These areas can act as a portal for many external constituents who are not familiar with academia but who would like to become more involved with the university. It is almost always the case that individuals who are initially attracted to one area of the university reveal broader interests and passions. A carefully designed university-wide development strategy can utilize these portals to attract involvement and support for a wide range of disciplines. A key component of this strategy is that all campus leaders adopt a philosophy that they represent not only their own unit, but also the entire university. If the appropriate university-wide collegiality exists, the deans of areas with wide portals can help match donor interests and facilitate gifts to other disciplines while also gaining support for their area.

Example: The business school as a portal

While I was dean at the Wisconsin School of Business a number of major donors to the school also expressed an interest in other areas of the university. During a meeting with one such individual, he indicated that his mother was a concert pianist and he had a desire to honor her by making a significant gift to support graduate students in the performing arts. Although we had been cultivating him for a multi-million dollar gift to the business school, I volunteered to connect him with the appropriate individuals in the School of Music and explained how he could make his wish a reality. Eventually, he generously donated a $20 million endowment for graduate fellowships in music performance. While he also made a significant contribution to the business school, I was delighted that I was able to help School of Music, even in a small way, receive such critical support. It was also gratifying to witness the delight of the donor as he honored his mother in this way. Over the course of my decade long deanship, while development in the business school was very successful, donors who were introduced to the university through the business school also contributed substantially to many other areas of the university.

The best possible outcome for any university derives from a universally accepted goal to create a joyful donor. As long as a gift is consistent with an established priority in the university's mission, each leader should work to ensure that the donor's wish is fulfilled. In some instances, leaders view themselves in competition with other units for claims on a selected set of donors. As described above, coordination across units is essential; donors can easily lose patience and connect with other organizations if they do not sense collegiality and common purpose across the university. If the university's mission is well understood and widely supported, then in all likelihood campus leaders will support one another and use portals effectively. This unified environment attracts potential donors and facilitates a productive atmosphere for successful development.

<u>One naming opportunity but two donors: the judgment of Solomon</u>: Finding one donor who is willing and able to provide a large naming gift is a challenge, but it can be even more challenging if two or more individuals step forward expressing an interest in the same naming opportunity. This scenario can become intense with potentially severe negative consequences. The best outcome is that both donors can be satisfied; one with the intended naming gift and the other with an alternative but satisfying opportunity. The donor whose naming offer is declined is likely

to be upset and withdraw from the university, at least temporarily. It is helpful to have a current supporter who is a friend of the individual serve as a neutral party, maintaining contact and relaying the apologies of the university. Over time, the DO can attempt to rebuild the relationship. In the meantime, an array of alternative opportunities can be developed and at the appropriate time can be presented. In some cases, it may not be possible to repair the relationship until there is a change in leadership.

Overly involved donors: Especially when considering naming gifts, the DO and the leader should assess the donor's intended level of involvement in the activity that is being underwritten. Misunderstanding what is expected and what is reasonable can lead to challenging and distasteful interactions. Some donors believe that their gift entitles them to a major role in determining the direction and activities of the unit. In extreme cases, even estate gift agreements can be written in such a way that the "dead hand of the donor" exerts a measure of control that can be unreasonable.

What level of interaction is best? A passionate donor who has a successful career usually has a vision for the unit that requires change and innovation. The individual may also have a deep network combined with an ability to get things done that can be beneficial. These attributes should be welcomed, but with caution. Early on, before the gift agreement is crafted, it should be established that the unit appreciates ideas and support but operates within the normal confines of faculty governance and university oversight. The translation is that the ideas proposed by the donor will receive appropriate study; some may be acted upon and others will not. The final say does not reside in the hands of the donor but rather in the hands of the university. If the donor adamantly disagrees with these guidelines, the university may do best to decline the gift. In some cases, even though discussions like the above occur, the donor becomes overly intrusive after the gift is made. In the example below, one way is offered to help calm tensions that may develop.

Example: When a donor relationship turns sour

This episode occurred at a large public university after a donor provided a multi-million dollar contribution to name a center. Before agreeing to the gift, he had reviewed and apparently agreed to the strategic plan, the financial structure for the center and the level of involvement that was acceptable. After the gift was made, he became a frequent visitor and engaged in lengthy discussions with the faculty member who directed the center. He openly criticized the curriculum, the teaching in the program and the emphasis on research. He asked the director to initiate major revisions. Not surprisingly, the director and participating faculty objected strongly, arguing that the donor's interest was to strip out the academic foundations of the program and transform it into a primarily applied program. At this point, the dean decided to intervene and discuss the situation with the donor. Although calm, the conversation was pointed and little common ground could be established.

The dean and center director subsequently decided that they if they could not improve the situation they should offer to return the gift to the donor. After considering a variety of options, they decided that perhaps the donor needed to be better informed about the participating faculty and students, courses and specific actions and results of the center's initiatives. They agreed to attempt reconciliation by organizing a two-day series of meetings between the donor and faculty, students, director and dean. The dean informed the foundation and chancellor, describing the situation and seeking their approval to return the gift if this reconciliation was unsuccessful. They received affirmation from the administration to do so.

The meetings turned out to be productive. Afterward, the dean met with the donor and set boundaries on future involvement by asking the donor to interact only by attending advisory board meetings, meeting quarterly jointly with the director and dean and attending invited events. The dean again strongly reinforced that while suggestions would be valued, the donor could not mandate specific changes in the program or activities of the center. The dean also informed the donor that if this scenario was not acceptable to the donor, the university had agreed that they would return the gift. Subsequently, the donor agreed to the conditions and although not perfect, the relationship improved dramatically. Today, over 20 years later the center continues to be productive and successful.

The above example is atypical. While the vast majority of donors provide support and advice in addition to funding, they also recognize the boundaries of their input. Donors often become frustrated with the glacial pace of change in academia, but they respect the leader's efforts for change and they applaud successes. David Grainger, who donated over $15 million to The Business School at Wisconsin during the 1990's provides a role model for a successful, productive donor-university relationship. He always welcomed interactions with the university and offered a vision and financial support for an area that he cares deeply about; supply chain management. But, he never sought a public podium nor did he wish to control any activities. During visits with the dean, DO or other university officials, he would listen carefully to updates, pose helpful questions and then react to discussions by asking "You don't want me to actually tell you what to do, do you?" The ultimate philanthropist, David carefully probed to assess how productive his gifting was and whether expectations were being met. He would offer help, but also recognized the boundary between the suggestions he offered and the governance of the university. The impact of his generosity and his vision are deeply impacting the School at Wisconsin today, over twenty years later and are likely to continue to have a positive effect for many years to come.

Another example of exemplary donors are Paul and Lilly Merage whose generosity is well known throughout the country and globally. After naming the school of business at the University of California Irvine, Paul Merage agreed to serve as Chair of the Dean's Advisory Board. He played a critical role in helping to shape the vision of the School while attracting other major influential individuals to join the board and support the School. External advisory board members who become ingrained with the university and are captured by the passion and ability of the leader can provide significant wisdom and support and become highly valued friends of the university.

Summary and Conclusions

Given the permanent reduction in public support for higher education, the need for supplemental funding is a top priority at every university. In the past, development was delegated to a dedicated staff and a few key academic leaders. Today, every leader on the campus is integrally involved in the development process. While for some traditional faculty members, the prospect of working closely with "civilians" in the outside community can be daunting, many who enter in these activities find them very rewarding. For most, these interactions become both educational and pleasurable. But development is not easy. It can be time consuming, frustrating and costly. Understanding the cycle and mechanics of development can help systemize the process. Ultimately, for the newly minted academic leader, working with a skilled development officer can help to build a set of skills that promote active listening, the ability to make an artful ask and, in the end, create a joyful donor. If done well, interactions with donors can be some of the most satisfying and enjoyable activities in an academic leader's career.

Key Takeaways: Chapter 7

- Through well-designed strategies, private universities attempt to develop a "cradle to endowment" relationship with potential donors.

- There is a science behind successful philanthropy but there is also an art to becoming a publicly admired individual who people trust and have faith in, so much so that they are willing to provide financial support for the individual's cause.

- A development strategy is not a stand-alone list of needs. Rather development priorities derive directly from the vision, mission and financial strategy of the academic unit and university.

- A reasonable strategy is to announce a slightly lower than achievable fundraising target and then outperform expectations. The alternative of not reaching a publicized goal casts a negative stigma that is difficult to dissipate.

- A key principle is "internal before external." Already busy faculty and staff are unlikely to be enthused about a new initiative if they have not been involved in its development.

- Philanthropy results when there is an intersection between the means to give and the passion for a cause. The ultimate goal of successful development is to create a joyful donor.

- Prospective donors are busy people. Do not waste their time. When preparing for a donor meeting, imagine that the donor is thinking "I will give you two minutes to convince me that I should spend another three minutes with you."

- Active listening is critical. Excessive talk on the part of the university rarely results in successful development.

- Never take away the donor's joy of giving. Asking too quickly robs the donor of the sense of pride that derives from offering rather than being asked to help.

- It is critical to determine how and when to create an environment where the donor understands that an ask is being presented.

For major gifts, you must earn the right to ask.

* For some donors, too little recognition can sour a relationship; for others too much recognition is unwelcome. The outcome of effective stewardship is a joyful donor who continues to contribute and bring other donors to the unit.
* The leader should ensure that donations are used and used properly. Donors are understandably upset when they receive a report that indicates the funds that the leader claimed were so desperately needed are now lying idle.
* Before accepting a gift, ask the following question: "Does this gift fill an existing hole or does it create a new one?"

CHAPTER 8

Personal Strategies, Tactics, and Pragmatics

• • •

If we don't plant the right things, we will reap the wrong things.

—Maya Angelou

Introduction

Inexperienced leaders, especially in their first position, have a tendency to dive into their new role and immediately become immersed in a plethora of activity. They often neglect pacing, act as if they are running a sprint and face the danger of quickly burning out. Before taking on any role of consequence, the leader should examine the expanse of the position and develop a personal strategy that serves as a framework for handling the volume of activity. The multitude of responsibilities requires adoption of both tactical guidelines for processing recurring, routine tasks and strategic principles for reacting to less frequent but more complex issues. The characteristics of the leader's personal strategy depend on career aspirations; "taking one's turn" implies different strategies from those chosen by someone who is attempting to build a career credential.

This chapter first examines day-to-day issues including prioritization, delegation and meeting efficiency. The discussion then turns to more idiosyncratic challenges such as reacting to unjust criticism, messy personnel issues and crises. The style of presentation is prescriptive, often directly addressing the reader and making suggestions. The caveat is that what works for one individual may not work for another; everyone naturally adjusts their style over time to best suit their own personality and ambitions as well as the environment they face.

Pragmatic considerations for new leaders

Table 8.1 highlights pragmatic considerations in the development of a personal strategy and corresponding tactics. These items need little discussion, still the leader can benefit from systematically addressing them. New leaders are often surprised by the multitude of tasks before them and they are wise to seek advice on allocation of their time. From the university's perspective, time should be allocated to those activities that add the greatest value in achieving the university's mission. From the individual's perspective, time allocation depends on the environment, status and ambitions of both the unit and the leader. Someone who views their role as taking one's turn can implement a strategic planning process "for show" that has little meaningful impact. These individuals usually continue to prioritize their research program and are less likely to become integrally involved in university-wide activities. Alternatively, individuals who view leadership as their career path are likely to deemphasize their research, teaching or clinical program and engage increasingly in university and community initiatives. They adopt a process similar to that described in Chapter 3 to develop a strategic plan that they are committed to implement. These individuals aspire to become campus leaders and gain national prominence. For the most part, the discussion here assumes that the individual is aspirational, building a credential for a career in leadership.

Prioritizing: Regardless of the path chosen, there are many priorities and the leader needs to make difficult time allocation decisions between them. While new leaders find it tempting to innovate by adding new initiatives and supporters, they should first focus on effectively handling the ones that already exist. Table 8.2 offers an overview of a suggested prioritization of key activities, each of which is discussed below.

Life Balance: Many of the interviewees urged that new leaders give top priority to life balance, which includes family and fitness. Several interviewees reflected that the felt they had not allocated sufficient attention to their families. They advised that simply showing up is not good enough; achieving life balance means being intimately involved with no distractions, especially from e-mails and texts.[71] Moreover, a sometimes difficult lesson, especially for workaholics, is that physical fitness and vacations are necessary components of sustained leadership. Set aside time on your calendar for both; you will be more productive and happier.

Example: Prioritizing family

Early in my deanship at the University of Wisconsin, I learned the day before a Dean's Advisory Board meeting that my daughter Emily's soccer team had advanced to a championship game on the next afternoon. The board meeting was scheduled to start the next morning and proceed all day, ending with a dinner. I attempted to contact the Advisory Board Chair but he was already travelling to the meeting. I left a message describing the conflict and seeking his advice on whether I could leave for part of the afternoon to watch Emily's game. I did not hear back from him until the meeting started the next morning. As the Chair opened the meeting, he indicated to the board that before proceeding, he wanted to bring an important motion before the group. He then said (paraphrased), Andy's daughter Emily has a championship soccer game this afternoon. I move that Andy leave us early and attend the game. All in favor, please say aye. The vote was unanimous. This incident provided a life-long lesson. I was struck that this group of CEOs and high level executives of leading companies and organizations had no hesitation in prioritizing family. For years afterward, many of the board members asked me about Emily first and the school second.

Internal before external: The allocation of time between internal and external activities is a critical strategic decision. As described in Chapters 6 and 7, implementing an external relations strategy can involve a considerable time commitment. If the academic reputation of the area is strong and the leader appoints a capable associate dean or assistant chair to oversee internal initiatives, then there is more flexibility to implement an external strategy. If the area needs to upgrade academic standards or if there is internal strife, then the external strategy can wait. It is difficult to present a strong case externally if there is weakness or lack of cohesion internally.

• • •

TABLE 8.1 Personal Strategies and Tactics

STRATEGIC CHOICES:

1. Importance of life balance with family and personal life.
2. The amount of time allocated to research and teaching.
3. The extent of your personal, national and global profile.
4. The extent of your community profile.
5. The extent of your campus profile.
6. How to prioritize the key ideas in the strategic plan.
7. What to delegate.
8. When to say no.
9. Who you need to meet with routinely.

TACTICAL ACTIONS:

1. Never lack the confidence to seek advice.
2. Keep track of your tasks.
3. Attach a priority level to each task.
4. Do what matters most first.
5. Update your list daily.
6. Travel strategically and productively.

• • •

Strategy: A new leader should take advantage of a honeymoon period to achieve early successes that make a difference. The first step is to implement a strategic planning process, as described in Chapters 3 and 4, that is financially sustainable. If done well, the process involves all constituents in an institutional effort. Establish three to five top priorities and work on them fervently and quickly. Providing leadership with passion to make a difference inspires confidence and leads to support.

Academic quality: One of the most important responsibilities of the leader is to ensure the standards and overall quality of both the faculty and learning environment. The decision concerning promotion with tenure is arguably the most critical activity that the leader oversees. Sufficient time should be allocated to analyze each tenure case with great scrutiny. More generally, as discussed in Chapter 5, faculty recruitment, development and retention require an ample amount of the leader's time. The leader's responsibilities also include oversight of the quality of the student body and the curriculum. To a large extent, the university determines the quality of undergraduate students. Still, some departments or colleges can dictate or at least provide advice on the acceptance requirements. For graduate programs, most universities delegate quality standards to departments, with oversight by the graduate college; chairs and deans play a critical role to ensure that quality matches the expectations identified in the strategic plan.

University leaders at all levels should maintain meaningful contact with students, and especially student leaders, either through teaching, regularly scheduled lunches, coffee hours or town halls. No one experiences the programs like students do; their perceptions and suggestions are critical components of maintaining quality of the learning environment. Department chairs should review teaching evaluations, including written student comments. It is also useful to examine student surveys conducted by the university. External input from peer and aspirational departments, alumni, recruiters and advisory board members also provides useful information for curriculum modifications and innovations. Feedback from these sources should be shared with appropriate committees; those that require action should be prioritized in the strategic plan.

• • •

TABLE 8.2 A Suggested Prioritization

1. Life Balance
   a. Family
   b. Fitness
   c. Vacations
2. Internal versus External
   a. Appoint a strong academic "second in command"
3. Implement a strategic planning process
4. Academic quality
   a. Tenure and promotion cases
   b. Faculty recruitment, retention, development
   c. Student quality and student interactions
   d. The learning environment
5. Develop an external relations strategy
   a. Engage the campus, community and profession

• • •

At the department level, the chair should strategically select the recruiting, admissions and curriculum committee chairs, choosing faculty who are respected and knowledgeable about the issues. The leader sets the charge for each committee based on the established strategic priorities and then meets with each committee chair to monitor progress. If significant change is being contemplated, the leader needs to take a more active role. Faculty members leading such efforts are rarely willing to confront controversial issues; the leader needs to maintain frequent oversight, placing concrete deadlines to achieve meaningful progress.

Compliance: Universities operate in an increasingly regulated environment. Compliance creates challenges, especially in a culture of faculty independence. Every university has developed training opportunities, usually available on-line, on such issues as prevention, identification and reaction to harassment; conflict of interest; FERPA obligations; cyber security; and institutional commitment. All leaders should pursue this training and understand the issues that can arise and how to react if they do. University policy usually requires relevant faculty and staff to undergo compliance training. Most of the responsibility to ensure that the faculty and staff do so falls on the department chair and/or dean. Leaders should expect some faculty to protest that in their particular case, the training is not necessary. Set an example by publicizing your own compliance and commenting on the usefulness of the training. Being forceful is important; as Mike Gottfredson observed during our discussions, "An ounce of prevention is worth a ton of lawyers."

Day-to-day organization: At this point in your career, you have developed a personal system to organize tasks. Still, the following suggestions, derived from both comments by the interviewees and personal experience, may be useful. First, set aside time for both life balance and meetings that require your attendance. Next, update your list of tasks daily, prioritizing each as high, medium or low. Then map these priorities into your calendar with an appropriate amount of time allocated to effectively address them. Part of this prioritization, which is often overlooked, includes blocking out time for creative thinking about strategic issues, research projects, upcoming presentations and external advisory board meetings. If there is a time of day when you tend to be more creative, reserve that time for these complex tasks. For meetings that your office schedules, choose times of the day that match your preferences. Some meetings are pro forma and basically only require your presence, even if you are running them. Others are strategic and require you to inspire direction.

Even after prioritizing and organizing, the reality is that there is never sufficient time to devote the desired amount of attention to each task. Compromises have to be made and an overarching strategy needs to be developed. The high volume of activity combined with the typically lean administrative infrastructure makes it a virtual certainty that there is always a problem somewhere. When issues arise, calmness and confidence need to prevail. Being able to provide direction and knowing how to pursue a resolution instills confidence in the leader. For problems that can be contained in the unit, the leader should appoint someone who has the ability to take charge and act prudently. This individual can be an associate dean, assistant chair, executive assistant or staff member who is trained and able to follow through on the resolution. Some issues, including crises and legal recourse, require expertise beyond that available in the unit. These cases are discussed in a later section in this chapter.

Inevitably, most leaders become overburdened. A common reaction is to devote many hours attempting to shorten an ever-expanding list. Setting priorities helps, but once you have done so, there is a great temptation to multitask. Being distracted has consequences. Whether at a meeting where participants perceive you are not interested in their perspective or at your desk working on a key issue, not giving your full attention is the best way to ensure an inferior outcome. Focus on one thing at a time and recognize that there will always be one more thing. After a long day, when you have the urge to work on one more thing, go home and don't bring work with you. You will be fresher the next day and the list will still be there.

Should you maintain an open door policy? While the leader should be available, it is also important to protect your time. A delicate balance needs to be achieved. Giving the appearance that you are barring individuals from your office can be perceived by the faculty as an affront to academic freedom and by the staff as being high-handed and aloof. One approach is to widely communicate that everyone is welcome to see you but let your administrative assistant be your gatekeeper. Individuals should then feel that the leader is approachable and available. Your assistant can shield you from random non-critical walk-in meetings and non-essential e-mails, phone calls and mail. All leaders should also have two university phone numbers and e-mail addresses, one that is directly handled by your assistant for public interaction and a second that is distributed to a much smaller group. An additional private account helps to maintain separation of personal communications from university related business.

Early in your tenure, work with your assistant to set the protocol for each type of interaction and for each constituency and then modify the prioritization appropriately over time. For example, a prioritization protocol for a dean's administrative assistant could include interrupting a meeting or contacting you immediately if calls are received from the president or provost, a major donor or the governor (a possibility at a major public university) or if there is a student, faculty, staff, campus or family emergency. Your assistant can also gain a sense of who should be allowed to "pop in" to see you and when to politely find another time if you need to focus without interruption.

Leading change: The department chair and dean should develop a keen sense of the external environment, especially monitoring changes in academic standards and curriculum innovations at peer and aspirational departments. One challenge is that the leader is expected to introduce new ideas knowing full well that the faculty is naturally resistant to changing a model in which they have sunk significant investment. An ample literature exists that describes strategies for leading change.[72] While that literature is not repeated here, one way to proceed is as follows: When you are absolutely confident that an initiative needs to be adopted but faculty dissent is rampant, try to "chunk down" the problem. Break down the components into smaller pieces and then seek individuals to support each part of the puzzle. Even significant change usually requires meaningful participation from only a small fraction of the faculty. By enlisting several respected faculty members to take on leadership roles, others recognize that first, they personally are not being asked to alter their current activity, and second, other credible individuals are supporting the change. Patience and persistence are the best tools the leader can apply in this situation. If the initiative is compelling and executed effectively, its success over time will convince other faculty members to consider joining the effort or, more realistically, to at least refrain from active opposition.

EXAMPLE: SCHOOL OF EDUCATION, UNIVERSITY OF COLORADO

Philip DiStefano, now Chancellor at the University of Colorado, served as Dean of the School of Education from 1986 to 1996. His main challenge over his ten-year tenure was to break down the two-tier system that existed on the faculty, with a goal to build a high quality research intense faculty that also valued excellent teaching. There was great resistance from a cohort of the established faculty that led to unpleasant faculty meetings and a tense atmosphere. He chose to meet individually with the faculty, openly listen to concerns and treat each individual with respect. Doing so built a trust among the faculty. Over his tenure, the school recruited high quality faculty and drastically changed the culture. Today the UC School of Education consistently ranks among the top graduate schools of education in the country. By "chunking down" the issues; that is, by meeting individually with the faculty, he gained a sense of trust and reached a comfort level among the faculty that allowed the necessary steps to be taken.

Effective leaders look past the negatives and proceed to get things done. Every novel idea generates resistance and doubters. Move past them and act, recognizing full well that not every initiative will succeed. If you have a failure, do not take it personally. Failures are soon forgotten if handled well. Admit the outcome, explain that you understand the consequences and that you have learned from the experience. Do not shy away from initiating the next innovation. You will be remembered and respected more for taking on difficult challenges than for overseeing the easy wins.

DELEGATION

A natural temptation for a new leader is to always be in control, making as many decisions as possible. Over time, recognition sets in that being too deeply involved is unrealistic and inefficient. But which decisions should be delegated? Even more importantly, which items should *not* be delegated?

In most situations, the individual who understands and has control of the budget is the person who actually runs the organization. During the first year in office the leader should work closely with the appropriate budget officer to gain a full understanding of the unit's sources and uses of revenue. Once the flow of funds is understood, a sensible policy is to establish a dollar amount above which the leader maintains control over all allocations. Allocations below this level can either be automatic or rest in the hands of an associate dean or assistant chair. In addition to significant financial decisions, other areas that should typically not be delegated include direct interaction with major donors, other university leaders and highly respected senior faculty who are being recruited. These individuals are not likely to respond positively if they believe the leader isn't actively engaged and supportive. Especially for major donors, the leader is the top development officer; it is rare that a major gift is received without heavy involvement of the leader. The leader should also be the point person in negotiations with the campus or if relevant, the board of governors and legislature.

George Daly suggested the following way to delegate, which is similar to how several other interviewees described their methodology. Items that can be delegated depend on their importance and the comparative advantage of the skills of the leadership team. New leaders should initially examine all major decisions to gain a sense of their significance and complexity. Over time, they can decide which items can be delegated and to whom depending on where the best talent lies to handle each issue both efficiently and cost effectively. The leader should identify the individual who has primary responsibility for each task and assign oversight of the activity to a different individual. Delegation of authority not only allows more efficient use of time but also provides an opportunity for the leader to develop the next generation of leadership.

EXAMPLE: EFFICIENCY THROUGH PRE-APPROVAL

There are many processes that require the leader's approval. Some of these are critical; others are pro forma. Systematizing those that require minimal scrutiny can save significant time. For example, departments provide funds to the faculty for travel to conferences and ancillary research, teaching and other professional expenses. An inefficient way to allocate these funds is to require each faculty member to submit a written application and then centrally review each request. A better way is to annually provide an amount for each faculty member that can be used for professional expenses that would normally be approved anyway. If a faculty member needs additional funds they can submit a request with a short rationale. This request can be reviewed and acted on by someone other than the leader. The system can be reviewed annually to ensure funds are being used productively. This approach saves considerable time by removing costs of making and evaluating requests that are almost always approved, while still providing accountability. Other similar processes within your control can also be routinized.

MEETINGS

The interviewees identified the volume of requests for meetings as one of the most frustrating aspects of a new leadership position. Many people want to meet an incoming leader and it is easy to lose control of one's calendar. During the first few months of any new position, it is expected that the leader respond positively to as many of these meeting requests as possible. But there should be a strategic outcome associated with this plethora of activity. The intent is to determine which meetings are required, which are useful and which are wasteful. The required meetings offer no option, especially for those chaired by the head of the next layer of administration. For a department chair, these meetings are called by the dean. For a dean, these meetings are called by the provost or president. If you cannot attend due to a conflict, inform the appropriate individual and ask for permission to send someone in your stead (an associate dean or assistant chair.) Do not ignore these meetings or treat them lightly. Your seriousness is noticed. For meetings that are neither useful nor required, express your apologies and ask for the minutes and materials in lieu of attending.

<u>Meetings under your control</u>. There is a routine set of meetings that are scheduled by and presided over by the leader. For example, the meetings under the control of the dean's office include regular meetings with

* The faculty;
* The department chairs or area coordinators;
* The external relations staff;
* Associate deans; and
* Donors and potential donors.

A sensible policy concerning meetings under your control is to cancel any regularly scheduled meeting if no action is necessary. For example, if the proposed agenda for a regularly scheduled faculty meeting is pure-ly informational with no action items, then in most cases, it is best to cancel the meeting. Any information that might have been distributed can be shared electronically. If the resulting feedback is controversial, then the issues can be discussed at a subsequent meeting. The faculty will appreciate that the administration values their time; they should be more willing to attend meetings when they are called and they are likely to take the agenda more seriously. Both attendance and the quality of the discourse at the meeting should improve when the faculty recognizes that meetings take place only if there are significant issues that need to be addressed.

EXAMPLE: THE INEFFICIENCY OF MEETING TOO FREQUENTLY

When I was a department chair at the University of Iowa a good friend in another department informed me that it was his turn to become chair. He dreaded taking on the role because faculty members always bickered at every department meeting. Several faculty members had long standing disagreements and since there were only twelve members in the department, the tension in the room was palpable. At one point he mentioned that the department met once every week. I indicated that I could not envision a situation where a department would have such a large agenda that the entire faculty needed to meet that frequently. He reflected that, in fact, there was not much real business that needed to be conducted in these weekly meetings. Most of the conversation related current issues to age-old controversies. We then discussed the possibility that department hold fewer meetings, with each focused primarily on items that needed an action. After pondering this suggestion, he thought that he could try canceling a meeting or two and see the reaction.

Over the next year, the group agreed to meet only once a month. The result was that the meetings focused only on action items and there was much less time for idle conversation and age-old arguments about marginal issues. The strategy to avoid unnecessary meetings proved to make the meetings more productive while fostering a more positive culture.

Meeting Dynamics: [73] There is no excuse for a nonproductive or wasteful meeting if you are presiding. Some of the factors associated with effective meetings are provided in Table 8.3. First, recognize that everyone's time is valuable. Arrive and start the meeting on time. Distribute the agenda prior to the meeting and define the purpose of the meeting at its outset. Do not discuss topics that are not relevant such as an article you just read, a meeting you just attended or a speech you just heard. Keep the discussion on topic. Bring the group together to talk strategy and solicit suggestions on important issues. Show respect for the participants; encourage collaboration and recognize and thank individuals for their input. It is also important to understand and implement Robert's Rules of Order. [74] The leader or leader's delegate should ensure that procedural issues concerning motions, voting rules and quorums do not become the center of discussion at any meeting.

Before any meeting that involves a critical discussion and/or vote, consult with the key players to solicit their feedback and discuss any controversial issues. Open the meeting with an overview of the agenda and ask if anyone would like to add any items; then request approval of the minutes, if any, from the previous meeting. If a strategic initiative is to be discussed, provide a brief opening overview and then ask the individual who is primarily responsible to lead the discussion. Allow the participants ample time for discourse, offering only clarifying comments; do not enter with substantive comments prematurely. In most cases, providing conclusions and direction at the end, rather than the beginning is a wise strategy. Take notes during the meeting to demonstrate that you care about what people are saying and that you intend to think seriously about their comments. At the end of the discussion, use your notes to summarize the main points, giving credit to individuals for the specific comments they contributed. Then conclude with an outline of the next steps.

Meetings of the faculty: Even after scrupulous preparation and attention to detail, many leaders still find faculty meetings to be particularly stressful and divisive. This aspect of faculty discourse may have its roots as far back as 2300 years ago when Socrates popularized a thinking process based on dialectical reasoning. De Bono (1999) points out that Plato, in reviewing Socrates work, found that in 80% of the dialogues in which Socrates was involved, there was no constructive outcome. Socrates viewed his role as identifying what was wrong. De Bono relates faculty meetings to dialogues that follow Socrates' approach. He concludes that one should not expect much to be accomplished at any faculty meeting. Still, while faculty meetings can sometimes emanate an almost hostile environment, the exchange of ideas is powerful. The most creative suggestions often arise from the most heated debates. The leader's role is to listen carefully, prioritize next steps and bring the discussion to a conclusion with appropriate actions. Arriving at a productive outcome requires that prior to the meeting, the leader engages in extensive behind the scenes discussion with individual influential faculty members. This political nature of academia is well known to any seasoned leader, but still can be very frustrating.[75]

<u>Your interactions at required meetings</u>: Usually campus meetings that require your attendance are those called either by the person to whom you report, another higher level campus leader or a chair of a committee on which you serve. Don't be an empty suit at these meetings. Have an opinion; add value to the discourse. At the same time, do so professionally. Respect is a top priority. Never belittle any of your colleagues or become emotional. And definitely, never try to outshine or aggressively disagree with your superior in a public forum. If you have a substantive disagreement, it is much better to wait to discuss the issue with your superior in private. There is always some chance you are mistaken, in which case you avoid embarrassment in front of the group. But if you are correct, you will gain the confidence of your superior who will appreciate that you had the good sense to raise the issue privately.

Try to learn from the interactions at each meeting. For example, you may notice that every so often one of the participants makes a point emphatically but receives no response. The individual then repeats the comment and if no one responds again, repeats the comment even louder. Eventually, the individual retreats but suffers embarrassment. If you make a suggestion at a meeting and there is no reaction, the least likely reason is that no one heard you. Don't keep repeating yourself and especially don't say it louder. Accept the fact that either there is no support for your argument or that the comment does not merit further discussion. Let the discourse proceed.

Finally, some required meetings are likely to be a poor use of your time. In this case, you can either attend as necessary, letting the status quo continue, or you can enlist other attendees in an effort to modify the meeting agenda to become more productive.

● ● ●

TABLE 8.3 Key Elements of Productive Meetings

1. Circulate the agenda at least one week in advance.
2. If there are no actionable items or critical items for discussion, consider cancelling the meeting.
3. Begin and end on time.
4. Greet attendees and make them feel welcome.
5. If individuals are new or new to each other, ask for brief self-introductions before beginning.
6. Review the work accomplished at the last meeting.
7. Ask for approval of the minutes.
8. Review the agenda; ask for any additions or questions.
9. Lead off the discussion, then hand off the substance to the person(s) leading the initiative.
10. Encourage relevant participation.
11. Intervene minimally, only to clarify and express appreciation for good ideas.
12. Keep the discourse focused on the agenda.
13. Take notes.
14. At the end of the meeting, use your notes to summarize key points and identify and thank the persons who made these points.
15. Draw conclusions and outline the next actions.
16. Leave when the meeting is done; otherwise the meeting will continue.

• • •

Example: Making meetings more productive

One interviewee described the meetings of the academic council at a large comprehensive public university. He noticed that over the seven years that he had been a dean, the number of staff members who were invited by the provost had grown to the point where there were now more staff members than deans participating. At each meeting, one or two staff members discussed informational material that could have been distributed rather than presented. He shared the desire for more productive meetings with the other deans. Subsequently, the deans unanimously requested that there should be regular meetings attended only by the deans and provost with a focus on strategic issues pertinent to the deans. At the first such meeting, the provost indicated that the state budget was once again in disarray and the chief budget officer needed to update the deans. After 45 minutes of detailed description of inter-legislative battles and technical jargon on various budget items, the deans, who were accustomed to this banter, were on their cell phones reading e-mails under the table. The Associate Dean from Engineering, an infrequent attendee who was substituting for the out of town dean, was visibly agitated. Finally, he could contain himself no longer and pointedly asked the budget officer (paraphrased);

> *Do you practice being this obtuse or does it come naturally? After 45 minutes, I have yet to hear anything that the deans need to discuss. Do we really need to be here?*

An interloper had the courage to say what the normal attendees were thinking; why are you wasting our time? Subsequently, the provost relinquished the agenda for every other meeting to the deans. They suggested topics, which the provost could then accept or modify. The meetings became more productive and more focused on useful dialogue.

BUILDING YOUR TEAM

There is no better wisdom for building you team than in the well-worn phrase: hire the best people and get out of their way. Still, the intent of the statement is sometimes misinterpreted. What is does not mean is that the leader should abandon the team after the individuals are chosen. When I began as Dean of the Business School at the University of Wisconsin,

Chancellor Donna Shalala said to me (paraphrased); Andy, the School is yours to run. Just call me when you need me. Donna Shalala believed in building a team of deans who could operate independently within the vision of the university, but she made it clear that they could always seek her when needed. I called upon her when school initiatives required the support of the University of Wisconsin System or legislature, when I was meeting with a significant donor or when we faced a politically sensitive situation. Many others have learned from the independence and leadership that Donna Shalala provided; several have indicated to me that she was the most influential mentor along their career path and I certainly agree.

As a leader, you should be there when a member of your team needs your advice and support. The first step in building your team is to maintain a high standard in the selection process. The best leaders hire the best people; weak people hire even weaker people. To maximize your effectiveness, choose individuals who complement your skills. Seek individuals who have an opinion. Anyone who always agrees with you is redundant. Recognize that it is impossible for the leader to have all the answers; the best answer does not always come from the top. Effective leaders facilitate the development of talented faculty and staff, where strategic leadership takes place among a diverse set of individuals who possess different talents. Although you should provide independence, it is critical to set goals and track performance. Don't confuse effort with results. A written list of responsibilities and goals with a timeline is essential. Regular meetings with your team allow you to monitor progress in a helpful way, offering praise to those exceeding goals and encouragement and support to individuals who may be falling behind.

Over time, as the team starts to gel, allow selected individuals the freedom to take measured risks and make mistakes. Carefully weigh the cost of failure and if not too significant, allow the individual to proceed. Even if the initiative fails, the individual is likely to be grateful that you allowed the attempt. The lesson learned by the individual is to better formulate future initiatives and assess the probability of success more carefully before bringing the next idea forward.

LESS FREQUENT BUT MORE PROBLEMATIC ISSUES

Reacting to unjust criticism: Any leader who confronts critical issues and follows through on "doing the right thing" is likely at some point to be confronted with unjust criticism. A measure of the leader's performance is not that criticism arises but rather how the leader deals with it when it does. In some cases, an antagonistic faculty member may offer criticism reflecting personal opinion with little basis on facts. The first reaction to this type of attack, even if it is broadly distributed, is to simply not respond. The protagonist wants and needs a platform. A response provides that platform. Not responding is likely to frustrate the individual; if it appears that no one cares or believes the allegations, the individual eventually runs out of fuel. If the attack takes place in public, perhaps at a department meeting, then responding in a non-emotional, factual way can disarm the individual and give a sense to the audience not to take the issue seriously. Resist fighting fire with fire; rather, fight fire with a hose.

If a written criticism is particularly painful, one way to proceed is to follow the well-known advice to draft a detailed response but then put it in your drawer. This approach can be therapeutic. Read it again the next day; almost always, the issue seems less important as time goes by. Even if you remain incensed, you should still throw it away. Again, the instigator wants a platform; don't provide one. There is at least one circumstance where a formal response may be required. If the attack is not only false but can cause some damage to the institution by compromising your principles, then again draft a response and let it sit for a day. If you still feel that the attack is sufficiently damaging and that a response can make a difference, then seek the council of others, including the university's legal counsel. If they agree that a response is warranted, proceed.

Difficult personnel situations: Relationships are great until they aren't. Typical problematic scenarios include underperformance, caustic behavior, or violation of university policy. One common fault, especially among new leaders, is a tendency to not act quickly enough when individuals are not meeting expectations. In some cases, it can be difficult for the leader to recognize the person's shortcomings. Individuals who excel at "managing up," can disguise true behavior and delay an accurate assessment by the leader. To avoid these situations it is useful to perform 360-degree or other performance evaluations and to obtain input directly from coworkers. An often elusive lesson for many leaders is that people don't change much beyond what they intrinsically are. The leader's challenge is to bring out the best traits and minimize the worst. Some of the interviewees indicated that they spent too much time attempting to influence behavior. They eventually recognized the low probability of success; in most situations, the only way to change people is to change the people. As Maya Angelou aptly advised;

"When someone shows you who they are believe them; the first time."

Reacting to a case of underperformance or poor behavior can be onerous and painful; there is a fine line between being honest and being brutal. You must be able to clearly send a message and deliver negative news in a respectful way without humiliating the individual. There are several possible reactions when someone receives a strong negative message. First, the individual might retreat into seclusion; while still doing the job the individual withdraws from the normal activity of the unit. This behavior sometimes leads to a peaceful coexistence, which may be tolerable if the individual is sufficiently competent. Alternatively, the individual may become belligerent and seek legal recourse. A further possibility is that the individual stays the course, not changing disruptive behavior and/or continuing to underperform. In any case, by opening the conversation about performance, recognize that the danger is that you create an enemy. In some cases, this outcome is fine; in others, you may rationally decide that it is best to either do nothing or request that the central administration intervene on your behalf.

The emotional stress of dealing with negative personnel issues can demoralize even the most effective leaders. Ultimately, if all else fails and the individual needs to be dismissed, the process required to do so can be long and distasteful. The more experienced and well trained human re-source and legal experts should be consulted as quickly as possible in these messy situations. The leader is usually asked to participate in a meeting to inform the individual about the action to be taken. It is critical for the leader to understand the legal ramifications associated with any meeting with the affected party. A cardinal rule is never to meet alone with the individual. In addition, the leader should be familiarized with how state laws apply to meeting interactions, including whether or not the meeting can be recorded, and if so, who is legally allowed to do so.

EXAMPLE: LEGAL RAMIFICATIONS OF MEETINGS BETWEEN AFFECTED PARTIES.

As Interim President of the University of Iowa, Gary Fethke faced a difficult decision to affect change in leadership in a sizable university operation. At a meeting attended by Fethke, the Vice President of Research and a senior member of the Human Resources staff, the then head of the operation was informed of the decision to terminate employment. The employee secretly recorded the meeting and subsequently presented the transcript at a court hearing where Fethke and the University were being sued for an unjustified firing. According to Iowa code, a secret recording of the meeting is legal, as long as the recording is not conducted by a third party. If prior to the start of the meeting, university personnel had asked whether anyone was recording the meeting and the answer was "no," then the recording would not have been permissible. As it turned out, the recording in this case actu-ally supported the University's defense and the case was decided in its favor. Still, the legal framework that governs meetings with the affected party can play a significant role in the deliberation of the case; not recognizing what is permissible in court can have serious ramifications.

Terminations and suits: When considering a termination, illegal actions that involve violation of university policy usually provide clearer grounds for dismissal than performance related issues. Still, justification for any dismissal can be legally difficult to defend. In the case of a performance-based dismissal, annual performance reviews need to document and be consistent with the reasons behind a recommendation for termination. If they do not, the goal changes from dismissal to relocation with the individual's approval to another position at the university. The intent is that with appropriate coaching the person can find a better home and new start elsewhere where no negative baggage exists.

If a suit is brought against the university, the relevant department chair, dean and provost work with university counsel to assess whether defending the case is worth the legal cost and emotional toll. Universities tend to be risk averse and are likely to suggest settling a case out of court rather than to pursue a lengthy legal battle. The example below describes a situation in which the decision was made to defend a lawsuit by a faculty member who had been terminated. Still, there are many instances where universities choose the easier path to settle.

Example: When settling is not the right solution.

A dean at a top university was informed that a full time female faculty member had accepted a second full time position at another university. As is the case at virtually all universities, the university's policy explicitly forbids full time employees from holding another full time position. Consequently, the university moved to terminate the individual's employment due to violation of university policy. About three weeks later, the faculty member brought a suit against the specific college and the university on the basis of sex and age discrimination. While the dean and others believed that the suit had no merit and that it was highly likely that the university would win in court, university officials suggested a settlement. As is frequently the case, the university preferred to avoid a long, distracting and expensive legal battle, even one that they would likely win.

After consideration, the dean argued to defend the case because in his view the termination had nothing to do with sex and age discrimination. He felt strongly that it was wrong for anyone to either violate university policy or make false claims and then be rewarded for doing so through a settlement. Giving in would send a signal that the way to obtain rewards in the system would be for others to follow a similar path. After considering the alternatives, the university agreed with the dean. Outside counsel was hired and as expected there was a long period of tense depositions, with multiple distasteful allegations. In the end, the dean and university were wise to defend their position. The judge dismissed the case on summary judgment and it never went to court.

In complex legal situations, universities tend to acquiesce and seek a settlement to avoid the distraction and cost of what can be a long, emotional process. Moreover, the possibility of media attention adds another layer of risk. Understandably, as in any litigation, settlement can appear to be an attractive path, especially for reasonable amounts. Department chairs and deans should be aware of the university's predisposition in litigious situations. Making bold statements based on principles without the backing of the administration is not likely to end well for the leader. Still, in spite of the costs of defending a suit, as demonstrated in the above case, there are times when the university needs to stand firm. Settling a case that attacks the principles of the university can set a precedent whose long run costs far outweigh the costs of defending the case in the first place.

Crisis management: Academic leaders are sometimes thrust into crisis management situations that involve complexities they are not prepared to handle. A crisis often results from events that lie outside the direct control of the leader, yet it is the leader who typically becomes the primary person expected to guide the organization through a tumultuous period. Crises at universities can range from national disasters, as occurred in the case of the impact of Hurricane Katrina on the universities in New Orleans, to the acts of violence that have occurred on several campuses. The most likely scenarios for universities are rules violations or personnel issues. These situations have the potential to damage the reputation of the university and can cause significant financial repercussions. When a crisis occurs, the leader is called upon to be the primary interface with the public and to make critical decisions over a relatively short time frame. Bad news does not improve with age; it is always best for the leader to inform the appropriate parties as soon as the facts are known. The leader should personally research the facts to the extent possible to be able to confidently build a data based argument.

Major universities have a crisis management infrastructure that includes public relations, legal, psychological and campus security expertise. David Ward pointed out that this team serves a number of critical functions. In addition to providing a skilled staff to address the complexities of the crisis, this group helps the leader survive what could otherwise be a very isolated period. He reflected on a difficult personnel situation that occurred when he was Chancellor at the University of Wisconsin. He recalled the feeling of being left alone to deal with the consequences, as academic colleagues close to the problem were understandably reluctant to become involved in a complicated, thorny situation. Thankfully, he was able to rely on skilled legal and other administrative staff for support. Depending on the complexity of the issues, outside consultants can also provide strategic direction and support. Suggestions offered by the interviewees concerning how to proceed when confronted with a crisis are summarized in Table 8.4.

Example: Alleged NCAA Rules Violations

In 2010, the University of Miami (UM) informed the NCAA about alleged violations concerning purported improper benefits given to players in the football and men's basketball programs between 2002 and 2010.[76] UM President Donna Shalala took on the role as the main spokesperson for the campus; she pledged full cooperation with any investigation into the matter. In August 2011, the NCAA's investigation was made public and President Shalala pledged to "vigorously pursue the truth, wherever that path may lead." She insisted upon 'complete, honest, and transparent cooperation with the NCAA from (UM) staff and students. The university continued its own internal investigation; when it turned out that some of the infractions were corroborated, President Shalala issued significant self-imposed sanctions including post-season bans in 2011 and 2012. Later on she indicated that the university recognized that there were significant violations and they wanted to take immediate action and not wait for the NCAA to finish their deliberations.

In February 2013, an unprecedented development occurred when the NCAA admitted that it had made mistakes during the investigation. NCAA President Mark Emmert indicated that the tactics used by the NCAA's enforcement staff had "failed" and "acted contrary to internal protocols, legal counsel and the membership's understanding about the limits of its investigative powers." President Shalala responded firmly but tactfully that the while the University of Miami believes in fairness and due process it had clearly been wronged in this investigation. Essentially the University, which was playing a cooperative and truthful role, had become victimized by a flawed investigation with inappropriate practices by NCAA staff. She called for no further sanctions to be levied beyond the already self-imposed punishment. In response to their own missteps, the NCAA made personnel and process adjustments.

• • •

TABLE 8.4 Steps in Crisis Management

* There should be one spokesperson for the university;
* All public communication should be the result of strategic consultation with a team of experts;
* There is a thin line between providing too little and too much information to the media;

 * Bad news does not get better with age--inform relevant parties as soon as possible but make sure you have all the information before commenting on significant issues;
 * Never appear to be defensive--publicly pledge your cooperation and the cooperation of all appropriate parties with the investigating entities to supply all evidence;
 * Pledge to aggressively investigate to find the truth and then to take appropriate actions;
 * Accept responsibility if the evidence corroborates wrongdoing; admit fault and follow through on appropriate punitive action.

● ● ●

In October 2013, the NCAA ruled that UM exhibited a lack of institutional control. The NCAA accepted the "extensive and significant" penalties that had been self-imposed by the institution. By taking these actions and tactfully but aggressively reacting to the mistakes made by the NCAA, the university had made an effective case that no additional serious sanctions were warranted. Although several additional penalties were levied, the athletic program avoided further significant encumbrance.

Lessons learned: This episode provides an excellent example of effective crisis management. When the allegations arose, the university immediately took appropriate steps. It appointed one spokesperson, openly shared the available information with the regulatory agency, pledged to cooperate and investigated the possible infractions. Later on, when violations were validated, the university took swift action to self-impose penalties, some of which were very painful to students who would miss a once in a lifetime opportunity for post-season play. In addition, when miscues were detected on the part of the investigative agency, the university took a firm position, asking who was in fact the victim. This prudent and responsible action provided the impetus for students, faculty, staff, alumni, donors and other members of the community to stand by and support the university at a challenging time. In the end, UM's aggressive reaction to the violations reflected an honest admission of error and a deep sense of commitment by the university to ethical and accountable behavior.

SUMMARY AND CONCLUSIONS

When taking on a new leadership position, developing your personal strategy is just as important as developing an overall strategy for the organization. A key consideration is whether your style is well suited for the needs and culture of the unit. Organizations require different types of leaders at different points in their development. A department that is outmoded with a deeply entrenched faculty needs dramatic change; the leader needs to be resolved, confident and impervious to criticism. Alternatively, for most situations, there is a wide range of personal styles than can be successful.

Should a leader be loved or feared? A Machiavellian would argue that feared is better, as long as the leader is not hated; people are more likely to take advantage of a leader who is loved rather than one who is feared.[77] But a charismatic leader who inspires individuals can fuel a passion for supporting the greater good. A charismatic leader does not instill fear but rather displays sincere respect for others and through actions and success receives respect from them. It is especially critical for a new leader to show respect for the faculty. Sometimes, when a faculty member shifts into a leadership role, the faculty serves as a convenient scapegoat. If goals aren't accomplished, it is because faculty don't cooperate, or even worse, they are blamed for not working hard enough. The leader takes a Machiavellian approach of threatening the faculty in an attempt to force the desired outcomes. In reality, the faculty collectively is likely to be highly productive and dedicated and can be the source of innovation and implementation of a strategic plan. Berating the faculty and displaying a lack of appreciation is likely to result in a short tenure in office.

Whatever leadership approach you choose, be a visionary and a pace-setter. When others observe your commitment and aspirations, they will either be inspired or conclude that they do not fit well. Some may seek other opportunities, which can be the best outcome. The challenge is re-acting to hostile individuals who remain. Innovation initially requires involvement of only a small percent of the faculty; chunking down the issues and gaining support of influential individuals is critical. Over time, doubtful faculty can be convinced when respected colleagues step forward and engage in successful new initiatives.

Personal style needs to be complemented by a pragmatic approach to the multitude of tasks that confront any leader who takes on significant responsibility. Even the most efficient leader recognizes that the high level of activity combined with the typical lean infrastructure makes it a virtual certainty that there is always a problem somewhere. Calmness and confidence need to prevail. Being able to recognize issues quickly and knowing how to resolve them instills a sense of confidence and trust in the leader. Avoid lots of analysis with no decisions; most situations call for swift, but carefully crafted responses.

A final piece of advice offered by one of the interviewees is to never become deluded by how you think the world should be or should work. Human beings and institutions rarely measure up to our best ideals. Don't sacrifice effort by complaining; rather, work to the best of your ability within the system while trying to change it for the better. For the moment, you need to play the hand that you are dealt. Over time, you can work to change either how the game is being played or what game is being played. If you believe the environment can be improved you shouldn't complain; you should act.

KEY TAKEAWAYS: CHAPTER 8

- Inexperienced leaders in a new position often neglect pacing and act as if they are running a sprint. The danger is that they quickly burn out.
- Simply showing up for family time is not good enough; life balance requires no distractions, especially from e-mails and texts.
- The volume of activity and lean administrative infrastructure makes it a virtual certainty that there is always a problem somewhere. When issues arise, calmness and confidence need to prevail.
- "An ounce of prevention is worth a ton of lawyers." (Mike Gottfredson)
- One measure of the leader's performance is not that criticism arises, but rather how the leader reacts when it does.
- Focus on one thing at a time and recognize that there will always be one more thing. At the end of the day, go home and don't bring work with you.
- In most situations, the individual who understands and has control of the budget is the person who actually runs the organization.
- Delegation of authority not only allows more efficient use of time but also provides an opportunity for the leader to develop the next generation of leadership.
- If you make a suggestion at a meeting and there is no reaction, the least likely reason is that no one heard you.
- Don't be an empty suit at meetings. Have an opinion; add value to the discourse.
- Resist fighting fire with a fire. Fight fire with a hose.
- The first reaction to unjust criticism is to not respond. The protagonist wants and needs a platform. A response provides that platform. If it appears that no one cares, the individual eventually runs out of fuel.
- "When someone shows you who they are believe them; the first time." (Maya Angelou)

- Bad news does not improve with age; always inform the appropriate parties as soon as the facts are known.
- If you have a failure, do not take it personally. Admit the outcome, explain that you have learned from the experience. Do not shy away from initiating the next innovation.
- You will be remembered and respected more for taking on the difficult challenges than for overseeing the easy wins.
- Never become deluded by how you think the world should be or how it should work.
- You need to play the hand that you are dealt. Over time, if needed, work to change either how the game is being played or what game is being played.
- If you believe the environment can be improved don't complain; act.

CHAPTER 9

Impact, Legacy and Life After Leadership

• • •

Even the mightiest of works may change the world only a little.
But to change the word a little, that is a mighty work.

—LYNDON BAINES JOHNSON

INTRODUCTION

WHAT WILL YOUR LEGACY BE? What would you like it to be? Whatever you think your impact may be, don't let your hopes expand beyond the reality of academic culture. Returning from a sabbatical after my third deanship and almost thirty years in leadership positions, I wandered into my newly assigned faculty office. As I contemplated my return or, as some would say, my move "up" to the faculty, a senior faculty member stopped by to welcome me back. We were having an amicable, engaging chat when he began discussing my successor. I quickly but diplomatically ended this line of conversation. Other than offering supportive comments, the previous leader should not welcome analysis of the new leader. After a brief silence, my colleague became reflective and revealed that he had considered becoming a dean earlier in his career; he chose not to because faculty members who are excellent researchers don't become deans. He further commented that if his research weren't so valuable, he could have become a dean since after all, he does work thirty-five hours each week. In fact, he said, sometimes he even works forty hours a week.

Some academic leaders might have been insulted or become depressed by these comments. I viewed them as more humorous than brutal. Many faculty members understandably reside in their own universe, framed by their research and teaching in highly specialized areas. They do not recognize the complexity of leadership positions or the volume of activity and the number of hours required. Moreover, they often see little connection between their mostly independent activity and the mission of the institution. Perhaps Clark Kerr described it best when he said: "A university is a place to bring together independent entrepreneurs who share one commonality, complaints over parking." The path to success for an academic leader is to do the things that bring the most value to the unit, university and society. Even with systematic communication, many times faculty members do not recognize or appreciate the value that the leader creates. They do not devote much time to issues that do not affect their daily activity and they argue against initiatives that on the surface appear to negatively impact their domain. One measure of success is the extent to which the leader convinces the faculty to willingly move in a direction for the benefit of the unit that they are not inclined to pursue on their own. In this sense, as the LBJ quote above implies, even a small innovation can be a significant achievement.

Legacy is a consideration throughout one's career, but it is especially important when contemplating the right time to step down. This chapter reviews some of the factors associated with the decision to end one's journey on a leadership path. The book concludes with an examination of the transition from a world of authority and responsibility to one of hopefully, fulfillment and reflection.

Stepping away from a leadership path

Chapter 2 describes some of the factors in the decision of when to step down from your current leadership position. The added focus here is on determining the right time to step away from your academic leadership career. One scenario is that you have attained reasonable success and are deciding when to announce your departure from what is likely to be your last leadership position. Usually, there are major accomplishments or key signals that the time has come. Some indicators include the following:

1. You achieve a significant milestone (campaign goal reached, new building, program or school approved, accreditation achieved);
2. You are losing interest in activities that once were your passion;
3. You are becoming impatient with individuals who are discovering for the first time ideas that you have seen many times over;
4. Your family interactions and life balance are suffering;
5. You are perennially exhausted;
6. You feel over networked and never seem to make progress on an ever expanding list;
7. It is simply just time to move on; as a mentor of Donna Shalala's once told her, "Always leave a job while you still love it."

Frequently, when a leader contemplates the right time to step down, the successful completion of a major fundraising campaign or the approval of a major new program or building are events that foster a natural end to one's term. In 2013, Donna Shalala completed her third university presidency after thirteen years at the University of Miami. She was asked to continue but felt she had attained her goals by overseeing the growth in prominence of the University of Miami to one of the top 50 universities in the country and spearheading two capital campaigns, raising collectively over $3 billion. If she stayed, she would be repeating what she had already accomplished; it was time for the university to seek a new leader. Several of the interviewees had similar experiences. Heading into my ninth year as dean at UC Irvine we had achieved academic and fundraising goals, but the defining moment to step down was the funding approval by the legislature for a new building.

While many former leaders leave the university, either to retirement or to a new endeavor, those leaders who remain on the faculty should carefully manage their behavior. Several suggestions below can serve as a guide:

1. Do not attend faculty meetings or strategic planning sessions that are run by the new leader until a reasonable period has passed;
2. Refrain from discussing the new leader except to offer brief supporting remarks;
3. Be available for the new leader but refrain from offering advice unless asked;
4. Do not be highly visible; and
5. Very importantly, when you no longer hold the position, stop doing the job.

There are many examples of individuals whose lives became defined by the position they held. Former long-term leaders sometimes have difficulty transitioning to a non-leadership role and they continue to seek involvement in the direction of the unit. Openly engaging in strategic issues after leaving a leadership position is not healthy for either the individual or the institution. As indicated in the example below, many times former leaders do not recognize the extent of their involvement and need others to gently help coax them to a more distant role.

Example: When you no longer hold the position, stop doing the job.

When my son Keith was about ten years old, we occasionally went to my office on a Sunday afternoon where he did homework while I caught up on some reading. One Sunday while taking the elevator up to my office he asked, "Dad, what does a dean actually do?" As I was contemplating an appropriate answer for a ten year old, I noticed that there was some dust on the ledge below the light indicator for the floors. I began wiping off the dust with my finger and told him that a critical role for any leader is to always strive for excellence. Leaders set high standards for the organization and then demonstrate how to uphold them. Sometimes this means taking care of key issues that others either don't notice or don't believe are their responsibility. I explained to him that the dusty shelf is an example of something that reflects badly on the school; one job of the leader to make sure that problems others are not addressing are solved.

The shelf dusting became a ritual every time we went up to my office. Ten years later I had stepped down as dean and returned to the faculty. At one point, Keith asked to see my new faculty office. He was now in college but to follow our tradition, when we entered the elevator, I raised my hand to dust off the shelf. As I did so, Keith pulled my arm down, looked me straight in the eye and said, "Dad, no longer your job." As humorous as his comment was, the message struck a chord. I recognized that I was having a hard time adjusting; whenever I saw problematic issues I had an urge to get involved. Keith had made me realize that when you no longer hold the position, stop doing the job. From that point on, I did exactly that.

Life after Leadership

What will you do next? When is it time to no longer explore the next opportunity? Whenever a successful leader steps down, others look to that person to take on additional leadership roles. How does one decide whether to do so? As is the case for nearly every such philosophical question, the answer is, "it depends." Leaders often feel they have more to give, but for most, a time naturally comes when they have fulfilled their desire for responsibility and authority. At that point, the passion to be creative and visionary leads to different channels through perhaps innovative teaching, research in different areas, membership on boards, not-for-profit activities, hobbies and most important, family.

Former university presidents are often sought after to apply their accumulated knowledge and leadership skills in a different environment. David Ward, after his tenure as Chancellor at the University of Wisconsin, accepted the leadership role at the American Council on Education (ACE), where he continued his record of significant accomplishment. Then stepping out of that role, he was called back into service as interim Chancellor at Wisconsin for two years. In 2015, Donna Shalala, who "loves a new challenge," accepted a position as President and CEO of the Clinton Foundation. As in the case of David Ward, former leaders are sometimes asked to step into an interim position, especially when the incumbent leader departs quickly or a search is taking longer than expected. Both Joe Alutto, at Ohio State and Gary Fethke, at Iowa, were drafted as interim presidents and they performed admirably. For some, the thought of returning to the helm can act like a seductive drug; but is the experience worth the heavy personal toll, especially if the opportunity arises at the last phase of one's career? Equally as important, if one does accept the role, how should it be approached? Should an interim be a placeholder, assuming the chair but not the role? Or should the office be used as an opportunity to invoke meaningful change, paving an easier road for the permanent leader?

Example: The role of an interim leader

Gary Fethke completed a successful thirteen-year tenure as dean of the Tippie School of Business at the University of Iowa. He was then called upon by the Iowa Board of Regents to assume the position of Interim President. He accepted on two conditions; first, he would not pursue the permanent position; and second, he would not act as a temporary placeholder but rather would make tough decisions that needed to be made. Over fifteen months as Interim President, Fethke took on a strategic role; he helped to reorganize University of Iowa Health Care; streamlined the office of the president by eliminating unnecessary administrative positions; oversaw the completion of the State Hygienic Laboratory; directed the hiring of an Athletic Director and worked to replace the basketball coach. He also supported the development of the remote Sport Medicine Clinic and engaged in other strategic initiatives. The advantage of a dedicated interim leader is the ability to take on controversial issues and fix problems that would be difficult for a new permanent leader to immediately address.

IMPACT AND LEGACY

Given that a major constituent base, the faculty, may have little appreciation for the role the leader plays, how will the leader's legacy be recognized? Your impact on an organization can be demonstrated in any number of lasting ways. The development of new programs, university collaborations, funds raised, new buildings, improved rankings and research accomplishments of the faculty can have lasting impact. Many of the interviewees achieved national and international acclaim through innovations they led at their own universities and also through leadership in national and global organizations. Some of the interviewees were recognized via rooms named in their honor, plaques that memorialized their contributions or scholarships that carried their name. Many especially realized their impact, both physically and emotionally at testimonial events as they stepped down. These celebrations allow university leaders, faculty, staff and others to express their own personal appreciation. At the same time, the leader can visualize the impact through the eyes of others in a way not possible in day-to-day interactions.

In the end, all indicated that their legacy relates more to the development, growth and success of the people they interacted with than to any other type of recognition. The individuals they recruited and those they successfully retained against tough competition brought a great sense of pride. It is especially meaningful when a faculty member who was once bitter and perpetually angry is swayed by the leader and becomes a supporter. In turn, what faculty, staff and students remember most is how the leader influenced their lives; the advice, mentoring or the help with a promotion. Leaders who play a meaningful role in supporting others can find themselves rewarded with life long friendships.

EXAMPLE: THE ENDURING LEGACY OF JERRY LEVEY

The comments by Jerry Levey provide an excellent characterization of most of the reflections of the interviewees. Both Jerry's greatest challenges and successes occurred as Vice Chancellor, Medical Services and Dean of the David Geffen School of Medicine at UCLA. He chose a talented team, treated them with respect and honesty, and together they accomplished what many felt could not be done. His philosophy is excellence; his vision was expansive but he always prioritized. Over his fourteen-year tenure at UCLA, he directed the design, construction and funding of five research buildings. With insufficient public support, he recognized that if he didn't raise the money, the building projects would collapse. Jerry recalls wondering at one point if UCLA was really a state supported university.

With his great success in leading the development of a world-class research facility and hospital, what Jerry remembered most fondly were his colleagues, mentors and individuals he had helped along the way. In the end, Jerry explained, it is all about the people. He expressed great gratitude and affection for the individuals who worked every day to support the initiatives that he placed before them. In Jerry's view, everyone is a player from the janitorial staff to the top layer of administration. Anyone who has ambition should attempt to build on it; if they made the attempt, Jerry would be there to support them. Jerry is now retired but his obvious passion and enthusiasm show no signs of waning.

IN THE FINAL ANALYSIS

There are often differences in the memories of people in the organization concerning what transpired during a leader's term in office. Never be surprised that the areas where you felt you made the most significant contributions are not what others recognize. Universities have a special variant of Attention Deficit Disorder with a very short-term memory; too few maintain a history of any of the units on the campus. Still, several of the interviewees recalled fondly expressions of gratitude and friendship when years later they accepted invitations to return for events at universities where they held key positions earlier in their career.

Looking back over their career, many of the interviewees shared the following sentiment. Always view the opportunity to hold a leadership position as the honor that it truly is. Recognize that your time as a leader is but a moment in the history of the university. Enjoy the moment fully; it will be gone in flash. When it's over, don't linger. Let the new leader shine; it is no longer your stage. As one interviewee reflected, it is a blink of an eye from when the leader is seen as a unique visionary to when almost no one recognizes him in the hallway. The interviewees recommend that former leaders dwell on the sense of pride in moving an organization in ways that would not have occurred without them. In the end, you will be judged on action, effectiveness, performance and results. But, the most satisfying aspects of a leadership career are not the personal accolades of the journey, but the successes of the people that you helped along the way.

Notes

• • •

1. See Gmelch and Miskin (2004).

2. *The Resource Handbook for Academic Deans* (2014) edited by Behling provides short essays by deans on topics including leadership style, personnel issues, curriculum development and interactions within the college and across the campus. Bolman and Gallos (2011) provide an eclectic approach to leadership, developing a conceptual framework and examples. Gmelch and Buller (2015) offer a well-conceived framework to create a program to prepare individuals for academic leadership. These works examine primarily the role of a leader in a traditional academic setting. Christensen and Eyring (2011), Fethke and Policano (2012) and Ehrenberg (2015) describe current challenges and offer recommendations for change. The above work falls short of analyzing the leadership tools required to invoke the innovations necessary in the current environment, which is the focus of this book.

3. The impact of this debate on the University of California is discussed in Policano (2014) and Kinkade (2013). UC Berkeley is facing severe issues: see Anderson (2016).

4. Over the decade 2004 – 2014 the cost of higher education as measured by the Higher Education Price Index (HEPI) increased by less than one percent above the CPI annually. The average rate of

increase in HEPI was 3.1% while the CPI average was 2.5%. See jhttp://www.commonfund.org/CommonfundInstitute/HEPI/Pages/default.aspx?RootFolder=%2FCommonfundInstitute%2FHEPI%2FHEPI%20Documents%2F2015&FolderCTID=&View={86E774 1D-E445-47E7-8DD5-7A168C4A701E.

5. The University of Michigan for example, has a published tuition rate that is about twice that of the average of public universities in the US, yet the average family income of student attendee's is less than the University of Iowa whose tuition is substantially lower. Moreover, student indebtedness is also lower at Michigan than Iowa.

6. See http://www.sheeo.org/projects/shef-%E2%80%94-state-higher-education-finance.

7. See Pollnow (2003).

8. See http://tucson.com/news/local/education/arizona-spends-too-much-sending-too-many-to-college-lawmaker/article_56663c2f-5928-5d32-a64b-2b737765f6ad.html.

9. See http://trends.collegeboard.org/sites/default/files/college-pricing-2013-full-report.pdf

10. See http://www.wildcat.arizona.edu/article/2015/06/budget-cuts-finalized-ua-in-process-of-deciding-where and https://azregents.asu.edu/legislativeaffairs/newsreleases/ABOR%20Statement%20Regarding%20FY16%20Budget.pdf.

11. Tuition rose from $4,487 in 2005 to $11,403 in 2015 while the rate of inflation over the period was 22.2%.

12. The University of California System has historically been character-ized by a growing disparity in allocations to the universities, where the oldest campuses, Berkeley and UCLA received an artificially high al-location due to their longevity in the system. Newer campuses suffered from starting at a low base where uniform annual increases provided less funding compared to universities that had built a larger base over time. The System recently completed a "rebenching" exercise that re-calculates the allocation of the state appropriation, with different fund-ing weights across academic programs that would apply to all campuses. Undergraduate, post baccalaureate, graduate professional and graduate academic master's students are assigned a weight of 1, doctoral stu-dents 2.5 and health sciences students are assigned a weight of 5. This reallocation recognizes the different costs of different programs and also signals the value of graduate and professional education. Still, this program was developed and adopted by the UC Office of the President and not by the Legislature who may have a different preference order-ing when comparing undergraduate and graduate education.

13. See http://theadvocate.com/news/opinion/12426711-123/lsu-president-chancellor-f-king.

14. See http://chancellor.wisc.edu/blog/

15. See http://www.ncsl.org/research/education/performance-funding.aspx

16. See Blank's Slate, http://chancellor.wisc.edu/blog/, July 17, 2015.

17. See http://www.aaup.org/about/history-aaup.

18. From the US Department of Education, (http://nces.ed.gov/pubs2005/2005172.pdf) the percent of tenured faculty has fallen as fol-lows: 1975, 56%; 1989, 46.8%; 2005, 31.9%; and 2009, 30%.

19. See http://www.aaup.org/report/heres-news-annual-report-economic-status-profession-2012-13.

20. The study utilized the results of many analyses of the differences in performance in the two frameworks; see "Evaluation of Evidence-Based Practices in Online Learning: A Meta-Analysis and Review of Online Learning Studies. US Department of Education (2009).

21. See http://khanacademy.org/.

22. See Anderson (2016).

23. See Fethke (2011) for an analysis of the relation between changes in the subsidy and access and quality.

24. See http://collegemeasures.org/4-year_colleges/home/.

25. The University of Florida implemented a responsibility centered management budgeting approach that incorporates the costs of program deliver. Essentially, student credit hours generated by each program were weighted by their respective cost of delivery to determine the budget allocations to various academic programs.

26. See http://wvtf.org/post/sweet-briar-college-has-240-students-and-brighter-future#stream/0

27. *Paying it Forward: The PhD Project* (2014) provides details of the program with personal examples of its impact.

28. An ample literature exists on these issues; all academic leaders should be well aware of the critical role of diversity in promoting an inclusive and productive environment. See for example, http://www.acenet.edu/

news-room/Pages/Diversity-Issue-Briefs.aspx and http://www.aacu. org/publications.

29. More detail about the dismissal of the ethics violation can be accessed at http://www.purdueexponent.org/campus/article_dc06e9da-1942-11e2-abe8-0019bb30f31a.html

30. See Russell et. al. (2012).

31. See "The Value of a Purdue Education". *Purdue.edu/PurdueMoves.*

32. The attributes of leadership are widely examined and will not be repeated here in great detail. Two excellent sources are Collins (2001) and Avolio (2004).

33. In the vast literature on leadership different schools of thought revolve around Plato, Franklin Delano Roosevelt, and contingency models. Table 2.1 draws from a variety of sources including Dallek (1971), Mitchell, Biglan, Oncken, & Fiedler(1970) and Takala(1998).

34. Jack Welch has widely talked about this concept; see for, example, Welch (2013).

35. Collins (2001) refers to this combination as Level 5 leadership; he finds that having a CEO with Level 5 leadership is a differentiating feature of great companies.

36. An experienced leader may wish to skip this section, which provides the basic mechanics of a search process.

37. The discussion both complements and extends Fethke and Policano (2012). There the analysis emphasizes how to define and measure of

value while the focus here is on the academic leader's role in the strategic planning process.

38. See for example Porter (1980, 1985, 1996.)

39. Christensen and Eyring (2011) describe the tendency for every private university to emulate Harvard. The fallacy is that while many universities propose to be like Harvard, very few have Harvard's resources. Moreover, the aspiration to achieve the same outcome leads to homogeneity of universities and thwarts innovation.

40. Ehrenberg (2015) provides a convincing argument that the transitions needed to take place in public universities are also critical at private universities.

41. The University of Iowa, for example, is facing significant stress under recent pressures to maintain low tuition while abiding by a mandate for all three of Iowa's public universities to increase resident enrollment. This constraint will most certainly decrease the research competitiveness of the University of Iowa, which currently attracts the vast majority of its graduate students from out-of-state.

42. See Fethke and Policano (2012) Chapter 10 for an in-depth discussion of university governance.

43. See Fethke and Policano (2012) for several examples.

44. The financial analysis of this program with projected enrollment, tuition and costs is shown in Chapter 3.

45. This statement is directly adapted from the "agreed upon" definition of strategy at the Harvard Business School: "A strategy is an integrated

set of choices that position a firm, in an industry, to earn superior financial returns over the long run."

46. See Fethke and Policano (2012) and (2013) for a more complete discussion.

47. See the 2015-16 Budget for Current Operations, University of California at http://ucop.edu/operating-budget/_files/rbudget/2015-16budgetforcurrentoperations_.pdf

48. A method for prioritizing research allocations is an implicit part of the strategic planning exercise discussed in Chapter 3. Each area describes (a) the relevance of its research for addressing social needs: (b) an assessment of quality: and (c) an estimate of the full cost of conducting its research program. Relevant parties evaluate the plans and each area is assigned a relative assessment based on these and other metrics. One outcome is that some areas may need to pursue less ambitious goals and eventually, may see a reduction in the size of their research faculty.

49. Valdivia (2013) reports that in 1979 only 30 universities had technology transfer offices; by 2012 the number had increased to at least 155.

50. Chapter 7 includes an extended discussion of the academic leader's role in the increasingly important area of development initiatives.

51. See Berkowitz, Upton, and Brady (2013).

52. Chapter 8 provides a deeper look at a specific difficult situation with the NCAA that Donna Shalala faced at Miami.

53. Many universities are making a concerted effort to develop new revenue generating programs either by offering on-line degree programs, new master's programs or non-degree extension programs. To

incentivize departments, some universities apply an RCM model for these programs, even if a CAM model is used for existing programs.

54. Chapter 1 examines the long-standing debate over the cost of higher education, tuition and access, and discusses the many misperceptions on which some of the arguments are based. Here the main point is increasing for the broad base of the student population, even when including a set aside portion for financial aid, can increase revenue by an amount that is likely to exceed any other source of funding.

55. See Fethke (2015) and Fethke and Policano (2012).

56. See ARI Labor Intensive or Labor Expensive Delta Cost Project.

57. Examples of RCM implementations can be found, for University of Florida, in The University of Florida RCM Manual (2011); and for the University of Minnesota at http://www.budgetredesign.arizona.edu/sites/default/files/UA-Full%20Model%20Presentation%2001-10.pdf.

58. Additional discussion of the non-productive impact of lobbying can be found in Fethke and Policano (2012).

59. This chapter focuses primarily on strategic issues. Analysis of day-to-day activities including prioritization, time management and methods of effective communication can be found in Chapter 8.

60. The determination of which areas to prioritize is discussed in Chapter 3.

61. Conley and Onder (2014) examine the research productivity of economics doctorates who graduated between 1986 and 2000. While one should be careful in extrapolating from one discipline to others, their results are provocative. They find that only ten to twenty percent of

top program graduates produce sufficient research to attain tenure at a medium ranked research university.

62. Rath and Conchie (2008) report the results of a Gallup survey, which show that when an organization's leadership focuses and invests in employee strengths the odds of an employee being engaged are over eight times higher than when the focus is elsewhere.

63. See Sample (2002).

64. Mark Twain and Will Rogers are two of the most well known orators, both famous for their entertaining, yet informative styles.

65. There are many books and materials that can guide a path to effective speaking; two particularly insightful sources are Weissman (2006) and Simon (2006).

66. The "payout" from the foundation on existing endowments varies across universities but is usually in a range between 4 and 5% based on a three to five year moving average of the market value of the endowment.

67. The overhead charge by the Foundation is discussed later in this chapter.

68. Two organizations that provide excellent sources of information on development are the Council for Support and Advancement of Education (CASE; case.org) and the Association for Fundraising Professionals (AFP; afpnet.org).

69. I am grateful to Don Gray, my Senior Development Officer at the University of Wisconsin, now retired from his position as vice president of principal gifts at the University of Wisconsin Foundation. Don

founded and has co-chaired the CASE Conference on Development for Deans and Academic Leaders since its inception in 1994. He is the originator of the graphic in Figure 7.2 of the Cycle of Successful Development, which is used here with his permission.

70. See the 2013 CASE survey.

71. One check on how well you are balancing your personal and professional lives, every so often ask yourself where you would like your ashes scattered after you die. If the answer is across your desk, it may be that you need to re-evaluate your life balance.

72. See Kotter and Heskett (1992).

73. Munter and Netzley (2001) provide a complete analysis of the dynamics of effective meetings.

74. See http://www.rulesonline.com/

75. For a detailed description of faculty culture and governance see Fethke and Policano (2012), especially Chapter 10.

76. See http://www.ncaa.org/sites/default/files/Miami%20Public%20Inf%20Rpt.pdf for the complete NCAA University of Miami infractions report.

77. See Machiavelli (1992).

References

• • •

Anderson, Nick. (2016, February 10) Berkeley is facing big budget trouble, "painful" measures ahead for nation's top public college. *Washington Post.*

Avolio, Bruce J. (2011). *Full Range Leadership Development.* Thousand Oaks: SAGE.

Behling, Laura, L., ed. (2014). *The Resource Handbook for Academic Deans.* San Francisco: Jossey-Bass. Third Edition.

Berkowitz, Steve, Jodi Upton and Eric Brady. (2013, July 1). Most NCAA Division I athletic departments take subsidies. *USA TODAY.*

Biemiller, Lawrence. (2015, April 03). To Resurrect a College, Supporters Need More Than Nostalgia. *Chronicle of Higher Education.* http://chronicle.com/article/To-Resurrect-a-College/229055/

Blank's Slate. (2015, July 17)http://chancellor.wisc.edu/blog/

Bok, Derek. (2013). *Higher Education in America.* Princeton: Princeton University Press.

Bolman, Lee, G. and Joan V. Gallos. (2011.) *Reframing Academic Leadership.* San Francisco: Jossey-Bass.

Bowen, William G. (2013). *Higher Education in the Digital Age*. Princeton: Princeton University Press.

Christensen, Clayton, M. and Henry J. Eyring. (2011). *The Innovative University*. San Francisco: Jossey-Bass.

Collins, Jim. (2001). *Good to Great: Why Some Companies Make the Leap... and Others Don't*. New York: Harper Collins Business.

Conley, John P. and Ali Sina Onder. (2014, Summer). The Research Productivity of PhDs in Economics: The Surprising non-Success of the Successful. *Journal of Economic Perspectives*, 28(3), 205 – 216.

Dallek, Robert. (1971). Franklin Roosevelt as World Leader. *The American Historical Review*, 76(5), 1503–1513. http://doi.org/10.2307/1870517

De Bono, Edward. (1999). *Six Thinking Hats*. Mica Management Resources, Inc. Originally published by Little Brown and Company.

Delta Cost Project on post secondary education Costs. (2011). "Trends in college spending 1999-2009." *American Institutes for Research*; accessible at: http://www.tcs-online.org/Home.aspx

Ehrenberg, Ronald G. (2014). What's the Future of Higher Education? A Review Essay on Gary C. Fethke and Andrew J. Policano's "Public No More: A New Path to Excellence for America's Public Universities." *Journal of Economic Literature*, 52(4), 1142 – 1150.

Evaluation of Evidence-Based Practices in Online Learning: A Meta-Analysis and Review of Online Learning Studies. (2009) *US Department of Education*.

_____, ed. (2004). *Governing Academia: Who Is In Charge at the Modern University?* Ithaca: Cornell University Press.

Fethke, Gary, C. (2014, May 8). One size doesn't fit all for regent schools. *Des Moines Register.*

_____. (2013). "A budget-consistent tuition-setting process," Working Paper, Department of Management Sciences, Tippie College of Business, University of Iowa.

_____. (2011). Welfare Effects of Subsidizing Higher Education When Access and Quality are Endogenous. *Economics Letters.* 112 (1): 45 – 48.

Fethke, Gary C. and Andrew J. Policano. (2012). *Public No More: A New Path to Excellence for America's Public Universities.* Stanford: Stanford University Press.

_____. (2013). Public No More Universities: Subsidy to Self-reliance. *Journal of Management Development,* 32(5), 525-536.

_____. (2012). The Precarious Profession of University President. *Chronicle of Higher Education.* http://chronicle.com/article/The-Precarious-Profession-of/132987/

Gmelch, Walter H. and Val D. Miskin. (2004). *Chairing an Academic Department.* Madison: Atwood Publishing. Second edition.

Gmelch, Walter H, and Jeffrey L. Buller. (2015). *Building Academic Leadership Capacity: A Guide to Best Practices.* San Francisco: Jossey-Bass.

Greenfield, James. (1999). *Fund-Raising: Evaluating and Managing the Fund Development Process.* New York: John Wiley.

Heppell, Michael. (2004). *How to be Brilliant.* Prentice Hall LIFE.

Jacobs, Peter. (2015, March 3). A College With an $85 million Endowment is Shutting its Doors, and People in higher Ed Should be Scared. *Business Insider.* http://www.businessinsider.com/sweet-briar-college-closing-2015-3

Kinkade, Tyler. (2013, October 19) University of California Budget Still Rocky After Years of Drastic Cuts. *Huffington Post.*

Kotter, John P. and James L. Heskett. (2011). *Corporate Culture and Performance.* New York: The Free Press.

Laffley, A.G. (2009, May). What Only the CEO Can Do. *Harvard Business Review.*

Machiavelli, Niccolo. (1992). *The Prince.* Dover edition. Translated by N.H. Thomson, as previously published in Volume 36 of "The Harvard Classics" by P.F. Collier & Son Company, New York, 1910.

Mason, Mary Ann. (2012, May 3). The Future of the PhD. *Chronicle of Higher Education.* http://chronicle.com/article/The-Future-of-the-PhD/131749/

Mitchell, T. R., Biglan, A., Oncken, G. R., & Fiedler, F. E.. (1970). The Contingency Model: Criticism and Suggestions. *The Academy of Management Journal, 13*(3), 253–267. Retrieved from http://www.jstor.org/stable/254963

Munter, Mary M. and Michael Netzley. (2011). *Guide to Meetings (Guide to Business Communication Series)*

The National Center for Education Statistics; accessible at http://nces.ed.gov/pubs2005/2005172.pdf

NCAA University of Miami Infractions Report. (2013). http://www.ncaa.org/sites/default/files/Miami%20Public%20Inf%20Rpt.pf

Policano, Andrew, J. (2005, September/October). What Price Rankings? *BizEd*, 26 – 32.

_____ (2007). The Rankings Game: And The Winner Is... *Journal of Management Development*, 26(1), 43 – 48.

_____ (2014, December 17). Tuition Increases Can Increase Access. *Sacramento Bee*.

Performance Based Funding For Higher Education. (2015, January 3) http://www.ncsl.org/research/education/performance-funding.aspx

Pollnow, Meagan. (2003, February 17). *Changing Directions: History of Tuition at ASU*. https://asuwebdevilarchive.asu.edu/issues/2003/02/17/campusnews/371339

Porter, Michael, E. (1980). *Competitive Strategy: Techniques for Analyzing Industries and Competitors*, New York: Free Press.

_____. (1985). *Competitive Advantage: Creating and Sustaining Superior Performance*. New York: Free Press.

_____. (1996). What is Strategy? *Harvard Business Review*. 74 (6), 61 – 78.

Rath, Tom and Barry Conchie. (2008). *Strengths Based Leadership*. New York: Gallup

Rein, Matthew. (2015, July 30) Budget Cuts Finalized UA in process of deciding where. *Arizona Daily Wildcat.* http://www.wildcat.arizona.edu/article/2015/06/budget-cuts-finalized-ua-in-process-of-deciding-where

Rosovsky, Henry. (1990). *The University: An Owner's Manual.* New York: W.W. Norton.

Russell, John; Sabalow, Ryan; Schneider, Mary Beth; Sikich, Chris (June 20, 2012). "Gov. Mitch Daniels pick called a coup for Purdue, but qualifications questioned". *The Indianapolis Star.*

Sample, Steven B. (2002). *The Contrarian's Guide to Leadership.* San Francisco: Jossey-Bass.

Simon, Eli. (2006). *Eli Simon's Power Speech.* Irvine:Whistler.

State Higher Education Finance http://www.sheeo.org/projects/shef-—-state-higher-education-finance

Takala, T. (1998). Plato on Leadership. *Journal of Business Ethics,* *17*(7), 785–798. Retrieved from http://www.jstor.org/stable/25073123

Tichy, Noel M and Warren G. Bennis. (2007). *Judgment: How Winning Leaders Make Great Calls.* New York: Penguin.

University of California Blue and Gold Opportunity Program. http://admission.universityofcalifornia.edu/paying-for-uc/glossary/blue-and-gold/

University of California. (2013). *Budget for current operations: Summary and detail, 2013-14;* accessible at: http://www.ucop.edu/operating-budget/_files/rbudget/2013-14-budget.pdf

University of California, Irvine. (2013). *2013 Facts and figures.* Accessible at: http://today.uci.edu/pdf/UCI_13_Facts_and_Figures.pdf.

University of Florida (UF), (2011). "RCM manual." Budget Office. University of Florida, Gainesville; accessible at: http://www.cfo.ufl.edu/rcm/rcmc/RCMManual08312011.pdf.

University of Iowa, Budget Task Force Report; accessible at: http://provost.uiowa.edu/work/strategic-initiatives/docs/tfreports/SITF_Budget.pdf

US Department of Education. (2009). *Evaluation of Evidence-Based Practices in Online Learning: A Meta-Analysis and Review of Online Learning Studies.*

Ury, William. (1991). *Getting Past No: Negotiating in Difficult Situations.* New York: Bantam.

Valdivia, Walter, D. (2013). University Start-Ups: Critical for Improving Technology Transfer. *Center for Technology Innovation at Brookings.* 1-22. http://www.brookings.edu/~/media/research/files/papers/2013/11/start-ups-tech-transfer-valdivia/valdivia_tech-transfer_v29_no-embargo.pdf

Weissman, Jerry. (2006). *Presenting to Win.* New Jersey: Pearson Education, Inc. publishing as FT Press.

Welch, Jack (2013) IoD Convention https://youtu.be/jVWAbqMdsJM

Whalen, Edward L. (1991). *Responsibility Center Budgeting*, Indiana University Press.

Wolken, Dan. (2013, February 18). Emmert: NCAA Failed our Membership with Miami." *USA Today.* Also available at http://www.usatoday.com/story/sports/college/2013/02/18/miami-ncaa-enforcement-investigation-mark-emmert/1928263/

Index

• • •

About the Author

• • •

ANDREW J. POLICANO IS FORMER Dean, Dean's Leadership Circle Professor and Director of the Center for Investment and Wealth Management at the Paul Merage School of Business, University of California, Irvine.

Policano is a seasoned leader with over thirty years of leadership experience at five universities. During three deanships he created innovative programs and enhanced academic excellence while developing financially self-reliant strategies. His endeavors at the University of California, Irvine, have resulted in highly ranked programs, a naming gift for the business school and an over 400 percent increase in the school's endowment.

Policano received his doctorate in economics from Brown University. His work in macroeconomics, higher education and media rankings has been widely published. He is co-author with Gary Fethke of *Public No More: A New Path to Excellence for America's Public Universities.*

Policano is a Distinguished Alumnus of Stony Brook University where he received his undergraduate degree in Mathematics. He has been honored by AACSB International for his leadership both as chair of the AACSB Board and in developing global accreditation standards. He has been inducted into the PhD Project Hall of Fame recognizing his leadership in diversity initiatives.